Behind These Eyes Such Sweet Madness Lies (My Life On and Off the Stage)

BRANDON ROSCOE MAGGART

Copyright © 2014 Brandon Roscoe Maggart
All rights reserved.

ISBN: 1502390566
ISBN 13: 9781502390561

Other books by Brandon Roscoe Maggart

My Father's Mistress

Dear Kate, Love, Henry

The cover photograph is by Annabel Clark.

The back cover photo is by Marcus Blechman.

The back cover painting, as well as all other paintings, are by the author.

Publishing rights to photos within the book were arranged through Martha Swope's collection at The New York Public Library. Other photos are from the author's private collection. Any objections to the use of certain photographs owned by private parties will be pulled by the author on request.

My thanks for knowledge and encouragement to: Gary Haber, Fiona Apple, Maude Maggart, Jennifer Maggart, Julienne Maggart, Spencer "Bran" Maggart, Garett Maggart, Kylie Wishart, Mona Abboud, Lee Roy Reams, Robert Donahue, Diane McAfee, Mary Cross, Jon Steely, Peter Palmer, James Gavin, Scotty Bowers, LuJan Fenton, and Annabel Clark. And, a special thanks to my many friends of the "Forgotten Musicals," the "Vintage New York Stage," and the "MUSICALS: STAGE&SCREEN" communities.

The Writer, the Old Actor, and the Mirror

I ask you the reader to envision an elderly bearded gentleman, who coincidently bears a striking likeness to this writer. He stares down onto a blank page. He will take a deep breath. And, he will begin to write. More than likely, he will write the first words that come into his aging, but extremely focused mind. His, is a mind that will allow him to, occasionally, speak inappropriately. His, is a mind that is oftentimes quick-witted and razor sharp. At other times, his is a mind that might seem to be vacationing in a distant soup of fascinating possibilities.

Personally, I find him to be, at least, honestly forthcoming, and at best, surely not without a certain amount of quaint charm for a gentleman of his advanced age. If a smile begins to invade his face, it is often about an interesting woman from his questionable past. (On one occasion, he had been in love with four women at the same time. This situation did not end well.) Or, better yet, just the right word has revealed itself and has fallen into its proper place on the page. Or, he is onto something that he thinks might help in solving an aggravating conundrum.

You can read from the page as the old actor begins to write: Six years ago, I was asked to contribute some of my writings to a Hundred Year Time Capsule, to be opened in the year 2108. What a great idea! This made me wonder what it would be like to have words, written by my Great-Great Grandmother, or G-G-G-Grandfather, and so on, back in time... Words about what they believed or doubted... Stories they told and laughed at; or, kept as secrets for fear of ridicule or worse... Words that might let me know who they were... Not just calendar dates of births, weddings, offspring, and deaths. This idea was especially appealing to me since I have not one word written by any of my ancestors. Even, a short poem would have been nice. I did have a postcard from my Dad. But, that one wee bit of writing from my father was lost somewhere along the way. I do remember the words. I can clearly see his handwriting: "I went to Yankee Stadium today and saw the Yankees beat the Red Sox. Be home Friday. Daddy."

Idea: Of course, there is a lot of inherent freedom in writing thoughts and opinions today what won't be judged for a hundred years. But, maybe, I should do this writing for my children and grandchildren as well as for any interested future generations to come... And, do it now... And, let them read it now. They won't be alive in a hundred years! At least, have it available for them to read. Possibly spark a dialogue... Questions and answers... Get to know each other a little better than just the role-playing of parent to child. At the very least, this might offer some insight as to who their patriarch, this old Actor, might be. Here; on these pages, I will have unabashedly done so to the best of my ability. I realize that some of these personal words might cause embarrassment to certain members of my family. Nevertheless, I have weighed those negative possibilities as opposed to a superficial attempt and have set out to bare my imperfect self. Although, I have no warts of the physical nature, I have had a few character warts. However, I do believe that they have been successfully removed. Admittedly, I cannot take full credit for this surgery: an advanced age does seem to have a considerable taming effect.

This aging actor of 81 years, whose sharp memory and physical capabilities have begun to diminish, creates a stage on which he lives, acts, writes, paints, and makes love. He manages this by using an ability (passed on, genetically, from both sides of his family) to be in more than one place and time at a time. He ventures from his *travel* chair while *traveling without leaving.* This *traveling* is done on the small attic stage beneath his brow and behind his eyes. Accuse him of self-mythologizing if you wish, but he creates his own work, holds soirees for his cast of fascinating and celebrated guests from times-past. And, he enjoys blissful intimacies with the beautiful and talented actress, Vivien Leigh. He explains this Utopian world by his ability to access his desired experiences through something akin to quantum entanglement; meaning a non-local connection.

Without having to use his *Travel* chair, the actor recalls and relates his personal history from, both, onstage and backstage, with Lauren Bacall, Carol Channing, Lynn Redgrave, Jerry Lewis, Soupy Sales, Tovah Feldshuh, Ronny Graham, Marshall Barer, Howard Keel, Jane Powell, Leonard Sillman, Madeline Kahn, Jack Carter, dozens of others, and in private council with Athena, Goddess of Wisdom.

He tells about his bizarre relationship with a famous guru to the stars who flew too close to the sun. Although, an award-winning operatic baritone, he confesses his winning of the National Hog Calling Championship.

And, he shares tales of his own family of performers: the celebrated cabaret and concert singer, Maude Maggart, the iconoclastic, Grammy-winning, singer-songwriter, Fiona Apple, and actor, Garett Maggart. Daughters, Jennifer, and Julienne, as well as son Spencer Brandon, are equally as interesting. Also, he writes about the devastating tragedy of losing his daughter, Justine Marie Maggart.

A sober alcoholic for the past 33 years, he confesses to his past excesses in the irresponsible consumption of booze and to the dancing of many tantric tangos with some of the most interesting and desirable of women in the arts. Politically and socially, he prefers the liberal minded… though, not exclusively.

"In the midst of winter, I find within me the invisible summer…"
Leo Tolstoy

Table of Contents

1. The Writer, the Old Actor, and the Mirror........vii
1. I've Been Waiting All Day for Vivien Leigh to Call........1
2. It's the Doing of It........9
3. Traveling Without Leaving........29
4. Athena, Goddess of Wisdom........35
5. Venice Beach........41
6. On Butterfly Wings to the Possum Spring Dance........49
7. The Wizard of Ooze........59
8. Damn Yankees and Lil Abner........65
9. The Upstairs at the Downstairs........69
10. Idle Thoughts........83
11. Children, Fistfights, Movies, and Booze........89
12. Auditions, Radio City Music Hall and…........101
13. My Agent at the Time........113
14. The Spring of 1968 and New Faces........119
15. Timing........131
16. Pain Management and Sad Songs........135
17. Different Laughter........143
18. The Foraging Wino and the Chow Chow in Drag........149
19. Sometimes it helps........153
20. Sherry Britton and Burlesque........159
21. Casting........167
22. Buddy and Jim on Sesame Street........171
23. The Theatre World Award........175
24. Applause........179
25. Lorelei and Carol Channing........191
26. Being on Stage with Tamara Long and Carol Channing........205
27. Oric Bovar........209
28. Wedding Band during Lorelei........217
29. South Pacific with Howard Keel and Jane Powell........225
30. Straws in the Wind........231
31. Saturday Night Live........233
32. Jennifer Slept Here........235
33. Brothers........239
34. Chicken Soup........243
35. Ronny Graham........249
36. America, Be Seated:........259
37. Marshall Barer........265
38. LuJan........277
39. Musical Chairs........281
40. Hellzapoppin' and Lynn Rachel Redgrave........283
41. Losing My Fastball........293
42. Rex Reed, John Simon, and Fiona Apple........295
43. Before I was in Africa........309
44. Soirees, Artists, Glitterati, Cognoscenti, and Me........323
45. My curtain speech........343
46. Before My Attic Stage........351

Rapture

To enter
To breathe
To walk into the light
To see her
To embrace her
To kiss her lips
To sing the song
To dance the dance
To know her
To love her
To win her
To paint the picture
To hear her laugh
To hear her cry
To lose her
To down the shot
To drink the quart
To write the song
To lose the light
To exit
To enter
To breathe
To find the light
To embrace the light
To see her

Rapture Redux

BR Maggart

I've Been Waiting All Day for Vivien Leigh to Call

The year now is 2014. I'm an eighty-one year old actor unsure of my lines. This is not good for conventional work in my profession. But, within my winter I find a cornucopia of ripened fruits for the plucking. I have a magical gift. From here in my *travel chair*, I *travel without leaving*. This fortuitous gift was passed on to me genetically from both sides of my family.

From this *travel chair*, with full mental acuity, I am able to revisit past performances on the legitimate stage, on the boards of burlesque, and in front of the television and film cameras. From here, too, each and every day is a day for new and experimental work without boundaries. Beneath the proscenium arch of my brow on this small attic stage behind my eyes, whether on canvas, parchment or by use of the spoken word; I attempt works of art. If the work is to be theatrical, I do my own casting. If painting, I choose the paints and the brushes, and I do the painting. I am the sole arbiter of all productions, both the new and the revisited. I am unencumbered by any fear of stepping into uncharted territory. The stage is mine. This is my realm. Here, the unconventional is king. For this artistic freedom, I am truly grateful.

Here, without endless backers-auditions… Without villainous critics spewing sulphur from their bully pulpits. Here, there are no more morbid opening-night exits from Sardi's after having heard The Times read aloud to all concerned.

After a full day of creativity, I enjoy the casting of interesting guests for my nightly soirees. Having completed that: I drop all selected ingredients into the pot. I, then, stir the plot what's in the pot… And, here, on my private, attic stage; the magic we call, Theatre, happens. Life is good.

I've been waiting all day for Vivien Leigh to call. Writing, painting, and performing on my stage are wonderful, but I have other needs. Having a close relationship with Vivien is like waltzing on a moving stage with a beautiful Tiffany bowl. However, the bowl is filled to the brim with nitroglycerin. Balance and dexterity along with one's unqualified appreciation for the unique beauty of this fragile bowl, are required.

I, usually, avoid television, but once a month, on a scheduled weeknight at 11PM, I make an exception. I cast three or four characters from a list of notables to gather around a solitary empty chair. Those from the list who are not onstage are seated in the audience. With anxious anticipation, we wait. After hearing the overture to *Candide,* and our urbane and witty host from Nebraska fails to appear; after a few moans and groans, someone will laugh: a spark to the tinder. And, that's when my soiree begins to roll into a wonderful evening on my small attic stage that will if necessary, expand to accommodate the size of the production. My guests begin to entertain themselves by the telling of tales and the singing of songs, and, especially, with good conversation.

Among this evening's guests, all possessing an abundance of wit, charm, and unpredictability are: Norman Mailer, William F. Buckley, Gore Vidal, Shelly Winters, Betty Davis, Katherine Hepburn, Janis Joplin, Anthony Burgess, Alistair Cooke, Orson Welles, George Burns, Jack Benny, Groucho Marx, Truman Capote, John Gielgud, Ralph Richardson, Buddy Hackett, George Carlin, Fred Astaire, Honi Coles, Richard Burton, John Cheever, Tennessee Williams, Beverly Sills, and Nora Ephron. This excellent cast, after being properly sated by the sharing all that wit, charm, and unpredictability make their exit. Mailer and Vidal are at odds as they tarry a bit. I usher them out and close the door behind them.

I'm still waiting for Vivien Leigh to call. If Vivien calls and comes over in one of her good moods, I will have my perfect ending. Unfortunately, as is the case with Vivien, I've found that many extremely talented artists do often totter on an unreliable edge. If Vivian is smiling when she enters, things will go well. In that case, I'll have either Glenn Gould caress us with a selection of Bach partitas. Or..., maybe, Antonio Carlos Jobim to soothe us with a feast of his bossa novas. Perhaps, both. After Jobim and Gould make their exits, Vivien, and I will more than likely get naked and enjoy sexual bliss with untethered abandon on into the wee hours. Totally spent, we will fall asleep wearing goofy, matching smiles. When I wake, Vivien will have made her exit.

I have come a long way to reach my present perch. I began acting and singing in high school and then in college before going to New York for a life on the stage. I joined Actor's Equity in the summer of 1958. That was the first time I had gotten paid for being an actor. Although, I had been paid for singing at Radio City Music Hall only a few months before. It seemed like a most enjoyable way to make a living. To sing, dance and act on the stage and to get paid for it… Sign me up.

My first Equity show was a touring company of *Damn Yankees*. Now, fifty-six years later, following a fairly respectable career, I have been spending most of my time painting and writing and remembering about when I had no problem remembering. But now, losing the ability to memorize chunks of new material, and, even worse, the fear that, at some inopportune time, a number of my neurotransmitters might fall asleep at the wheel, is daunting to me. Also, not being able to stand and walk about the stage very well due to a troublesome back problem, can be another problem for a working actor. But, fortunately, not a problem for me.

I, now, have the situation well in hand. I am in control. What's more, I have elevated my current situation to near Utopian heights. I am the author of my own life and my own shows at my own pace and from my own theater.

In the larger part of this book, from memory and writings done at the time, I indulge myself in the telling of my personal show business stories. One featured story, told, without embellishment, concerns a huge Broadway personality and her husband-manager and a year-long national tour in preparation for a year's run at The Palace Theater on Broadway. (My second show at the Palace) This story is included for personal reasons, and as a lesson about how a sharp manager protects, sells, and uses his star. Another story is about my first musical at The Palace. It was a much more fulfilling experience, involving yet another big star.

Out of necessity, my creative mind tricks my brain into defying logic and most laws of physics. By doing so, I construct a fascinating and readily available playground for the restless mind of an aging actor. This has been a saving grace at times of creeping ennui. It's been said (by those rascals who say things) that I am, at times, unusual, inappropriate, bizarre, eccentric, strange, a professed galactic transient by way of quantum entanglement, and at times, a brazen bender of recognized truths. I voice no argument in rebuttal; with one caveat: I write my truth as I perceive it on this holy stage beneath the proscenium arch of my brow. From here, I am able to conjure and to experience and to relate the comedies and dramas of life as I see them. I do this without fasting, sleep deprivation, or by the use of hallucinogens.

At times, I am prompted to blend time and space; interweaving these thoughts and facts into extended perceptions and fabric. As with many actors, I live with any number of alter egos. Over the years, I have improved and refined my technique so that I do not have to leave my home and my *travel chair* in order to appear on a Broadway stage or to be in close communion with exceptional actresses, dancers, writers, singers, humorists, ecdysiasts and a few amusing free thinkers in the realm of the occult.

With my *traveling without leaving*, physical space is not in the equation. No matter how far we are apart, we maintain our relationship; as in quantum entanglement: A non-local connection. Considering quantum entanglement; every wee bit of energy has a twin somewhere in the universe. Geometrically, I see this as twin circles sharing a common radius. I seem to be able to be in two (or more) places at the same time. For performances, on this small stage behind my eyes, I call upon players, both the living and the previously-living, to inhabit these theatrical larks of mine. Most importantly, I remain a sympathetic and grateful audience for my own sweet self and my various productions as I trod the storied boards of my cherished attic stage, where quantum leaps abound.

In other words, I spend lots of time living inside my head. It's free. It's convenient. And, best of all, there are no imposed rules. Total freedom… Without restraints… With the powers invested in me, you, the audience will experience these productions through my eyes and my words… Words, written here, on these pages before you.

Leo Tolstoy said, "The kingdom of God is within you." I have respectfully considered these words. Indeed, I ask myself, "What must it be like to be God, to be the sole author of everything; and, at the same time, to wonder if you even exist?" One would necessarily flirt with any number of insecurities. I am everything… I am nothing… I am schizophrenic.

I am still waiting for Vivien Leigh to call. I could just write on this page: "Vivien called. She's on her way over." But, I don't. I do want it to be her idea. So, I write: "I'm still waiting for Vivien to call. Maybe, she's on her way." Even though, I do the writing, certain women do have an alluring power over me. Do I allow that? I wonder. I am the author, am I not? At the moment, am I, indeed, doubting my authorship?

Consider this: A young boy is without a father. So, the boy fantasizes a father. In order to impress himself and his friends, the boy lets it be known that his father is a pro football quarterback, a scientist, a baseball pitcher, an astronaut, a deep sea diver, a poet, and is seven feet tall; but he lives in another country. On the other hand, what if the father does exist, but he is not any of those things. If the father considers coming home to his son, does he think about what a disappointing shock that might be to the boy? He knows that the boy has placed him as being a giant. And, yet the father is much like any other man. Maybe the boy would eventually accept him as his dad, albeit, just an average dad. Yes? Maybe it would destroy the boy's world. Should the father take that chance?

On the other hand, what if the father would turn out to be even more than the vaulted image the boy had created? Maybe the father deservedly owns the reputation bestowed on him by his son.

Should you walk right in and say: "Hi, son. You have been right all along; I am God."

It's the Doing of It

It dawns on me that writing, in many ways, is an archeological pastime; digging into one's psyche, unearthing and confessing the findings to the world. With that in mind, on these pages, I will be coming to you from this sacred temple and living quarters behind my eyes. I maintain these living quarters for those who might, following one of my soirees, desire to stay overnight. Presently, and in the foreseeable future, it's only Vivien who stays over. Vivien is about all I can handle.

You can't see me now because you are looking at this page on which I am currently pushing the pen. Actually, I type. At eighty, my handwriting is less than serviceable.

For my today's endeavor to make art, come with me. Read as I write. Today, I shall take on multiple roles concerning the weightiest of subjects. Be seated with me in the audience. I am in seventh-row center. It will soon be revealed that while I am in the audience, at the same time, I am on the stage... Quantum entanglement be my mode of travel. I am in two places at the same time. Three, considering that I am the writer... All this without the use of hallucinogens. Did I not say unto you that I am the observer and the observed? (I think I said that.) As I write, and you read; you and I are aware that the houselights are down, and the stage is dark, except for enough backlight to offer a distinguishable silhouette. After a pause that begins to make me and the rest of the audience a bit uncomfortable, I, in silhouette, speak to us from the stage:

"You're looking for me, I believe."

We, in the audience, are hooked.

"I've been watching you all the while you've been looking. I couldn't stop watching you if I wanted to. You're fascinating. I made a place for you, and almost as soon as you got here, you started looking... Looking for me. I must confess; I like that. I appreciate that. However, some of you smart ones have deduced that I'm not here; that I am not now nor have I ever been here, pointing out that no one has ever, actually, seen me. But, you keep an eye out just in case; which leads me to opine that some of you eggheads feel there is something missing in your math... Small windows... Small cracks that bother you. You can't quite square the circle. You can't exact Pi. Might I be tucked away in something like that? Something infinitely smaller than where your imagination might take you, or the opposite: something of a magnitude that lies beyond your limited scope?

"Others of you are pretty dog-gone sure that I am here. But, you don't like me; because, in your opinion, I've been doing a lousy job... Not living up to my billing. That, I will say, is a plausible assessment. Most of the rest of you know for sure that I am here and that everything I do is somehow, always, for the best. No matter how wretched your life gets, you believe that if you stick with me, there will be a happy ending.

"So, we have the ones who deny that I'm here… The ones who think I'm here but don't like me… And, the ones who know I'm here and know that I know what the hell it is that I'm doing. And, we have others who are stressed out, and way too busy to give it much thought. And, there are some who just don't give a rat's ass one way or the other. Truth is; I'm equally fond of all of you. You are, indeed, fascinating. That's why I watch. And, you? You keep looking. I like that. I find that to be enormously encouraging.

"But, hold onto your hats; I'd like to, or rather I need to, shake things up a bit. I am going to make a public appearance; otherwise, there's no point in all of you sitting there in this theater, and looking up this way. This puts considerable pressure on me to take the leap, and to settle things, once and for all.

"Now, I'm trusting that my public appearance won't be so shocking as to cause widespread panic, heart attacks, strokes and such; especially amongst the smart ones who contend that a masterpiece can just happen by itself without authorship… Without guidance. I have to straighten that out. Clear that up.

"Hopefully, unless you're dumber than a stump, you will come to see and understand that I am the creator and the created. I am that I am, plus, I am that I am perceived to be…, which is troublesome… But, not always. For instance, the fellow we're dealing with here; tonight's actor (That'll be me, as well), who will be working along with us; he does perceive me to be: BIG ROOSTER. (And, yep. That's me too.) That might sound odd to you, but this works well for me. This translates into something I can use... What I can use is fear. He perceives me to be the BIG ROOSTER because, when our actor was a very young boy he was introduced to the emotion of fear, a near paralyzing fear, by one large, cock-of-the-walk, bad-assed, barnyard bully of a rooster.

(This is true. I was there)

"This BIG ROOSTER would announce his dominance at first light, from on high, flapping his wings, crowing, strutting, flashing his long, sharp, intimidating spurs; implying a swift and violent flogging and possible death to one who might offend him in some way. Many is the time that the bullying BIG ROOSTER chased the boy around the yard, pecking at his heels and ankles; with the boy barely making it to the safety of his front door. This scared the crap out of our young boy. So our fella, tonight's actor, is a BIG ROOSTER fearing man."

(Still in silhouette, I take a moment to consider. And then, I lay it on the line)

"A long, long time ago, before the beginning, there was another beginning... A beginning with great promise. I was creating everything from scratch, and it was working. And the doing-of-it was joyous. That's exactly what it was. It was joyous. Now, here's the thing. Please get this... It is the work... The careful hands-on-doing-of-it that fills the cup. And, filling the cup by your own artistry, in your own style, is the whole point. Even for me. Especially, for me. On the flip side, if it starts going south on you, as this genesis did, it's discouraging.

"I reacted poorly, unacceptably. I had me some of the fury that you might have heard about. And, I smashed it! I smashed my creation, and I flung it into the bottomless pit. And, I watched my hard work; my very promising efforts disappear, adrift into the infinite nothingness. Bummer; taking me to an overwhelming ennui that I could not bear. I pulled myself together, and I retrieved, from the bottom of that bottomless pit, all of my essential ingredients. And, I began again. I gathered every scrap of my creative energy and packed it into a singularity of infinite power. And, I released it...

"And, the evening and the morning were the eighth day... Or the ninth... Not really sure. Took a nap on the seventh day and slept right through. And I woke, and behold, I saw everything that I had made. And, it was... Not bad... But, not a masterpiece. You see, I was counting on a masterpiece.

"A couple of days before, on the sixth day, everything was looking top notch. But this? This was not what I had in mind. Again! Again! I was about to unleash me some of my hellish fury! I could feel it coming on, when I noticed that what I had created was, itself, creating... On its' on! All over the place! No order whatsoever! But... But, hold on ladies and gentlemen... Even though it was all mistakes and adjustments..., and not a reassuring sight; it was fascinating! Fascinating! That's when I, really, started watching and seeing that my failure wasn't necessarily a failure. In fact, failure seemed to be quite essential to this incredibly violent dance of these tiny, string-like energies, vibrating in waves... Waves and particles... Dissonances and harmonies... And vibrating strings of uncertainty..., and unpredictability.

"A whole lot of *shakin' goin' on* with a determined sense of rhythm and direction towards, of all things..., beauty and elegance! Who knew?? Well! This would be an imperfect masterpiece at best. But, Yowzah; the damned thing was working; almost imperceptibly at first, because of the violence and the time involved. But, taking "time" out of the equation, and the evolvement was obvious. Albeit trial and error. I was back in business! Joyous! And my cup did, indeed, runneth over. It runnethed over for a brief instant. And, I realized that I also had, pretty much, taken myself out of the equation.

"Where was the hard-work-hands-on-doing-of-it needed for my sense of personal accomplishment? I was all set with hammer and nails and lightning and thunder and wind and rain... That was the whole point; to do the work myself! This...? This was alchemy! Like, I'd taken a match and a stick of dynamite, and made a chicken. -- Or, I'd opened a door, and a chicken created itself! – Or, did I create a door, and thereby create a chicken?"

"I dealt the hand. But, the chemistry, the playing of the hand, I must share with offspring that I, myself, have created?!? Design by committee? Oh, no! Heaven forbid! But, ladies and gentlemen, like the lumpy camel..., which, you might have heard..., is really a horse designed by committee... This violent, lumpy awkwardness was stumbling and slouching on towards a promising, imperfect, masterpiece!

So, what do I do now? Here's what I would do. I would dance with the camel what brung me. That's what I would do!

(As a member of the audience, I'm liking this)

"It's like this; BIG BANG... Huge blank space or gestation period. Got born... Grew up... Went about the business of living a life... Parked the car... Walked in here and sat down. This is as far as you've gotten. Me too... This is as far as I've gotten. And here we are, together, you and I, in the same wagon, riding this fine, fine, ever-moving edge of *now*. We find ourselves in a symbiotic relationship. And, together, we need to fix our wagon. We need to fix our wagon afore the wheels come off! After all, we do not want to flirt with my rashness..., my hellacious and destructive furies. Do we? I don't think so... We do not want everything to be slung into an irretrievable oblivion!

"Here's what I'm thinking. I'm thinking that just a slightly closer alignment might do the trick... And, only slightly closer... Avoiding familiarity by all means. I'm loathe to completely give up my *mysterious ways*. Nevertheless! One hand should be a little more aware of what the other hand is doing.

(I look around at the audience beside me, and I see glazed-over eyes. But, there are some, including me, that have eyes as big as saucers. Yes, I'm liking how this is going)

"Out of darkness and void and in the spirit of this slightly closer relationship, I will create the Actor in my own image. He'll be in my image, but he's on his own. My job, at this point, is pretty much a supervisory position, keeping an eye on the sparrow while trying not to interfere. And you: the audience (that's us), you're more than just an incredibly organized bag of transient particles that took fourteen or fifteen billion years to get here, park your car, and sit down. You're players as well, although, at this performance you will remain where you are. You will remain seated and quiet, if possible. I abhor unruliness. Plus, I cannot abide being upstaged. You have nonspeaking but very important roles.

"It might be comforting to remember that in the scheme of the "Imperfect Masterpiece," everything is recycled! Everything stays in the mix. Everybody dances! No wallflowers! You "flowers" do fade; but, you're perennials. You'll be back.

"The neighbor's Rottweiler will piss on you. This odd camel of a thing will spit unpleasantness onto your face. But, you will persist through pain and excrement and awkward rhythms that befoul your footing! And, you will all return in different roles, each and every one capable of bringing forth beauty!

"Are you buying this? I hope so..., because that's pretty much how this imperfect masterpiece works! I'm serious. And, yes, there are many critics... Many, many critics... And, rightly so. I did say it was imperfect. The irony is; it's the imperfections that drive it and make it work. Let's face it; the miracle is; that it works at all. So, let's give it our best shot and not toss it just yet."

(I exit. And, like magic, I reenter as the Actor. I am donning a hat and a cape. I'll lose the John Barrymore hat and cape during the following speech.)

"So, this is where I live. I am pointing to my front door… Then, the bedroom… Bath… Kitchen. And here, in front of me, we have the Fourth Wall, which you can't see right now because you're it. When I say, 'I might as well be talking to a wall,' that's, usually, the case. This Fourth Wall is a self-organized representational mural. A lot like those haunted house portraits, where the eyes follow you as you go… Like now… It's doing it now as I walk about. It doesn't scare me. I look at it, and it looks at me… Lots of eyes. Tonight, as always, it's still defining itself. As I define myself.

"I see wonderful individual portraits. Nice warm countenance. Sometimes, though; rows of fish on ice, with mouths agape… Eyes wide. Right now, there are some wonderfully warm people… Some cold fish… And, the rest seem to be from Missouri.

"Too bad you can't see it. You could come up, one at a time, like Japanese tourists, snap a mental picture and go back; but, that wouldn't exactly streamline the evening. I'll keep moving here until I sit and begin to peruse the morning paper…

"There's a story here about a fight I saw on television. Good fight. In the interview after, the winner gave 'thanks' and 'all the glory' to BIG ROOSTER. The loser, who had been knocked down three times and knocked cold in the ninth, looked like he'd been chewed up and spit out. He, also, gave a 'thanks be' and a 'glory to' to BIG ROOSTER. BIG ROOSTER'S got a 'win-win' deal goin' for himself, here.

"When I wake in the morning I need to know what other people were doing while I was asleep. A long time ago, 'what other people were doing' was passed along by stories told around campfires and pictures drawn on the walls of caves... And, later recorded in books. Like the famous book that starts off: 'In the beginning...' Although, there were a few problems getting the various translations squared away, it's still a very good book.

"As a very young child, I wondered why everything was about me. I seemed to be the center of the universe. Why? Did all the other people have their own show that was just about them? Where was I before I was born? I had to have been somewhere. I couldn't imagine not being somewhere. I seem to remember..., almost remembering... Like having a vivid dream..., waking up and almost..., but not quite remembering... Just out of reach... Behind something. A few years later, while lying on my back on our rooftop on starry summer nights, I became obsessed with, 'If you go out there as far as it goes; where does it end? And what's on the other side of that?'

"I couldn't stop thinking about it. You might call it an obsession. I took this obsession of mine to my father, and he gave me the sure-fire remedy that I must use at once, or I might live a tortured life! He said that I should go out... Right now... And get a job! That having a job would put a stop to any kind of esoteric thinking. I did, and it did help some.

"Contemplating infinity, I found to be painful. My Aunt Ella said, 'The one thing that doesn't begin and doesn't end is the circle. It never begins and yet it's here. Think about that.' Maybe there wasn't a beginning. Maybe it just always was… Kind of a circle-like-thing. Those few words have been with me for the rest of my life. And, certainly, in the beginning, I would contemplate Aunt Ella's circles for hours… Look at stars for hours… Slowly evolving from circles to spirals…, to spheres…, to spheres spiralling…, to parallel spheres spiralling; Yins chasing Yangs chasing Yins… Wheels within wheels… Endless… Like a what? Like a circle.

"As I got older, it became a little more sophisticated; adding a musical underscoring; like an expansive collaborative symphony of the spheres… Mozart, Beethoven, Bach, Puccini, Gershwin, Handy, Sousa, Glass, Reich, and some Tibetan Bowl sounds; all of which, somehow, would blend into a soothing drone. Then… Hold on… Out of that soothing drone, I saw two circles sharing a common radius… Eventually, I saw one of the circles fading away, with the remaining circle attaching itself to a new circle and sharing its radius… Like musical styles coming and going and, eventually, coming back. This gave me the feeling that when one circle dies away, the soul might attach to a newly formed person… And, maybe come back around later. Just a feeling… A feeling that gave me some comfort. Flimsy…, to be sure… But, I could easily ride that horse around an oval track… Or a large spherical earth-like orb."

"There were lots of things to think about when I was a child. My sense of wellbeing came with things I could count on... Destiny. There was a beautiful and orderly destiny that existed when I was a child, at least in my perception. A poetry of events. Things would work out like they were supposed to. God already knew which girl I would someday marry. That would be my destiny. When my grandmother died, I was told that she would be waiting for me in Heaven... And, that God was in Heaven and, 'His eye was on the sparrow.'

"But, when you think about it that means: absolutely no privacy. He's always looking at you and the sparrow. You can't shake your 'willy' without Him knowing about it. So, that means BIG ROOSTER knew I took my friend's marble... The big blue one I really liked. I felt badly about it and wanted to return it. But, I buried it. I couldn't get up whatever it would take, to give it back. And, I buried it. And, it bothers me, even now, that I can't make amends. I buried it in my backyard. And, there's a paved parking area there now, where my backyard used to be. And that land belongs to a real estate agent.

"When I buried it, I knew I was being watched. I felt it. And, I knew who it was. He put a pavement over it so I would have to carry the guilt for the rest of my life. Why would BIG ROOSTER do that? And, what made Him have such a need to be feared and worshipped... Almost like a schoolyard bully or a father with low self-esteem? I wondered when BIG ROOSTER, Himself, as a kid... Was His Father like that? And, did He ever cry when bad things happened to people? Especially tragic things, like earthquakes, floods, and fires; that He, Himself, was responsible for? Was He considerate of His wife's feelings? I was pretty sure BIG ROOSTER had a wife... Although, He never mentioned her by name.

(I make a note here that from now on, the Actor will use the word, God, instead of BIG ROOSTER)

"And God said; 'let us make man in our image, after our likeness.' That's what a man and a woman do, isn't it? They make babies that have their likenesses. So, when Jesus comes along, was there a Mrs. God, at the time? And, if so, was she upset when God had a child with another woman, who already had a husband? Even if it was for a good cause, you know, like: 'Saving the world!' Well, 'Saving the world?' HA! What's she going to say if it was the only way He could save the world?

"Mrs. God and Joseph were both 'on the spot.' Now, Joseph! Now, there's an understanding fellow! But, they didn't make a big deal over it, and the world got saved. Good for them! Good for us!

But, when God kicked Adam and Eve out of the Garden of Eden saying, Adam had become like 'one of us.' Who was 'us?' What kind of crowd did God and Mrs. God hangout with? More than likely; that talking snake and his crowd.

"Years later, I realized that God needed the Devil for dramatic conflict... The Light defining and conflicting with The Dark. It's His show. He is the author.

We didn't have TV back then, so there was a lot of time to think of things like, 'Where did Cain's wife come from?'

"In my Sunday school, we were learning about Moses. God, actually, spoke to Moses, who had just killed and buried a man in the sand. God said, 'Moses, you better get out of town. Take a hike into the desert.' But, God didn't give Moses a map. And, sand looks pretty much like sand. So. I guess lots of Jewish folks spent forty years walking around the desert looking for a place like Miami.

"Moses asked God what to tell people when they ask what God's name was. 'And God said unto Moses, 'I am that I am.' I guessed that God wasn't about to give out His real name after sending those folks on that forty-year hike through the sand. But, I am that I am... I am that I am? I-yams-what-I-ams! Now, that sounded familiar. And it hits me. I, of course, inform the class that, 'God is Popeye!!' After church, I see my teacher, Mrs. Butler, talking to my parents.

"We're walking home and my mother starts making sounds, covering her mouth with her handkerchief, and laughing and peeing at the same time. Then, the three of us were laughing. The more we laughed, the harder we laughed. I wasn't sure, but I figured it had something to do with Popeye! That was one of my earliest really 'fun' times; laughing with my parents. A wall came down. It made me feel closer to them in a way. Not familiar… But, closer. And, making people laugh was better than eating a cold slice of watermelon on a hot summer day.

"I told Uncle Oscar and Aunt Ella about it, and Uncle Oscar said he wished he'd been there to see my dad laughing. He'd 'never seen a republican laugh really hard.' Uncle Oscar always had something funny to say, but Aunt Ella was the smart one. Aunt Ella walked into my room one day and asked, 'Whatcha readin'?' I said I was reading my bible. And, she asked, 'You understand it?' I said, 'Not everything.' That Psalms, I liked. Kind of like Shakespeare… Lots of really useful bumper-sticker-like-sayings, you could live by, and be a better person. Aunt Ella said, 'Well if you want to look at it that way; the Bible means…, and she starts in on squeezing the bible. It means be nice.' Wow! My Aunt Ella squeezed the bible down to a bumper sticker; like reducing a mathematical equation.

"But, if Aunt Ella was that smart, she probably knew I buried the Blue Marble. There was something about the Blue Marble that haunted me. I gave it all the thought I could muster. And, then, it hit me:

"Of course, the Blue Marble was perfect, and I was flawed. And, I was supposed to be in His image, the Creator, BIG ROOSTER; who spoke to you earlier: You know, 'Bang… Live… Park… Sit. This is as far as you've gotten?' When He's out here in the dark, I can hear him talking about *His Masterpiece*; or His *Imperfect Masterpiece*.

"The nearest thing to my idea of a masterpiece was Billy Buxter's mother walking out of her bathroom, stark bare-assed naked and standing there, frozen in my memory, for the rest of my life. I was, I think, thirteen. That was a world I'd only dreamed about while looking at the women's undergarment section of a Sears and Roebuck Catalogue. I will never, ever, ever, ever, ever forget that occasion. The rest of that story does often take place here on stage in the attic behind my eyes. It keeps coming back like a favorite song. If God created Mrs. Buxter in the image of Mrs. God, I don't see how, in His right mind, He could ever leave home to lie with another woman; even if it was the only way to save the world.

"As a matter of fact, my whole family was kind of freaky-funny. My Grandpa said I reminded him of his Grandpa when his Grandpa was a little boy. Now, that did seem to be a pretty near impossible feat. Grandpa had quite a remarkable imagination. But, Grandpa insisted he'd seen his Grandpa when his Grandpa was a little boy playing with a pet 'coon named "Washy." And that was before Grandpa was even born. And, he said his Grandma was Cherokee with certain powers. My friend, Baxter Key's dad, said that she was Choctaw.

"Anyway, I do, sometimes, hear the Creator when He's out here talking about His *Imperfect Masterpiece*. Then, He puts me out here as the actor, and He puts you to work as the audience. And, He watches. If it's good, He'll expect 'praise and glory' for what we come up with. If it's bad; He'll just try something else; which is okay, because it's His show."

And... Curtain.

I take a bow, and we in the audience applaud me; some more than others. A rather heavy-set man, sitting beside me, slept through the whole thing. I'm thankful he didn't snore. The audience as a whole was not overly enthusiastic. Some, I could see, were smiling and nodding approval. I liked it. It gave me a lot to chew on.

I must say that we were the quietest audience I've ever played to... Like auditioning a show in front of the Shuberts, in their office. The Shuberts were brazenly noncommittal. They might like your show, and might back your show, but you wouldn't be able to tell by the audition. Later, if they call, you might have a theater and some backing.

I did, recently, play a King in a Broadway musical, which was pretty close to playing God. But, when playing the role, I made myself more vulnerable than I could while playing God. At least a hint of vulnerability is always attractive to an audience.

However, the last time I played the role, it was pretty much a disaster. No, it wasn't. Now, that I think about it. After surviving a near disastrous performance, I had a glorious death scene at the end, wherein I actually ascended into heaven to spend eternity with my first love; fulfilling a vow I had taken 169 years earlier. Very moving. If I'm not mistaken, I played a fiddle at the end, without ever before having played a fiddle. I stand on our front porch, fiddling to "Cotton Eyed Joe," while Kate dances an appropriate jig. Heavenly.

And, as I recall, I did subject my Kate, and my previous self and his wife, to my three-hour solo production of *Ahab and Moby Dick*. Quite often, I do indulge myself with that half-hour pas de deux in the second act, in which I dance both roles of Ahab and Moby Dick. Very funny, and sad. Daring to break *the sacred fourth wall*, I allow myself to make smart asides to the audience during the tragi-comic ballet. I haven't done that whole show in a while. I'll do it again within the next season or two. Recently, I did do the *pas de deux* at one of my soirees. It was reminiscent of auditioning for the Shuberts. Tough house. I need to rewrite some of my asides.

Notwithstanding some of my efforts, usually, my soirees are quite successful. I have interesting guests drop by and perform for me and the other guests. Only last week, Frank dropped by and sang a few numbers; joined by Dean and Sammy romping through a half-hour set. Ella always sings anything she wants to sing. Two nights ago: a velvet song or two from Jo Stafford and "The Velvet Fog" himself, Mel Torme. Dorothy Loudon did the eleven-o'clock-number with "Fifty Percent," from *Ballroom*.

And, for a closer, Frank sang, "In the Wee Small Hours of the Morning," and from *Guys and Dolls,* "My Time of Day."

When they left, Vivien and I got naked.

On other nights, Ronny Graham might do a number or two... maybe, his "Vera the Vending Machine." Sir Noel Coward will swap funny, sophisticated, show business stories with Leonard Sillman. Christopher Hitchens might expound on any number of topics. Ruth dove will serve some of her famous pork and beans. Marshall Barer will insist on telling about how he got banned from The Comedy Club. For a change of pace, Walt Whitman might recite from his *Leaves of Grass*:

"...re-examine all you have been told at school or church or in any book, dismiss whatever insults your own soul, and your very flesh shall be a great poem and have the richest fluency not only in its words but in the silent lines of its lips and face and between the lashes of your eyes and in every motion and joint of your body."

Robert Frost might favor us with *Birches*. And, Thoreau with *Walden Pond*. As the evening draws to a close: Everyone will begin to make their exits just as Marcel Marceau takes the stage. Then, he too, will appear to be leaving.

And, then, of course, after all have departed, Vivien and I will get naked.

Traveling Without Leaving

And Tater Stretchin'

The term, *traveling without leaving* was first documented in letters written by one of my G-G-Grandfathers, to his *intended* while crossing the desert on his way to California, back in 1849. And, I have written about it in my novella, *Dear Kate, Love, Henry.* Henry was one of the hordes of optimistic young men rushing west to find the gold that was purported to be scattered around the ground and in the streams just waiting to be picked up and brought home. It was called the Gold Rush. It was a mess.

My first acquaintance with *traveling* in this manner came as I was meditating one morning at the beach here in California. For some unknown reason, my thoughts took me to Tennessee and to my bedroom I had when I was a child. I was sitting on the side of my bed looking around the room. I saw the night table beside my bed. I saw my Bible that I used to read each night (Mostly Psalms and Proverbs). I stood and began to walk around the house... Opening doors that I hadn't opened for over half a century... Going up to the attic... Past my mother's dressing-table mirror where I checked to see if I had grown any during the night. Into the kitchen... Then outside, and on from there to all around our farm... And anywhere else I wanted to go. I seemed to be about ten or eleven years old. I was amazed at how easy and convenient it was. Places, rooms, smells, fears, thrills, wins, loses, friends, relatives, and sweethearts that I hadn't seen in all those years. From there, my *travels* developed and expanded from that one fortuitous morning at the beach to a gathering of my life experiences by just *traveling* there. There was a door that had been there all the time. And, I had just not been aware that it was available to walk through and into my times-past.

Having out of body experiences, or *traveling without leaving*, was not unusual in our family. At my father's funeral as I stood looking down at his lifeless form, I touched his cold hand; my father was not there. He had left the premises. That was just a carcass, a stuffed mammal, or something akin to one of Madame Tussaud's Waxworks. I heard a crackling noise behind me. It was Uncle Herbert and his hearing aid. Uncle Herbert informed me that my Dad had visited him that morning, and had told him that he "had to go now," but would see him later. My father had passed away two days earlier, and twenty miles away. Another relative said that he had been transformed into a horse and had been ridden by children on several occasions. And, my grandpa was full of such stories of family lore, which might be categorized as *Tater Stretching*: Exaggerating the facts, hopefully, to make a better story. It's said that one of my ancestors, after his death, became an owl, and during the daylight hours, became a butterfly with the eye of an owl on each wing.

My Grandpa likes to tell about the time his Grandpa had two big ol' grizzly bears coming at him... "Smackin' their lips... and hungry as two bears." He knew he only had time for one shot. He would shoot one, and then try to sweet talk the other one. He fired his ancient weapon, and both grizzlies fell dead. He had killed two grizzlies with one shot! Impossible, but true! So, they say.

He could have been more famous than Daniel Boone, who had become famous by carving his initials on a tree saying that he had "killed a bar" thar. But, Boone only killed one "bar" b-a-r. And, he couldn't spell b-e-a-r "bear." But Grandpa's Grandpa could not prove his amazing feat because both grizzly kills were stole from him; stole from him while he was down to the creek washing the stink out of his britches. Evidently, the incident had created havoc within his intestinal tract.

But, when Grandpa's Grandpa gets back to where he shot the two grizzlies; there are just two dead possums lying there, and a bunch of yellow speckled butterflies fluttering around and yapping about an Indian called Two Bears, and a white man called Two Tongues. And, all of a sudden, the two lifeless possums arose from the dead and danced a jig down the mountainside! Lord, have mercy!!! Then all the speckled butterflies gathered together into one big yellow ball, and feathered out to be one "great speckled bird" that stared a hole in him, like that bird was trying to talk to him without words. Then, it flew away.

Grandpa's Grandpa stood there... Froze in his tracks... Shaking like a leaf for the rest of that day and all that night and on into the next day. When he sobered up, he went home.

Grandpa's Grandma, God bless her, said she'd once heard a preacher mention something about a "great speckled bird." He was reading from the Good Book at a revival service. She asked him about that great speckled bird, and the preacher said he'd be glad to explain it to her, later, out behind the barn. Grandpa's Grandma told him she didn't need to know that bad.

Years later, on his deathbed, Grandpa's Grandpa whispered, "That great big speckled bird wanted to tell me something. I never figured out what it..." And, his eyes got real big, and he said, "Jeremiah. It's from the book of Jeremiah in the bible." The preacher opened his bible, and, right away, found the quote: "Mine heritage is unto me as a speckled bird. The birds round about are against her." And Grandpa's Grandpa shouted, as best he could, "Praise the Lord! Praise the Lord! At last!!! But, what in the hell does it mean?"

And he looked down at his arms and hands, and his eyes got real big, and he said, "I am covered with golden speckled feathers." Then he looked around at everybody and said, "And, you are all against me!" And, Grandpa's Grandpa flew out the window. His body was still there, but something like maybe his soul flew out that window. There was the preacher, plus a bunch of family members that witnessed that, and did swear to it.

Afterwards, they were all sipping from a special jug of Grandpa's whiskey, when one of the small gold speckled butterflies flew into the room and out over the old man's lifeless body. It was fluttering around a bit like it was making an assessment of the situation: Then back out the window, where it stopped and hovered like a glittering hummingbird. With its piercing black eyes staring in at the preacher and the family, and that old man's empty shell of a body... Like he was taking a long look back over where he's been. Then, with his wings going faster and faster, all his gilded speckles flew off... Flying through the air like lots of little shooting stars that burned brightly... Then, flamed out. And, it was gone. The preacher and the family all stood in stunned silence until one of them began to laugh, and they all laughed, and they applauded. And, they finished off every last drop of Grandpa's whiskey.

An Indian called Two Bears, and a white man called Two Tongues wept beneath a mighty oak tree in the front yard.

Athena, Goddess of Wisdom

In a more recent past: I have been privileged to know a magical and wise spirit, who, for a time, took residence in the attic behind my eyes: Athena, Goddess of Wisdom. That she became available to me, was my good fortune. She came and went for reasons known only to her. She is always welcome to return.

I did not do drugs. I once had a very nightmarish experience with a wee half-tablet of mescaline. My feet turned into two fish that were flopping around on the deck of a boat; with waves of depression that kept getting darker and closer together. I was afraid I was going to die. Then, I was afraid I was not going to die. It was horrible. Finally, the toy soldiers came marching in… In color!!! I was truly out of my mind. That episode lasted for what seemed like an eternity, but I'm told that it only lasted for about an hour. That experience turned me off any drugs forever. So, what was this recent experience about? A couple of times before, I'd gotten a little spacy from the fasting. A few times, there were events that I wrote off as fantasy, but nothing like this:

While sitting in front of my easel in the field where the large tree, known as Big Oak, stands; lording over the beautiful vista on all sides, something extraordinary happened. I had been without food, for four days; while drinking only water from the nearby spring; when in the late afternoon of the fourth day; I went somewhere new… To another place. I separated from my physical body, and I danced! I danced, and I floated with dust particles and pollen over the alfalfa green and the crimson clover, and up into sky-blue hues, with swirling colors and shapes… Very, very Vincent. And, very starry, as Glen Gould played *Goldberg Variations* in my head, (The second recording… Not the earlier, crisper version) I sailed over treetops… Smiling happy tears.

Now, standing in front of my canvas, with my palette of primary colors; I'm slapping paint onto the canvas. Suddenly, I'm very thirsty. I walk to the nearby spring for water. The spring is within a patch of elm and maple trees. As I approach the spring, I see a beautiful woman. She stands on a rock beside our pool of cold spring water. I see a butterfly with the eyes of an owl on each wing… A turtle sunning on a log… And, a large green frog stationed at the woman's feet. That's it; I'm about to hallucinate a frog joke! I've painted several frog jokes but… Okay… Let's have it, frog! It's probably the one where the frog says to the beautiful lady:

"Kiss me and I'll turn into a handsome prince."

And the beautiful lady says, "No. I don't think so. I'm quite happy with a talking frog.*"*

I like that one. But, this frog just sits. A beautiful woman and a frog, and no joke!?! Odd! Maybe I'm supposed to do something. I'm thirsty. I take the dipper and fill it with the cool water to quench my thirst. I am very thirsty, but, I offer my water to the beautiful woman. She immediately becomes very small: a tiny version of herself, and she sits on the lip of the dipper. Then, she slips into the water in the dipper. A very large and homely woman, with missing teeth, stands by the frog and says "Drink." And, I drink. I drank the tiny lady! I did! I didn't mean to swallow the tiny lady. I didn't think about it. It just happened. She is inside my body and into my digestive tract!

Still, nothing comes from the frog. Sometimes, a frog is just a frog. Now! Here we go!! Now, I'm seeing her inside my body. She's roaming around. She's taking a tour! I'm watching her visit all my thoughts and desires. I'm a little embarrassed. She nestles in my right eye for a while, then my left eye. She's dusting... Cleaning... She's washing my windows. She's into my mind where she straightens up and tosses out a few things that tend to clutter. And finally; she's making a cozy little space there with a little bed and some little female furnishings. She's moving in.

I spring from the spring; straight up, and I am doing something like the *Starry, Starry,* orb thing... Up... Into deep space... And back... And over the trees... And back up the hill... Resting on a limb, high up in Big Oak. She exits the attic behind my eyes and; from there; she slowly drifts down, like a bubble, to a spot a few feet in front of my easel. I watch her as she drifts onto my canvas. And, I'm falling...

It's morning. I'm crumpled at the foot of Big Oak. Seems I've bled a little from the top of my head. I manage over to my easel for a look. And I see her on my canvas… Just as I had seen her amongst the swirls and down by the spring.

Now, I recall that the Greek God, Zeus had eaten his pregnant wife. And, out of his split head had come the fully grown, Athena, Goddess of Wisdom. I walk back down to the spring. Nothing. I go home.

Next morning, I wake with a slight headache. There she is… She's sitting on the foot of my bed.

"Yikes! Who are you?"

She looks over at the painting on my easel, then back to me and smiles a warm, disarming smile.

"Were you with me up by Big Oak and the spring yesterday?" She smiles. "And did we fly together, across the sky together?" She smiles. "And did you walk into my painting?" She is smiling.

ATHENA, GODDESS OF WISDOM

Athena, Goddess of Wisdom

I'm hungry. I walk down to the Fat Tater for breakfast. No one notices that there is a beautiful companion with me. At least she isn't a big white rabbit. She goes with me... everywhere. Sits with me while I paint... Shops groceries with me and sleeps on the bed beside me.

What should I do about this? Hire a *shrink* and have her removed? I have to ask myself: "How do I feel about this?" And my thinking was; that it's nobody's business, but mine. And that I have every right to enjoy, and even pursue the relationship. Why not? She's certainly low maintenance. We go to the movies on one ticket. And she doesn't have that annoying habit that some women have of jabber-jabber-jabbering all the time. And the sex!! The sex is incredible, but always at "her place," in her room; in *the attic behind my eyes*. And, she's always with me. In my belfry. Wherever I go, fishing, hunting, watching sports on my big screen TV... Under Big Oak... In church... She's with me... Life is good.

After a few weeks, when everything was going so well... Suddenly, she's gone. She's gone! My attic is clean and empty... Her bed... Her furnishings... Everything... All gone. I tried fasting again but; nothing. I had been dumped by an imaginary woman. I believe my mind entertains itself. My mind has a mind of its own.

Why did she come? Why did she go?

Recently, while watching the end of *Casablanca* on the Movie Channel, I watched her get on board a plane and fly away; leaving me alone with Claude Raines. I knew that didn't happen. That was Ingrid Bergman. I repeat; I do not use drugs.

Venice Beach

Eventually, with Athena gone, I left the farm, and I moved here to Venice Beach by the ocean. I like living here where in the early morning hours from my bedroom window I can hear the waves slapping the shore. How long have the waves been slapping that sandy beach? And, I wondered when people first saw the big sailing ships disappearing on the horizon; with the ship's sails being the last to go, did they think the ships were sinking? And what did they think when the ships came back?

One typically beautiful morning I was sitting here in my rather small front yard, with my lone lemon tree, thinking about the Owl Butterfly and Natural Selection segment, I'd seen on the Khan Academy website. And, I heard what sounded like Vivaldi... Maybe not... But quite nice. For some unknown reason, I looked into my long-vacant attic... And, there was a piano trio... Steinway grand, violin..., and she was playing beautifully on cello. I listened and watched as they played several very interesting pieces... Very soothing... Transporting, even. As I mentally applauded, my long-missing friend looked out through my eyes... at me... And, then assembled herself, full size, directly in front of me... And, without me fasting.

"Vivaldi?" I managed, expecting a *yes* smile or a *no* frown. She did smile, but she said:

"No. We do play the masters, but mostly, we play deserving composers who were never widely recognized. The politics in the music world, through the ages…, you'd be surprised how many…"

"I heard you speak. You spoke!"

"I do quite a lot of it… As do all my sisters. We were never formally introduced… I'm 'Athena.'"

"I'm Zeus."

"No. But, I am your Athena."

"You left without saying a word. Why? Why did you come into my life and let me be so happy? And then…, why did you go? Why did you suddenly absent my belfry…, when things were going so well?"

"Maybe you only needed me, as you desired your woman to be, at that particular time… Silent and accommodating."

"You walked into my canvas without invitation… You gave me perfection… And, you left without a word."

"Today, I'm making a follow-up call. I'm very fond of you. I accept you, just as you are."

"I'm healthy, and usually quite centered, thank you. Honestly, I've missed your company... I've missed you very much."

"Your attic is relatively clean for a man of your age. You are doing well. And, dear friend, I'm sure that down deep you know that you, yourself, created me: Your Athena. I am an aspect of you. Think about it. You needed refuge and validation that could come only from yourself. Let me ask you: Do you sometimes feel that people are watching you and expecting great things from you?"

"No. Not sometimes! People are watching me all the time. I've always been on stage... in one way or another. It seems I've been put here to live out my existence behind the "fourth wall"... No, that's not true... Sometimes, I do break the wall. There are eyes that follow me as I move about... On stage or off... It doesn't bother me. It feels like my natural habitat... My home. The audience and I have a relationship... Sometimes, better that other times."

"And for what purpose?"

"I think it's to understand... To appreciate... And, to constantly uncover some of the nooks and crannies of existence... To dig for truth... And to relate as much as I can in my allotted time... Before the act curtain comes down... Before my show closes. My answer is a bit theatrical, isn't it?"

"That's okay. That's who you are. I'm going now, but I'll be around... in case of emergency."

"I like it better when you're here!"

And, she's gone. Women are good at that: slipping off into another dimension and becoming unavailable. But, I do know that, now, I can call on Athena in case of emergency. And, maybe she's right; maybe I did just want a woman to be agreeable, to comfort me, and not complain that I don't take her to new places. I needed refuge, and that's what Athena gave me... Refuge. I've never had a consistent idea (other than physically) of how to please a woman, without losing myself.

I am not alone in this. Even Stephen Hawking says that the greatest unsolved mystery in the universe is "woman." According to Hawking: "They are a complete mystery."

I have always been more at home living in my head or on stage or painting or falling in love. I love falling in love. But, it seems, with a limit of about two-year chunks at a time. And, after about two years, women finally realize that's about all I have to offer. I begin to repeat my repertoire. I don't change enough over to their ways of doing and living. Who could blame them? They want to travel. I do most of my traveling in my head. They've heard all my stories... Seen all my charms... I become disposable... Honeymoon over. Believe me, I can understand that. I don't stop loving them, but I love them in a different and less painful way. And, that is a blessing.

And, thinking that I'm the cause of someone's unhappiness is a heavy, dark, and rotten feeling. I hate it. I want to run to someplace where I won't cause misery. That would usually be to a smart, interesting, and desirable woman who would find me fascinating. Being rejected in show business is a given, hammering you until acceptance comes along. It might come along in the form of a new and exciting role to play, or a mysterious femme could arrive to nurse the fragile ego. Sometimes, both. Often, the new woman would ask: "How did you become such a good lover?" Of course, I learned to be a good lover by being with and listening to other women. I seemed to make them happy... for about two years.

Oh, and I'm forgetting, or leaving out, about my history of heavy drinking. My consumption of the fermented spirits was never a plus in any relationship. And, I didn't drink to have a good time. Finally, I drank to get drunk. Not charming. Not healthy. Not good for a marriage or any other relationship.

Before I had to rely on my *travel* chair, I managed the life of an actor striving to make a living in New York and Hollywood. I did well. I cannot complain. I always scraped by, but with many very close calls. At one time, my apartment on Riverside Drive in New York burned... Everything lost. Due to other circumstances, I had less than two hundred dollars in the bank. I was responsible for seven children. No prospects. I had failed my responsibilities. I was ashamed of my inability to provide for my family. My career was dead in the water. Oh, and I had suffered a major heart attack just four years earlier. Then, out of the blue, I got a television series that lead to another television series. Whew!

During the early years, being father to a family of seven children, there was always a big nut to crack... Every month...

Consecutive waves of bills... And pressures. LuJan had not signed up for this. From the information I had given to her, she assumed we would live much better. But, she stayed, and stayed, and stayed, delivering to us four more children. That she was unhappy was painful for the both of us. By the time she had gotten somewhat used to life with me, I was already gone. I was a drunk, and my infidelity was rampant. When LuJan was eventually married to a much better mate, I was ever so relieved and happy for her. She certainly deserved her happiness.

In the meantime, Diane had come along. We, of course, had two daughters. Our relationship was troubled from the beginning. My drinking peaked along our rocky road. She had an affair while on a national bus-and-truck tour of Applause, which prompted a series of assignations on my part. I was no angel. I was called a drunk and "a third-rate Lothario," but, a third-rate Lothario "with a heart of gold." The quote: "a third-rate Lothario," was given to me by Diane. "With a heart of gold," was given to me by Himself. Somebody had to do it.

I dare not venture further reasons or excuses for my debaucheries. But, in the world of musical comedy; beautiful, talented, sensitive, and affectionate women were everywhere, and often in need of attention and comfort. Especially, on out-of-town tours. Anywhere from two weeks to a year on tour, with only a few straight men and many gay men; it became but a traffic problem in managing my dalliances and affairs. I will say that more often than not, the woman was the aggressor. Not that I put up a fight. I usually succumbed.

My disasters came when lavished with affection; I would think I was in love. And, once I bit that apple, I ate the bushel. Along with that, I drank. I drank. I drank. And, I was a goner, until a belligerent New York taxi driver took offense and assisted me in making a decision…, the decision that saved my life.

On Butterfly Wings to the Possum Spring Dance

Here's something I'm working on that I'd like to take a good look at. It was inspired by a magnificently disturbing dream I had, following a fretful night of dozing, awakening, and finally drifting into rhyme and music. I'll sit in the audience, and I'll give it a good look and listen. I am sitting center stage in my *traveling* chair and addressing me here in the audience:

Many miles and lots of years from my old hometown... on a quite possible, wildfire-mudslide-earth-shaking California night... It occurred to me that the world was a bit off kilter... It wasn't spinning quite right... A world on the wobble... on the imbalance... with way too much injustice, hunger and pain... too much or too little rain... plus the looming possibility of human extinction spinning around in my severely overcrowded brain... Tho' far from insane... I do fear for my brain... It teeters and it totters as it circles the drain... With the world on my shoulders... at least in my head... it's clear I'm not Atlas... more... Sisyphus instead...

This would be one more exhausting night without sufficient sleep... Facing unknown dragons tomorrow... tonight... I shepherd lost sheep...

BEHIND THESE EYES SUCH SWEET MADNESS LIES

My Dear Miss Bo Peep... I have found your lost sheep... They run and they leap over fences quite high... Over hedges, they fly... Tho, for me, slow to slumber, takes a much greater number of sheep after sheep jumping free and, my God, over gate and façade... towards the Far Land of Nod... So, leave them alone... You won't have to find them... I'm herding them home... I'm awake... Right behind them...

Yes... I was surely off my feed... in need of some repairs... when... there came to me a way – Sent by an Angel, I suspected – A way to purge these unrelenting and all-consuming dark thoughts and stressful cares... This Angel came to me, as in a dream, tho it did seem to me that I was wide awake in the vortex of a swirling mess of endless stress... A parallel "between" is my ventured guess...

For calming my mind, so's to let me be... This sweet Angel's voice instructed me to fly... To soar aloft on butterfly wings... Where possums dance... And the willow sings... Between me and you... I might have a loose screw... But this is what I'm determined to do... I will soar aloft on butterfly wings... And attend, perchance, the Possum Spring Dance... And listen enrapt as the wise willow sings... Awake... Or in a dream... I go pleasantly-dreamily-somewhere...... Somewhere "between."

In my dream, I see the river... flowing gently past the town...

> *There's a whispering breeze in the willow trees*

And every now and then from where the river rounds the bend

Comes a whisper through the trees… "Sit you down… Sit you down…

Sit you down by the river… Sit you down… Watch it flow…

Give your cares to the waters… Cast them out… Let them go

With the magic of this willow tree… Let your troubles drift away to the sea

On the banks of the Warioto… Ease your mind… Let it be."

(The Warioto, I believe, was the Cherokee name for the Cumberland River… I grew up on that Cumberland River.)

So, with things as they are… And the Cumberland quite far… Morphing me some Monarch wings… I take to flight… Homing eastward towards a hint of new light…

Up over the mountains… And I'm on my way… Out over the desert… to the coming of day… Now, I see the Colorado… Streaks of red rock down below…

Carving deeply through the canyon… Winding south towards Mexico. And, there's the mighty Mississippi… Mister Handy's "Memphis Blues," And, I do believe that's Graceland… "Love Me Tender" – "Blue Suede Shoes"

I'm goin' home… Yes, I'm goin' home… I'm goin' home to get some home repair So, you'd better lookout… I said lookout now… "I'm Moving On," I'm almost there…

I'm hearing Nashville… Down there below me… There stands the Ryman… That's it I swear…

The Ryman Auditorium… WSM… Nashville Tennessee… Look at that… She's wearin' that hat with the price tag still on it… And she's so proud to be there… So glad she could come… But the rest of 'em… Start right in… Making me want to cry, eat peanuts, and drink way too much beer… And I'll start wallowing in it; **"I will always love you… I can't stop lovin' you… Crazy… Walking after midnight… Why don't you love me like you used to do? I'm walking the floor over you…… That last long day you said good-bye… Oh, Lord, I thought I would die… And, Lord help me, there stands the glass… But this true-lovin' daddy ain't comin' back… I'm movin' on… Keeping on the sunny side… Still I'd like to know; was it God or somebody else that made them Honky Tonk Angels?"**

Fiddles and banjos fill the air… I see my river by the Forty… And the lushest green I've ever seen… It's spring and "My, oh, Lordy," I will soon be at that very spot… That very spot that God begot… By the willow trees not far from town… I will breathe that air…

And I will sit me down… And I sit me down… And I look around……

I see river bottom land... Hickory trees...

Fish from the river and honey from bees...

There's buttermilk biscuits and blackberry jam...

Red-eye gravy on Tennessee ham...

Home sweet home... Tennessee home... Years gone by... Now here's where I...

Sit me down by that river... Sit me down... I'm watching it flow... Giving my cares to the waters... I cast them out... I let them go... And now..., a light goes on inside of me... Lifts me up... And turns the tide for me... On the banks of the Cumberland River... Ease my mind... And let me **be**...

Yes, I'm home... Smith County home... Oh, Lordy me... Look at what I see...

There's Ma in the kitchen baking three or four pies... Granny keeping' busy swatting' pesky ol' flies... Church on Sunday... Dinner on the ground... All day singing and gather all around

Grandpa telling' 'bout way back when

Raisin' up a family in Horseshoe Bend

Granny, four kids and nine hound dogs

Built that cabin outta fine oak logs

Grandpa tells all the family lore... Every tale is true... Plus a little bit more...

Somewhere between madness and clarity, old King Lear said: *"Let us pray and sing... And tell old tales... And laugh at gilded butterflies,"* and marvel at the *"mystery of things."*

So, I sat me down... I watched it flow...

And I tossed my cares... I let them go...

In the magic 'round the willow tree... Let my troubles drift away from me...

From the banks of the Cumberland River... Easing my mind and letting me be...

And the river flows... As the river flows...

All the worry goes... All the worry goes...

My Ma and my Pa... they had...

Two smart girls... Two big boys

Two could sing... Two made noise

Some got chiggers... Some got fleas

One baby poops… Another one pees

Yes ma'am, no ma'am, thank you ma'am, please

Carve that turkey and pass me the peas…

Four was enough… But I got born

Hay got wet… Pa drank corn

The hay did rot… Pa drank quite a lot

Drank a lotta corn by the Cumberland River

Said he wouldn't drink no corn no more

No… He wouldn't drink corn no more…

…Whoa… Pa never said that before

Then my Pa went down to the river and he sat down by the willow tree… And he watched the river flow… And he emptied all his whisky into the Cumberland River… Poured it out… Let it go… Soon after… All Pa's friends came… And they sat down beside my Pa… And, like pouring gasoline on a fire… They brought a considerable amount of corn whisky with them to that magical willow tree… And they shared it with my Pa… And it turned into a wake… And they told stories… And they sang songs… And, yes sir, it was magic… On the banks of the Cumberland River… Drinking corn by the willow tree…

Lord, the corn did flow… And the tears did flow…

'Til there was some doubt… What they cried about…

So, they all went fishing… Had a big fish fry

They fished and they laughed… And they slept… Bye and bye

So, that was my red-eye flight on butterfly wings…, to where possums dance and the willows sing… With catfish, ho cakes, Ma's apple pie… Grandpa's tales… And my, oh, my… Went back a few years… And I cleared my head… Said my prayers… And I slept like the dead… Enough said.

I smile at myself in the audience.

On stage: I take a brief curtain call and ask:

"What did you think?"

So, what did I think? I confess that I really liked it… Especially, the use of the titles of those iconic country songs in perfectly describing how I was feeling… Taking me back to every bar where I ever sat on a barstool: "Making me want to cry, eat peanuts, and drink way too much beer… Then, I'll start to wallow in it;

"I will always love you… I can't stop lovin' you… Crazy… Walking after midnight… Why don't you love me like you used to do?"

Yep... Been there... Done that way too many times. Honestly, I liked what I'd done with it so far. Sure did. Although, it's difficult for me to judge my own performance. I thought I was certainly... a good and respectful audience.

I'll let the piece sit, and take another look at it in a month or so. But, I do like it.

The Wizard of Ooze

My son, Garett told me about his encounter with grunion here in Venice. It made an impression on me. Why? I would investigate this, and write something akin to this in my reclusive workshop nestled in the attic behind my eyes. This was to be fertile ground. I took the same walk that Garett took. A fishy story, indeed. Here goes:

About a week before Easter of this past year, I was walking along the beach here... Alone... Late at night. And, I happened upon a *grunion* run. Grunion are little fish that spawn in the wet sand at high tide. There was a huge moon playing peek-a-boo, making the night really bright then totally black. Now, if you're expecting a grunion run and you attend with that in mind, that's one thing. But, if you're not expecting a grunion run... You've never seen a grunion run... And suddenly... Grunion are running all around your feet...; it's mildly unnerving. Grunion! - Millions of them... Squiggling all over the place. Then, they are gone! Just like that. Mother Nature giving phantom, fishy kisses in the night. I stood there for some time thinking about how various species survive and multiply... And, I thought of that finger of coastline. I knew it was out there, but I couldn't see it, due to darkness. But that big, near-full moon popped out, and I got a glimpse of the finger, pointing between the dark sea and sky.

That's when the show started. From a point just beyond the tip of the finger came a small pinpoint of light; like the finger had placed it there. Then everything became an old black and white film, with hues of blue. The point of light rose above the water and gave off a beam or cone of light that came towards me and stopped about thirty or forty yards from the shore. Out of a breaking wave, emerged a rather B-movie, translucent, bearded, ghost of a fellow, gliding over the water to hover in front of me. And did he look angry!?! He was pissed! Like he might explode with anger! I tried to yell, but nothing came out. I couldn't move my arms... *I must be having a nightmare. That's it! I'll just have to ride it out.*

He then raised one arm and made a motion like pulling a light switch: BOOM! Circus Lights! The whole beach lit up like night baseball at Dodger Stadium! And the surf was filled... Oh, my God... Filled with hundreds of his pals; a gathering of a "Pissed off Dead Sailor's Society." And, they all began to make wildly contorted silent screams, along with the Head Spook.

And me too!!! Surely, a scene inspired by that Munch painting, "The Scream." And, just as the *poop* was about to be in my pants, the Head Spook pulled the invisible light switch again and... Lights out... Just like the grunion; they were here, and they're gone. And, on cue, the moon popped out and lit up the beach. And, I was alone..., except for one woman. I looked up the beach and saw a young woman. We stared at each other for a second and then she ran. Boy, did she run! I yelled out, "Did you see that?" But she was kickin' sand. Now, maybe she did see it, and it scared her, or, maybe there was nothing, and she ran because there was a weird sound to my voice, and I was yelling at her. I don't know. Was this a dream? Or, maybe, a little psychotic episode? Was I on a *ley* line? I was definitely at the beach because I had some of that oil, tar shit on my shoe..., from offshore drilling... or leakage from passing tankers. It seeps up and onto the beach in globs and globules.

The question is: Did I perceive that energy, channeled through my visual vortex? Or, did I manufacture and perceive the event inside the belfry behind my eyes? When people hear voices, get messages, see movies at the beach that no one else sees, it's only natural to suspect a possible malfunction in the belfry. Joan of Arc heard voices, and she went off to fight for what she believed. But, serial killers sometimes hear voices too.

Imagine Abraham's dilemma? If a voice said to me:

"This is God. I want you to sacrifice your child on a burning altar."

I would have to say, "Look, God, my incoming messages have been a little unusual lately. On the slightest chance that I might be picking up the wrong channel, I'll have to pass... And, with all due respect, I would need to see two forms of identification. And, by the way, couldn't You have come up with a better way to achieve what You wanted, without letting Your only Son to be crucified? That doesn't make sense... Does it? Maybe, to You, it makes sense... But, not to me."

I painted what I had seen at the beach: The Wizard of Ooze.

BEHIND THESE EYES SUCH SWEET MADNESS LIES

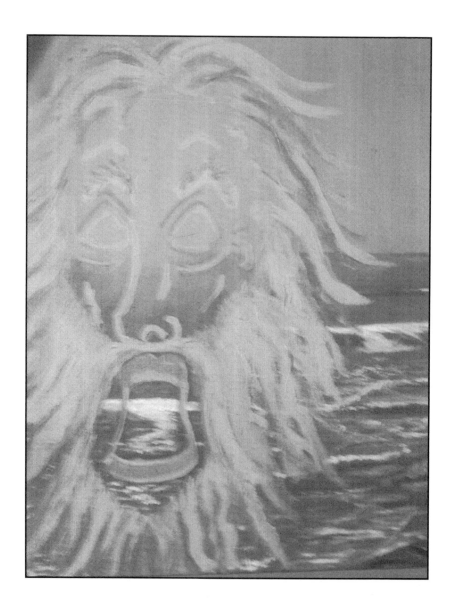

At home, in my chair, in the midst of some fitful dozing, I became aware of gentle, caressing strokes across my forehead. Athena! She began sweeping up debris, righting some overturned thoughts and giving a general sprucing-up to my attic. She kissed me on the lips… And, before leaving, she played a beautiful Chopin Nocturne on her Steinway Grand… Heaven… In the morning, I awoke with a smile on my face.

Damn Yankees and Lil Abner

That first summer, when I toured in *Damn Yankees*... I quickly learned how to make a scene to be all about me. During "Whatever Lola Wants," Lola (Patty Karr) was dancing, very seductively, in a follow-spot while we, the ball team, observed from the semi-darkness. I was smoking a cigar and each time Lola did one of her sexy bumps, I would make my cigar glow in the dark... Big laughs!

The director/producer, Stanley Prager was called to rein me in, and I quickly learned how *not to* steal focus. There were plenty of other laughs. Doing Damn Yankees each night was an eye-opener for me. Certainly, for me, this musical comedy thing was much more fun than opera. The show was like riding a wonderful horse. All you had to do was to hop on and ride that mother for two hours. Great fun. I don't recall ever having a bad audience. We just showed up... Jumped onto that horse's back and let'er rip. Yahoo! I expected this to happen with every other show. Not so. *Damn Yankees* was an exception. However, *Gems of Burlesque* with Sherry Britton was even better. More on that later.

The following year that same Stanley Prager hired me to star as ABNER in a touring company of *Lil Abner*. I made sure there were no cigars onstage behind me. I had learned my lesson. But, my three-year-old daughter, Jennifer, played the matinees and stole the show. In Dogpatch, we had to come up with something…, anything that could be deemed as "necessary," or else Dogpatch was going to be blown to smithereens by an atomic bomb. Little Jennifer made a "cross-in-one" in her little Dogpatch costume, holding a "potty." Huge, contagious laugh from the matinee audiences. When the audience laughed, Jennifer wore a big fake smile across and into the wings. The next scene I had to come on and sing a ballad. The audience would sometimes still be laughing when I started my song. Drat! Upstaged by my own little girl. I should have called Stanley Prager.

My Daisy Mae was Kitty Dolan. Renee Taylor was Appassionata Von Climax.

Later, Prager hired me for an episode that he was directing, of *Car 54; Where are You*? I later worked for producer/writer, Nat Hiken with Phil Silvers in a TV musical *special* called *The Ballad of Louie the Louse*. One day, I called Hiken aside and suggested to him how he could rewrite a particular scene. Hiken gave me a rather stunned, quizzical look, and walked away, shaking his head. I, wisely, made no further suggestions. Prager went on to direct Neil Simon's first Broadway show, *Come, Blow Your Horn*.

Only one agent saw me in *Lil Abner*. He came to Fort Lee, New Jersey to see the show, and told me to come see him in New York, when my tour was over. Yowzah! We had another month on tour, but as soon as I got back to New York, I went to see the agent… 200 West 57th Street… Just across the street from Carnegie Hall. Finally, here comes my big break. He seemed glad to see me; telling me that I would someday be a well-known Broadway performer. Stop. He also told me that he was getting out of show business and was moving to Greece… On Thursday. Following that encouraging possibility with a bad ending, my next line was, "May I take your order?"

The Upstairs at the Downstairs

37 West 56th Street, NY, NY

The first time that I uttered the words, "May I take your order?" was back in the fall of 1958. Julius Monk had seen me on that tour of *Damn Yankees*, at The Theatre by the Sea in Matunuck, R.I. And, he had hired me to cover the three gentlemen in the show. It was a time for satire, hobnobbing, and late hours. Which means... We were poking fun at politics and rich people... And sitting around, getting drunk after work. This began, for me, just after Labor Day, at 37 West 56th Street, The Upstairs at the Downstairs, where six actors were rehearsing the new fall cabaret revue under the supervision of debonair impresario, Julius Monk. The name of the show was *Demi Dozen*. The performers were accompanied by Gordon Connell and Stan Keen at twin pianos. The talented performers were Ceil Cabot, Jane Connell, Jean Arnold, George Hall, Jack Fletcher and Gerry Matthews. They were all good, especially, Jane Connell and Gerry Mathews.

And, I could not take my eyes off Ceil Cabot. Besides her talent, energy, and that enormous smile; I realized that, in many ways she was a much younger replica of my mother. For example, they both had a problem controlling their bladder when they laughed too hard. "Lookout for the wet spot on stage right," was a known warning when following Ceil on stage. As I say, I was to "cover" the three men. Estelle Parsons, who later went into the show, was to cover the women. I, also, got to wait tables, where I made more money than the actors I covered. The actors didn't appreciate that. The next year, I begged off covering the actors, so I could be free to take other acting jobs.

The rehearsals and the attendant figures were fascinating. There was, of course, Julius, the gentleman fashion plate who spoke and gave direction with a soft, totally indecipherable combination of British and Southern accent; partnered with the "not soft spoken," and micromanaging owner, Irving Haber. The two were definitely an odd couple. Some people disliked Mr. Haber, but I liked and admired him in many ways. He could be quite imposing at times. Whereas Julius Monk was elegant, Irving Haber was not elegant. With Haber, came Doris, his second in command.

Previously, Haber had owned a small, basement club called The Playgoers on the corner of 51st Street and Sixth Avenue. Morey Amsterdam had been the original star attraction there. Plus, small cabaret revues were presented in the basement; beginning with a show called, "Four Below," with Gerry Matthews, Dody Goodman, Jack Fletcher and June Erickson. There were three revues done there, and gaining in popularity, and joined by impresario Julius Monk, Irving Haber, moved the operation to its new incarnation: the old Wanamaker townhouse on 56th Street.

Besides owning The Upstairs at the Downstairs, Haber owned a string of six Gypsy Tea Kettles, where tealeaf readers offered their time, wisdom, and comfort to those who would have tea and a sandwich. To me, it seemed to serve as a poor man's "shrink." People were lined up in the morning waiting to see their favorite reader. The star reader was a man, apparently, from India. He wore a fashionable turban. He always had a cue waiting to see him. Can't remember his name.

In the main Tea Kettle at 200 West 50th Street, the entrance was between Broadway and 7th Avenue and Haber's office looked out on 50th Street, while the restaurant, where the "gypsies' did their thing, looked out on both 50th Street and 7th Avenue, caddy-corner to the Roxy Theatre and around the corner from Lou Walters' Latin Quarter.

As I walked into Haber's office one afternoon, Mr. Haber was at his desk doing some apparently very interesting work. Usually, when I came in, he would be his usual in-charge-full-throttle-bigger-than-life self. That day was different. It was as if he was in a deep meditation. He was quiet and peaceful. With a sharp lead pencil, he was carefully entering little numbers into tiny squares on a ledger. Eventually, he looked up, smiled, and said, "Hi, Buddy." Then, he went directly back into his meditation... His work: Putting things in order. I had never seen him like this. It was as if I had witnessed a miracle. A transformation. I exaggerate, but I was impressed... Nicely so.

The waiters at the club on 56th Street..., (All actors, including Maitre D and leading Strasburg proponent, the very droll Bruce Kirby) helped a work crew put the final touches on the place. I helped lay the carpet. The policy for the service staff was an actor's perfect situation: You could leave to do a show or a film and get your job back immediately on return. I was able to take advantage of this several times. I once left for three months to do a film in Germany, and when I got back, my job at the Upstairs was waiting for me. At the club, I worked mostly as a waiter, bartender, or Maître d'hôtel before writing and performing there in two of the shows. The shows in the Upstairs room ran for an eight-month season. Fortunately, with the usual good reviews, business was good. At the time, this was "the only show in town" for smart, topical, sophisticated humor.

During my first month at The Upstairs at the Downstairs, I would see a man with curious eyebrows that lofted at odd times; like, on being greeted, "Hello," his eyebrows would rise to great heights, and he would lean back a bit to get a better view. Upon assessing the greeter, he would make a decision to grin slightly... Or to just stare..., with eyebrows frozen in a pointed and apprehensive arch. He would come to see the attractive and talented young Ceil Cabot, who also, had eyebrows, equally as interesting. But, her eyebrows moved up and down as two straight lines as two window shades... Going up and down, and finally, knitting together in the center, reflecting her bemusement or "confusment." She was rather small in physical stature as compared to the fascinating, very tall man, with his well-travelled eyebrows. He, being tall, very tall, with receding hairline chasing back fairly long blond tresses. And when I say, "receding hairline," I don't mean a retreating line of rabbits, which is the grade school joke book definition of a *"receding hairline."* Although, there is a rabbit in the story, and there might have been a few rabbits up his sleeve, or in his hat, but if they came out, they came out *soooo* fast that no one could ever see them.

The tall man's piercing saucer eyes made judgments over a nose of generous dimension, creating an aura quite magical. Yes, all in all, a magical presence indeed. And, he had a magical secret. His secret was... He had a rubber chicken, and with that rubber chicken, he could cast a spell; an amusing and loving spell that would last a lifetime. The tall magic man had focused his seductive spell on the attractive and talented young woman who sang a song about a rabbit... A rabbit, who, alas, did not have the *rabbit habit*, in a ditty sung by the talented Miss Cabot. So, being no fool, the young beauty was definitely *pickin' chicken*. And, together they raised eyebrows, and laughter and children, and they lived happily ever after.

They were Ceil (Cabot) and Carl Ballantine. Carl, The Amazing Ballantine, could nearly always be found at the "track." Carl and Ceil named their two daughters, Saratoga and Caliente, after the two famous race tracks.

The Amazing Ballantine was a very funny and unique slapstick magician whose tricks, by design, never worked. His act was, in a way, like Bob Williams and his Dog, Louie. Louie would ignore Bob's extremely enthusiastic coaxing to climb a ladder, or jump through a hoop. With Bob's very loving, but ever increasing enthusiastic urgings, Louie would finally…, finally…, stroll, slowly, *under* the hoop. You get the idea. I was told that Bob Williams had amassed quite a fortune in real estate, in Malibu and Las Vegas… All done with a dog that seemed to perform not much of anything.

When working as Maître d'hôtel, one New Year's Eve, I was called from the Upstairs room to come quickly to the Downstairs… Trouble… As I rushed down, I saw Billy, (Haber's brother), who was the regular bartender there, facing a big problem. A man, obviously drunk, was leaning on the bar and pointing his finger at Billy. I approached the man from the side. While looking at and pointing his finger at Billy, he said, in a low growly accent: "In two minutes, you are going to die."

He then turned to Billy's wife, Gloria, who ran the cloakroom, and repeated the same finger-pointing, and saying: "In two minutes you are going to die." Then, noticing me standing beside him, with eyes ablaze, he pointed his finger, almost to the tip of my nose, and repeated: "And... In two minutes, you are going to die."

Being New Year's Eve, and towards the end of the evening, and after having a few drinks myself, and after seeing that the man had no bullets in his pointed finger, I took his finger between my thumb and forefinger, and as I was walking him out, I said, softly: "Don't ever come back here. And, never let me see you again... Never." I walked him out while still holding his pointed finger between my thumb and forefinger. This was apparently somewhat sobering to the "would-be-assassin." As he shuffled down the street, I called out, "Never again!"

What I am about to tell you now, I am not exactly proud about, but I was without self-control, or so I tell myself:

There was, on the corner of 56th Street and Sixth Avenue, Al Green's diner. Ronny Graham, Jimmy Catusi, and I, with one or two others (I can't remember who) from the club were having our 2 AM, New Year's Day breakfast there at Al Green's. While telling about the man with the unloaded finger, lo-and-behold, out the window, I saw the same man carrying on a rant with himself... And walking briskly towards Al Green's front door. Here came a fastball down the middle of my plate. I said to Ronny, Jimmy, and the others: "Watch this."

The entrance to Al Greens was in two stages. First, you entered into a square vestibule and then, through another door into the diner. (This was to keep the frigid air out during the winter months, and to keep the air-conditioned air inside during the hot summer months.)

I waited just inside the inner door until he entered through the outside door. As he came in, I opened my door and shouted: "I told you... Never!" The man had seen the devil. He ran for his life into the city that never sleeps. It was great fun for me, to do and to tell about... But, then, I felt sorry for him... And, ashamed. What if the man's wife had just left him, or his mother had just died, or he had just lost his job, or he'd been told that he had two weeks to live. The poor man surely had problems... And, I had been a bully. As much fun as it was, it haunts me. It would be a great relief for me to know that his life had since improved after that unfortunate finger-pointing episode.

A list of performers and writers who had worked at The Playgoers and The Upstairs at the Downstairs contain many of the very best sketch and songwriters of the time. Dare I list?

Some of the writers were Rod Warren, Tom Jones and Harvey Schmitt, Cy Coleman, Ronny Graham, G Wood, Woody Allen, Michael McWhinney, Sam Pottle, David Axlerod, Bill Weeden and David Finkle, Jack Holmes, Jack Urbant, Herb Hartig, Bill Dana, Claib Richardson, Murray Grand, James Shelton, Jack Yellen, Lily Tomlin (Her own monologues), Fannie Flagg, Bill Brown, Louis Botto, and your humble servant (Mostly, my own material). Those few, immediately, come to mind, but there were many other excellent writers.

A few of the performers over the years were Gerry Mathews, Ronny Graham, Lily Tomlin, Linda Lavin, Fannie Flagg, Betty Aberlin, Ceil Cabot, June Ericson, Jack Fletcher, Marian Mercer, RG Brown, "Fred" Macintyre Dixon, Dick Libertini, Mona Abboud, Jane and Gordon Connell, Billy McCutcheon, Carol Morley, Marilyn Child, Virgil Curry, Mclean Stevenson, Bill Hinnant, Jane Alexander, Phil Bruns, Pat Stanley, Dixie Carter, Ruth Buzzi, Mary Louise Wilson, Estelle Parsons, Freddi Weber, Judy Knaiz, Janie Sell, Bud Cort, Judy English, Christina Pickles, Bob Kalaban, Jenny Lou Law, Dody Goodman, Ellen Hanley, Del Close, Blossom Dearie, Annie Ross, Lovelady Powell, George Furth, Nancy Dussault. Madeline Kahn, Jim Catusi, and Himself.

Some acts in the Downstairs room: I saw Mabel Mercer, Joan Rivers, Tammy Grimes, Milt Kamen, Jackie Vernon, Will Holt and Dolly Jonah, Rose Murphy and "Slam" Stewart, Larry Blyden, Alice Ghostly, Ronny Graham, Barry Manilow and Jeanne Lucas, and Bette Midler. Middler did a New Year's Eve show in the Upstairs.

The rotund, constantly sweaty, deadpan comic, Jackie Vernon was a favorite of mine… To be honest, it was one particular story of his that was one of my favorites. His story was about a teenage Indian girl and a young Indian boy. They fell in love. They were from different tribes. One tribe lived on one side of a lake, and the other tribe lived on the opposite side of the lake. Their families forbade their marriage. Heartbroken, the two young lovers swam to meet each other in the middle of the lake; He, from his family's side of the lake, and she, from her family's side of the lake. And there, while embracing in the middle of the lake, they went under; ending their young lives. Recently, commemorating that tragic drowning, the lake was named, "Lake Stupid."

It was here, at The Upstairs at The Downstairs that I first saw and made friends with Ronny Graham. And, Mabel Mercer would often be playing that Downstairs room. Both, in their own unique ways, were revelations to me. I must say; it took me a while to appreciate the artistry of Mabel Mercer. Mabel was already past her prime, vocally. She sat on a high-back chair... A throne; where she did appear to be quite royal in both style and demeanor. Audiences sat enrapt, savoring her every word and gesture and whim. By and large, these audiences were rather regal themselves. But, I soon was an admirer. Ronny was another animal, altogether... A madman. A brilliant madman.

Also, I learned a lot by watching Joan Rivers improve her act from one night to the next by recording each show to review what worked and what didn't work as well. Always honing and perfecting the act.

I must pass along this following story that I witnessed, about how Mabel appreciated her fans just as much as her fans loved her. Mabel had done two sold-out shows in that small room (The Downstairs) on this Saturday night. She was exhausted, and was leaving the club for her home on 110th Street, just north of Central Park, when a couple breezed through the front door, saying they had flown from Majorca just to see Mabel. Mabel said that she was sorry but was finished for the night. The couple could see that Mabel was very tired, but they persisted; explaining that their plane was late and that they had reservations for both of her earlier shows... Which they did.

Sam Hamilton, Mabel's piano accompanist, was still standing at the bar holding his usual glass of club soda. Mabel did an about face and whispered into Sam's ear. Sam nodded, and they reentered the small room. The couple was then ushered to a table. Mabel joined them at their table, had a cup of tea and did a private show just for the two of them. It was as if three friends were chatting at a table in a darkened room... Only, here, one of them was singing for the other two.

We, who staffed the club that night, watched from the bar area, as a debt was being paid to a loyal audience of two. We were in awe as Mabel sang and then nodded to Sam to go into the next song after song after song. It wasn't the same show that she had done twice earlier. She sang songs that were favorites of her two fans.

Mabel wished them a "Goodnight" and went home. The couple from Majorca was, at this time, a mellowed and happy pair. So were we who had witnessed that extraordinary early Sunday morning moment in a small club in New York, New York.

Of course, Mabel was world famous and was worshipped by many, but as most show folk know... When one doesn't get the bookings, and the flow of money stops, times can get hard. Such was the case with Mabel in her later years. Several years after Mabel's passing, Marian Mercer (not related; other than being the best at what they did), Marian told me about one of those "slow" times. Mabel was in dire straits, but, before the final curtain, Mabel won the New York Lottery: Obviously by the hand of God... Or Deus Ex Machina. I believe she said it was for $50,000. Sometimes, things do go right.

Himself and Mabel Mercer at her home "Up Country."

I had fallen off the turnip truck and landed in the middle of a fairy tale. Definitely, not a fairy tale was the Cuban Missile Crisis in October of 1962. Immediately following one of the preview performances there, in the Upstairs room, a man stepped onto the stage and began to make an announcement. He seemed to be official, and quite somber, saying:

"Ladies and gentlemen; may I have your attention, please. I have an official announcement: In case of an atomic attack, please follow these three simple steps: Place your right hand on your right knee… Place your left hand on your left knee… Bend over as far as you can… And kiss your ass goodbye." The audience reaction was mixed.

Idle Thoughts

In recent years, by carefully honing my *traveling without leaving* technique, I have been able to revive some of my favorite performances onstage and elsewhere. Also, a few of my least favorite productions deserve their return. Again, mind you, I experience these theatrical adventures without leaving this comfortable chair in my attic home. I will, indeed, be in two places at the same time: in my chair and at some distant venue. In the beginning, I suspected that I might be dreaming. But, dreams cannot compare. I have no control over dreams. Here, while *traveling*, I focus and participate as I intend.

With our various techniques, we actors inhabit our on-stage characters while our twin-self observes from nearby. (Another case of two circles sharing a common radius) One friend says that she watches herself from the Lincoln box. In my case, I have learned that the physical distance between the two of us does not affect our relationship. I might remain at home in California while acting in one of Tom Topor's two short plays atop Riverside Church in New York. After seeing the play, Harold Clurman will drop by our apartment, (*as he did*), and offer his assessment.

I had met Clurman at The First Annual Playwright's Conference in Aspen, where he was a revelation. He was our resident celebrity director. He began each day by talking to us about writing, and acting, and committing to a purposeful life. His usual style was to begin on a low key... Then, slowly inspire himself into a passionate crescendo; at times, seeming to elevate himself off the floor. Amazing! We didn't need coffee to get on our feet after that.

Clurman and I shared our experiences of having had heart attacks within the past year. (And, here we were in Aspen at 10,000 ft.) Having vivid memories of a heart attack is understandable, but Clurman said that he clearly remembered every day of his life. He was totally in touch with the whole of his life. I have since learned that there are a few other people who have that ability. I won't forget Harold Clurman, with his contagious passion for life; and, especially, for a responsible life in the theatre.

(Confession: A question pops into my mind. Suddenly, I have doubts about why I am writing this book... To shake my cage about being such a rotten husband and a sometime-absent-father? I don't think I'm trying to justify or explain my actions through confessing my guilt... Or, am I? I have used the term, "Self-mythologizing." Am I trying to romanticize a life that should not be romanticized? At present, I am totally confused. Maybe I should finish writing the book... Get it out of my system..., and drop it into my trunk in the attic... A personal archaeological find to be filed away. No doubt, I am trying to validate myself in some positive way. I am clearly unearthing something. What? And, why? Am I slinging paint onto a canvas in hopes of getting some sort of abstract picture of my life as art? Will it turn out be a worthwhile painting...? A worthwhile picture of a worthwhile life? Obviously, I do have my doubts.)

I continue:

This popped into my mind: When revisiting some of my early years, I think about Johnny Jordan, when he and I were about five years old, and listening to an older boy, named Vernon, telling us about the sex act. An eighteen-year-old boy telling five-year-old boys about the process of the sex act can be difficult for the five-year-old boys to grasp. We had no idea. He told us all about it:

"That's what your Mommy and Daddy do at night, when you're asleep."

Johnny started crying. "My mother and father don't do that! You're making that shit up!"

"And that's what you'll be doing when you get old enough."

"You're a liar!"

"And you'll like it more than anything else you do."

Johnny said, "Bullshit!" And, he was crying and punching Vernon in the stomach. It didn't bother Vernon. I didn't know what to think, but it didn't seem right to me. No. That couldn't be right because those parts were used for peeing.

But, Vernon was right. And I do, very much, enjoy revisiting intimate encounters I've had with some of the most desirable women imaginable. Realize that, presently, all of my delicious Tantric Tangos for Two take place only in the attic behind my eyes, by way of *traveling without leaving,* across time and space. Nevertheless, they are real, to me. Even though, many of my best and dearest partners have *passed over…*, I resurrect them with all their beauty and talent for each and every affair. I smell them, touch them, laugh with them, dance with them, adore them, and am quite often confused by them. However, I do find it fascinating that, while making love, I can usually tell whether a woman is a Democrat or a Republican. One is liberal, in every sense, and the other is conservative. And that about sums it up.

Of course, with my ego, I note that they all seem to enjoy our indulgences with total satisfaction. As I was chatting backstage with one of my cast mates, while in rehearsals for a new show, although, we had had an assignation or two, she said she couldn't recall them. So, she wasn't impressed. She was a former drinker, too.

I appreciate that what few complaints they have are admittedly well founded. Those complaints usually stem from my own embarrassingly shoddy memory. It doesn't go well to say, "I love you Mary," when you are caressing Susan. There's no easy way of getting around such unfortunate lapses. One mustn't call Joan Fontaine, Olivia. Oops. Or, tell, in front of Rose and guests, how much you've always enjoyed Rose's blackberry pie, when Rose points out that she has never made a blackberry pie in her life. Oops. (That was Lucy, who had made such delicious blackberry pies.)

Sometimes… Sometimes…, the best evenings are spent with just being together and listening to good music… Bach, Mozart, Gershwin or Puccini; or some favorite recordings by Jo Stafford or Sinatra; followed by Chopin nocturnes and sweet sleep… Followed by a nice brunch, with eggs benedict for Vivien.

(Notwithstanding that earlier self-condemnation about me being a "rotten husband and a sometime-absent-father," my daughter, Julienne said to her children: "Papa is not great at being a husband but he's amazing as a father. He's been more present living 3,000 miles away than some dad's that live in the same house." Julienne will never know how much that meant to me. My children and grandchildren are foremost in my heart.)

Children, Fistfights, Movies, and Booze

About thirty-five years ago, I began to have a few rare premonitions. One vivid one was when taking the New Haven train to Darien; I flashed on my son Brandon (Bran); drifting, motionless, under ice, along the bottom of a lake or river. It was shockingly vivid. However, it never happened as I saw it. But, when I got to Darien, I found out that Bran had fallen through the ice on a pond, along Five Mile River, earlier that morning. His sister, Justine, stretching prone across the ice, had given him her hand. He was wet and cold but alive. I can't explain that, at all. Bran was usually the one who took care of his brother and sisters.

Once, while in San Francisco while, in a meditative state, I saw my Justine in Connecticut. She had a stomach problem. I phoned, and she did have a stomach ache. I saw what she was wearing. Jennifer said that it was what I described and that Justine rarely ever dressed like that. Now, I can't recall what it was that was so unusual about how she dressed, but, her stomach problem passed. Can't explain that either.

Occasionally, I make a very brief recollection to my days of moonshine (the kind that came in unmarked bottles)... Plus, scotch, bourbon, gin, vodka, beer, brandy, cognac and other fermentations. I guess I do this as a reminder. Those recalls are thoroughly enjoyable for about a minute. After that, the darkness of a hell on earth returns as the reminder. I usually drank late at night, and at home: not a social drinker. My father did not drink. My mother and her whole family were prone to falling victim to the overindulgence syndrome. Although, on her death certificate, it says death due to heart failure, it was in fact cirrhosis of the liver.

My drinking wasn't in full swing until I was into my late thirties. At one point, I was playing the lead character in a film called, of all things: *Christmas Evil*. I never drank on the job, but after work on location, and on my fairly long limo drive back to my home on Riverside Drive, Jack Daniels was my steady companion. The film was written and directed by a very intelligent and dedicated young man named Lewis Jackson.

I took the job because I needed a job. I auditioned, and I won the role. That's why I took the job. Many actors say they take jobs only after much scrutiny and debate. I happened to be watching the wonderful Maureen Stapleton being interviewed on an afternoon news show on the local NBC station in New York, when she was asked how she chose her roles. She thoughtfully considered the question and said, "First, I read it. If I don't throw-up, I take the job."

But, in this case, the role was a wonderful psychological study about how a young impressionable boy, who had been told that Santa Claus was "good," comes to a tragic end. From the first scene, when the boy, thinking he hears Santa downstairs, finds a shocking scene taking place between his mother and Santa, we know that this will not end well. The boy rushes back upstairs to his room and in a fit of rage accidently cuts his hand. On a close-up, we see blood trickle across his hand. It is red. It is the red of rage. There is much red throughout the film.

(One of my daughter Fiona's many wonderfully written lyrics very well describe her color red:

"But he's been pretty much yellow / And I've been kinda blue / But all I can see is Red, red, red, red, red now / What am I gonna do")

The young boy had been told that Santa rewarded all the good children with nice things and that bad children would receive either nothing or something on the dark side a la lumps of coal. In mythology, the German Santa Claus was a figure that rewarded "good" and punished "bad." Children were told that Santa and his helper, Black Pete, would visit all parents and ask if their children had been either good or bad. If the parents said they were good, their children would receive presents. If they had been bad, they might be stuffed into a sack and hauled away to who-knows-what end.

When the troubled boy becomes a man, and not being the sharpest tack in the box, he carries that ingrained idea of good and bad to extremes. Guess what? The now young man's job is working in a toy factory. While being a dedicated craftsman and making the finest of toys at home in his own workshop, the factory where he works turns out shabby toys. Becoming increasingly more disillusioned and enraged by all sorts of bad behavior around him, he resorts to violence and murder. At a tipping point in his troubled mind, he becomes Santa Claus: While observing himself in the mirror, and while spirit-gumming his Santa beard to his face, he makes the fateful transition... He takes on the responsibilities of being Santa Claus... A vengeful Santa Clause.

After a stressful night of mayhem, Santa sleeps in his van.

He paints his van to look like Santa's sleigh. And, lookout, bad guys! In Santa's bag he has a hatchet, a soldier with a sword, and other toys for violence. Ironically, he uses those toys in the killing of some rude people as they are leaving their church on Christmas Eve. In another case, he dispenses his rage with the star from the top of a Christmas tree. He cannot fathom why people don't appreciate the difference between "good" and "bad." Whether, literally or in his mind, the frightened and disillusioned Santa is chased through the streets by crowds of villagers bearing torches, who want to kill Santa. The final scene is a most magical exit made by Santa as he soars off into the night, crossing the moon at its fullest, and exclaiming to the world:

"Merry Christmas to all… And, to all a good night!"

Before shooting began, Jackson sent me to a private screening of Fritz Lang's film, *M*, starring Peter Lorre. The reason being that some humanity is within a man even though he has committed the vilest of crimes. When cornered by the enraged townspeople who are about to kill him, Peter Lorre's character pleads his case: "You are capable of making the decision to kill me or not to kill me. When I kill, I cannot help myself." Because pedophiles have no choice? But, in my case, Harry (Santa) was doing what he thought he was obligated to do. And, he couldn't understand why the angry torch-bearing townspeople couldn't see that he was doing what he was supposed to do… Reward the "good" and punish the "bad."

There were scenes that I couldn't relate to. "How do I do this?" The first time I approached Jackson about my problem, he gave me the perfect direction: "It's abstract." I was home-free after that. "I'm the paint in this picture." Jackson is the painter.

Watching the first screening of *Christmas Evil*: I did have mixed feelings about the film, especially, due to one scene in which the police gathered all the fake Santas for a line-up. (The only scene in the film that I was not in) Some people liked the scene because it was deemed to be funny. It was not laugh-out-loud funny. It was "irony" funny. But, for me, it hit a wrong note. In the spirit of full-disclosure, I have to admit that I also found it hard to think of *Dr. Strangelove* as being funny. Also, for me, the pace of the film, at times, was lingering too long on the task at hand.

Not being a "horror film," commercially, the film was a failure, but it later surfaced and, according to some, has become an "official cult classic." The film is shown during the Christmas season most every year at selected movie houses for the occult. Maybe Jackson didn't come up with the film he had in mind, but, under the circumstances, he did a pretty damn good job. Lewis Jackson says, "It's a film that will not die."

I worked six weeks straight on *Christmas Evil*, six days a week. During that time, I had a two-day window that I used to work on the film, *Dressed to Kill* starring Michael Caine, Nancy Allen, and Angie Dickinson, directed by Brian De Palma. I was not in great shape for those two days, but we filmed one short scene and a second long scene with me and Nancy Allen in a hotel room. In the scene, Nancy was playing the hooker, and I was her John... a John who only wanted to talk. I wasn't aware that the scene had not made the cut until I saw it in a theater. I had nice billing, but my on-screen time was about ten seconds. By itself, the cut scene was a good scene, but it did not belong in the film. Most of the scenes in the film were short and well-paced. Nancy lobbied to have it put back in for the European market but lost to her husband, her director, Brian De Palma.

CHILDREN, FISTFIGHTS, MOVIES, AND BOOZE

A few months after filming *Christmas Evil,* I began work on *The World According to Garp,* starring Robin Williams, Glenn Close, and John Lithgow, directed by George Roy Hill. I played the wrestling coach, Garp's father-in-law. My daughter was played by Mary Beth Hurt.

The World According to Garp was shot mostly on Fisher's Island in The Long Island Sound. Fisher's Island is a small private island with its own airport. Otherwise, it could be reached by ferry from Connecticut. A beautiful place. And rich. With one bar. One bar was all I needed. In the bar, there was our makeup artist. I did not see him, but early next morning, in makeup, he told me that he had seen me tossing back quite a few. He said that he recognized himself in me. Only, that now he no longer drinks. I worked for two weeks and then had six weeks off before resuming interior shots at the studios in Queens.

During that six-week layoff, I hit my "bottom." (Actually, I landed on my bottom) I have now been sober for thirty-three years. On May 29th, 1981, following a fist fight with a New York cab driver, in the presence of my two youngest children, Maude Amber and Fiona, I terminated my relationship with John Barleycorn. Otherwise, I would have missed the last half of a wonderful life.

I was not drinking at the time, but I was terribly hung-over from the previous two nights. I had picked the girls up from a playdate, and we were walking along Broadway and crossing 111th Street. As we were crossing, a taxi came screeching around the corner onto 111th Street, heading towards Riverside Drive… I was holding my daughters by the hand… One on each side.

As the cab driver made his fast and reckless turn, I had to jump, holding onto my girls, to avoid getting hit. Other pedestrians scurried out of the way and yelled at the driver. I yelled: "Hey! Jackass!!!" At least, that's what Maude Amber says, I yelled. I thought I had yelled, "You son-of-a-bitch!" But recently, while telling the story, Maude Amber, who was six at the time, said: "No, Daddy. You yelled something like, "Hey, Jack." So, "Hey! Jackass!" is probably what I did yell.

Apparently, it was offensive enough to cause cab driver to screech to a stop. The driver got out of his cab and came walking at a stride towards me. I knew it was on. There was a young man standing on the sidewalk. I asked him to please hold my girls that I had to "attend to this." He said something like, "No, sir. I can't do that kind of thing." Maude Amber says that a woman held her in her arms, and another woman held Fiona. All this was happening very fast, but I noticed that the driver resembled what Franco Harris' younger and bigger brother might have looked like. (Franco Harris was the fullback for the Super Bowl Champion Pittsburg Steelers.) He was huge; with a large afro, and I remember seeing rings.

Neither of us spoke a word. We went at it. Although, I had been a boxer in my youth, I began flailing roundhouse rights and lefts with everything I had. One of his punches, along with one of his rings, made an imprint on my noggin. We wrestled to the pavement. And, right away, he jumped up, scrambled back to his cab and sped off. I guess he was afraid the police might show up. They didn't. In my hung-over state, the cabbie had made short work of me.

I was on my back in the middle of 111th Street, looking up at a circle of people that had gathered around me. I was looking up, and they were looking down. I don't remember what, if anything, was being said, with the exception of one elderly African American gentleman. It was Fellini-esque. With his light brown skin, sparkling eyes, and warm smile, framed by shiny silver hair, he spoke in soft, measured tones: "You shouldn't do that in front of the children."

I collected my girls. Maude Amber was crying because she thought I had been cut from my forehead all the way down the side of my face. It was just a trickle of blood coming from a cut near my hairline. There was a drugstore on the corner, and some nice citizen escorted us inside and had me cleaned up a bit. Maude Amber stopped crying. For the life of me, I can't remember Fiona's reaction.

I walked the girls with me over to nearby St. Luke's for a few stitches. It was early Saturday evening, so the emergency room was already crowded. It seemed that every time we were next-in-line, another emergency came rolling in with victims of gunshot wounds and stabbings.

I was proud of my girls. They never complained even once about being stuck in a crowded emergency room with me for over two hours. Finally, the girls watched as I got a few stitches from a nice nurse who explained to the girls exactly what she was doing. The girls got a good ER education that Saturday night on the upper Westside of New York City. On the other hand, they probably got more than little girls need to see from their father's display. But, honestly, there was no way out of the situation.

I never had another drink after that. I was sorry the girls saw the fight, and I hated the fact that I was so hung-over that I was not up to my fighting best. It's a male thing. Sometimes, fist fighting is the only alternative. Falstaff would disagree, but to run, never entered my mind. Not much entered my mind. It was on. Notwithstanding all the negative aspects, I thoroughly enjoyed it.

Lying on my back in the middle of the street in front of my children served as my "hitting bottom," I guess. So, the incident did serve a purpose. Unlike Lewis Jackson's poor character in *Christmas Evil*, I did not die after facing a "torch-bearing mob." Maybe, the taxi driver wasn't evil. But, why in the world would he, being in hot pursuit, (or being hotly pursued,) interrupt that chase to take issue with someone who has called out, "Hey! Jackass!" Maybe, that day he was "hitting bottom," and I gave him an excuse to go berserk. He drove away. I got sober. For me: thirty-three sober years and still going strong. For him: Did that incident change his life? Does he remember as I remember? For the young man standing on the sidewalk who might have been traumatized with the possibility of such a responsibility; did the incident cause him to have some version of "hitting psychological bottom?" His frightened face haunts me. The old man who told me that I "…should not do that in front of the children; is he still alive? Probably, not. I would like to thank him. Maybe he'll walk into one of my soirees and surprise me. I'd like that. I would like to give him a big hug. And, how did that incident affect Maude Amber and Fiona's psyches?

As John Cameron Swayze used to say about his Bulova Watches: It "takes a licking but keeps on ticking."

Thankfully, so far, I keep on "ticking."

Auditions, Radio City Music Hall and...

So, here I am. How did I get here? Luck? As the ancient philosopher said: "Good luck is what happens when preparation meets opportunity." The first time I heard that quote, it was from Tom Landry, the old football coach. I believe he said: "Success is what happens when preparation meets opportunity." In my case, it was "unique, or unorthodox, preparation for specific jobs." One size does not fit all.

After doing plays and operas, and winning the coveted Grace Moore Award at the University Tennessee, and after I had spent a couple of summers in New York studying voice and dance, and having been given high praise and encouragement by an old Hollywood character actor (Olin Howland)..., I figured show business stardom would be a snap for me... And, that it might take me a full two weeks to get my first Broadway show. Oops... First, I had to audition... And, with a few exceptions, audition I did, for the remainder of my career.

In the meantime, I had to get a job to support me and my wife, LuJan and our baby daughter, Jennifer. I got a job at NBC, in the guest relations department... I gave tours of the studios...

Supplying sound effects with an improvised narrative, I made sixty dollars a week. Luckily, our rent was sixty dollars a month.

I wasn't in the Actor's Equity Union, so I found that I had to go to open calls for chorus jobs. "Chorus jobs!?! I don't want a chorus job. I want a featured role and then on to stardom." It's that old story: You can't get a job without an agent, and you can't get an agent without having a job. The agents have to see your work before they can work for you. Plus, I had no idea that there were so many hopefuls from all over the country wanting my spot at stardom. Drat! Why hadn't I figured on that?

There seemed to be only one chance: After the Equity union members had their auditions, the producers and casting agents were required to hear non-union members. Many times, the lines were around the corner. I, also, had no idea how good some of them would be. After getting inside and waiting in the wings, I heard some of the best operatic voices I'd ever heard… And they were auditioning for a chorus job. Back then musicals had principals, dancers and singers. In my category, there were usually two slots available for baritones. Two possible jobs available out of maybe twenty to thirty baritones all lined up, just like me. Eight bars and you're out. Sometimes without even looking up from their note pads or newspapers. A perfunctory, "Thank you," let you know that they had no employment for the likes of you. Ugh. This approach was a dead end. Plus, I wasn't as good as I thought I was. There had to be another way.

I had to be different. I wasn't good enough to be in the chorus. I had to get a featured role. I had to get their attention. One of the first specially conceived auditions in that happy vein was a bit I did with a wadded up paper sack in my pocket. When announced, I walked onto center stage. Faced the darkened theatre, and stood there, without doing anything, until the denizens in the dim distance looked at me. Then, slowly, I would express a look of: "I've got a secret in my pocket." No words. During this, I would see that at least one of the six to eight people involved with the audition began to look at his or her audition sheet, presumably, to check for my name, and any other information, such as, "Watch out for this one. He's a nut case." They noticed me. I slowly pulled the crumpled sack from my pocket; while facially expressing, "I'm about to show you a secret; a really special thing that I have in my paper sack." I put my searching hand into the bag. Empty. Disaster. Dumbfounded and crestfallen, I broke into "Somebody Stole My Gal." Ending with tearing the sack into bits, proclaiming: "He ain't getting' into the sack with her!" And a big ending with, "Somebody... somebody... somebody... Somebody stole my gal!!!"

"Thank, you." And, "Next."

At least I got their attention. I would be difficult to forget. I wrote special material for several auditions; and got my first Broadway musical that way... Not in the chorus, but in a featured role. The show ran for one performance, actually two. We had a matinee and an evening performance. At the time, it was the biggest flop in Broadway history.

Auditioning for Radio City Music Hall was different. I had to sing two arias for that job. They needed a replacement right away, and I happened to be next door at NBC. I got it. And, I was beside myself with pride and happiness.

It was my very first job in my chosen career. This was in 1958. I was hired as a singer at Radio City Music Hall, making seventy-five dollars a week... four shows a day... seven days a week. I was on top of the world. This was fifteen dollars more per week than I had made working across the street as a tour guide at NBC. At the Music Hall, I felt somewhat comfortable and assured of having a steady job and good pay. This was really big, for me. I was making a living by singing! The *Men's Glee Club* was a New York City highlight and tradition, especially for tourists... And, it had flourished there for the previous twenty-five years. Jan Peerce and Robert Merrill, along with several other opera stars, had worked in the *Men's Glee Club* while studying and learning roles. In between shows, we could use rehearsal rooms to vocalize and work on repertoire... or play duplicate bridge, which was very popular. Having the Rockettes, the Corps De Ballet, and exotic specialty acts around didn't hurt either.

For one show, there was an amazing male Flamenco dancer and a beautiful young woman dancing to Ravel's *Bolero.* This man had the Rockettes and ballet dancers entranced. Several of them stood in the wings and swooned as he did his rapid fire stomps and spins. The young ladies were practically drooling. After his number, it looked like a lawn sprinkler had been onstage. His sweat and whatever product he had in his thick shock of hair caught the lights as he would spin and shake his head... and it really looked like he was watering a lawn from his sprinkler head. The ladies of the ballet and the Rockettes found that to be very sexy... Go figure.

Crap!!! Disaster!!! After only a few months, we got our closing notice. I was very depressed. After twenty-five years??? How could that be??? Luckily, our apartment rent for LuJan, me, and our young daughter, Jennifer, was only sixty dollars a month. But, what was I going to do? Panic! In the New York Times, on the same day we got our closing notice, there was an ad offering a "generous monetary award" for their "Champion Hog Caller," sponsored by Merkel Foods. Hog callers in New York??? Clyde, the bass, from Texas, said, "Come on..., you might pick up a few bucks!"

I even had to audition to be a hog caller: I had a voice lesson between shows, and was walking back to the "Hall" for my next show, when I remembered that the contest was being held in Nola Studios, a half block away, on 57th Street. It began to rain... Great. I had never called hogs in my life, but I had about a half hour to kill, so I ducked in and went to the assigned studio on the third floor..., just for a *look see*. When I stepped off the elevator, I could see through an open door... lights and cameras... with a small group of men gathered outside, apparently there to call hogs. What about my career in opera!?! This was bizarre. I was told to sign in. I told the stage manager that I couldn't sign in for several reasons, and the main reason was that I had to hurry back to the Music Hall for my next show. He said, in that case, he could get me in next. I couldn't believe I was doing this. Although I had never called hogs, I had heard my Dad, and my Uncle Oscar, call hogs many times. It wasn't advanced calculus.

I walked into a room crowded with *suits*, a panel of judges, set-up with lights and cameras for the occasion. I noticed that two of the judges were wearing overalls and checkered shirts. I recognized them as cast members from *The Music Man*, currently running on Broadway, starring Robert Preston (later to become my friend while shooting *Mark Twain's The Man That Corrupted Hadleyburg*.) I stood there in front of the panel until the stage manager said... "Okay." I said, "Okay what?" He said... "Call hogs." I said... "What kind?" The room stopped, dead, still. I knew, at that moment that I had a room full of hog-calling-phonies here. That moment was one of the most delicious moments ever. Checkmate. I knew I was the only one there who knew anything whatsoever about calling hogs. I said:

"Do you want me to call Poland Chinas or Durocs? Do you want me to call little piglets from not too far away, or shoats and sows, say, as much as a half-mile away?"

They became immensely interested. I went through a series of various calls that I improvised on the spot. I won. I was Merkel Food's National Hog Calling Champion! Their PR people got me on the Jack Paar Show that very night... and on the Today Show on NBC... and the Robert Q Lewis radio show, the next morning. On the Paar Show, I explained to Paar and the audience the whole story. And, that if you blew your car horn while feeding the hogs, they would eventually develop a conditioned reflex to the car horn. They would become *Pavlov's Hogs*. The segment went over quite well. I even called hogs in German: "Kommen sie here swine!!!" (Big laugh)

About a week later, I saw Jack Paar on Fifth Avenue, and I blurted, "Hey! Mr. Paar! I *was on...*" Paar looked at me as if I were a serial killer... and scurried away. I was puzzled and worried that I had frightened Jack Paar. I had been just glad to see him. My hog calling bit had gone over really well. And, I really enjoyed getting some big laughs. He'd been very warm on the show. Right after that, within ten minutes, I got on an elevator with Otto Preminger*!* And did he ever look mean and threatening!?! This just wasn't to be my day. But, when Preminger saw me, he greeted me like I was a long lost friend. What a strange juxtaposition. I found out later that Jack Paar had a fear of being recognized and approached in public. Wish I had known that at the time.

My picture was up in all the butcher shops in New York, including in my neighborhood shop. And, they spelled my name incorrectly. But, the *biggie* was when the Knoxville News Sentinel carried my picture with the caption... "He's in good voice, OINK!" I had sung with the Knoxville Symphony Orchestra and performed several leading roles in operas while there. Plus, I had won the prestigious *Grace Moore Award* only the year before. By the way, for my first movie, *Armored Command* with Burt Reynolds and Howard Keel, my name was misspelled on those credits, as well. I'm off to a rousing start. Years later, there was a full page ad in *Variety* touting my starring role in the cult film, *Christmas Evil*. Guess what? They had also misspelled my name. In that case, I didn't mind.

A story that happened at The Music Hall that probably should not to be told in polite company:

One of the other singers at the Music Hall, Clyde, the bass from Texas, consistently won the farting contest in our dressing room full of twenty men singers. He held that honor in perpetuity… even though, several others were constantly practicing. What's more, they really enjoyed "cutting one" on stage. If I saw someone's shoulders start shaking up and down, I knew that someone had launched a big one. They enjoyed it even more if we were standing there and singing something like *Kol Nidre,* the *Day of Atonement.* All that farting wasn't amusing to me. In fact, it bugged me somethin' fierce… especially Clyde, who dressed right beside me. One day, just as *places* was being called, I'd had enough. I said, "All right you sonsabitches… Everybody, stop! I've got something for you…" Everybody stopped. I had a big one in my arsenal… ready to launch… and I let loose. Whoops!!! Disaster!!! I blew a major poop into my tux trousers. I heard the fellows laughing down the stairs to the stage. I missed the show. I had only one pair of tux trousers. Believe me, I will never participate in that gentlemen's activity again. The telling about that experience is much more fun than it was to live it.

At present, from my *travel chair,* I do sometimes enjoy doing some of those well used and often successful audition bits.

I have never been a harsh self-critic. I have always done my best at the time. But, now, there are times when I like to vary the experience. For me, that's what keeps these attic performances alive and exciting. One of my favorite bits, that I created and often turn to, I call "Casey." I walk from the wings onto center stage and stand there; looking quite ill at ease.

After standing there for a little too long, my pianist plays my introduction. I don't sing. He tries again; repeating the introduction. I sense the audience becoming somewhat confused, when I don't begin my song. I see them turning to each other; wondering "What's this?" Much like the "Somebody Stole My Gal" turn. The third time he plays the brief intro; I begin to sing; shakily so. As soon as I hear any reaction from the audience, I sing with a bit of confidence and gratitude. Trying to ingratiate myself, I smile. The more the audience reacts; the more I react. I begin to sing robustly, and with great enthusiasm; hitting and holding a high C at the end. So full of myself, I hold the high C for way too long. (Can't do that these days without my traveling chair) The piano player tries to cut me off several times. Finally, my accomplice, using his stage manager's blank pistol, steps from the wings and shoots me with a loud, "Bang!"

I come back, later in the show with the same bit, only with confidence this time. I hold the high C like before. My accomplice doesn't enter on time. I'm still holding the high C and glancing into the wings. As I'm about to croak, he steps out from the other side of the stage and shoots me in the back: "Bang!"

Oh... I call it "Casey," because the song I would sing was "Casey Would Waltz with the Strawberry Blonde, and the Band Played On." The high "C" came at the end: "...and the band played O-O-O-O-O-On!!!" BANG!!!

I used "Casey" to audition for the *Hellzapoppin* with Soupy Sales. It blew the roof off. I was sure I'd gotten the show, but

I had to audition a second time. Oops! The surprise is gone. What to do? That's when I added the button of shooting me in the back from the opposite side of the stage. Bang! I was later told that my audition was better than the show.

Ideally, I wanted to round the gag off with a crowning third bit. Although, it was never performed at the time; with my *traveling without leaving productions*, I perform it with great success. Sound systems can be and have been rigged to give the impression that an airplane is coming from the balcony to and over the stage.

This time, as soon as I start to sing, the plane is coming towards the stage. Closer and closer it comes and finally opens fire, with machine guns blazing. I scurry about trying to avoid death and destruction. And, as the plane noisily swoops low over my head, from a prone position, I leap and scurry off stage. In the last Alex Cohen production of *Hellzapoppin*, we had the plane coming in and swooping over me, but without the first two bits and the machine gun bursts. The machine gun fire completes the triptych. Nevertheless, what it could have been!?! But, it wouldn't have saved the show.

We, with Lynn Redgrave and Jerry Lewis, closed at The Colonial Theatre in Boston... once again, without reaching Broadway, with much internal conflict involved. More on that later. As I said, we had tried *Hellzapoppin* once before, ten years earlier, with Soupy Sales. Soupy was a dream to work with. Ready for anything. Lots of fun, but... No Broadway. No matter... I can, and do, use all three bits from my nice comfortable *travel* chair. And, I get enormous laughs. Although, I admit, I do often enjoy bombing. Weird. I could say it's like a strange *out of body* experience within a *traveling without leaving* experience. Weird. Sometimes, when the audience doesn't laugh (crickets), I laugh. Weird.

My Agent at the Time

My agent, for a time, was Peter Cereghetti. Peter was very enthusiastic about the theatre and his job in it. He said to me that his favorite part of show business was going to auditions with me. An enthused agent is a wonderful asset. Peter called me and said that there was interest in me for the male lead in a new Broadway play. I caught his enthusiasm and was eager to read the script. It was written by a playwright who currently had a big hit on Broadway. (I'm leaving out names.) When the script was delivered, I could hardly contain myself. After work (Yes, I was still working as a waiter,) when I got home, I sat down with a glass of scotch, and I began to read. The audition was to be the next afternoon, so I had work to do.

I read the script. I read it again. I read it through once again. I read it through, maybe, a dozen times. It's terrible. It's awful. This is going to be on Broadway? No. Oh, no... Not this piece of shit? No. I am so terribly disappointed.

I read it again, and again. Maybe I'm missing something. And, suddenly... suddenly... it hits me: "Yes!!! This is a *send-up* of recent films about lonely American women going to Europe and falling in love with dashing race car drivers!" I read about one, with Doris Day. Ripe for parody. Genius. Perfect. I can't believe it took me so long to see it. Now, I'm really excited… and a little drunk.

It's almost two o'clock. I arrive at the stage door. Peter is here with his new secretary. The young man is thrilled to be here because he has been told by Peter that he will be seeing just how it's supposed to be done.

The stage manager announces me to the denizens of the darkened house. I can feel the tense excitement from those four or five people sitting out there; waiting for me to save their show.

I can't believe I'm doing this, but before I begin my reading, I address the denizens of the dark; who would be the producer, the director, the writer, the casting director and a few others. I begin by relating my whole experience from last night. I repeat my disappointment and my eventual realization that the play is genius. It is a parody… and… Crickets. Oops! I may have made the wrong call.

There is silence… A big, big, fat, fat…, silence. I take a brief look into the wings where my agent and his new secretary are making a hasty retreat. I do the reading. There is the same deafening silence. No one says a word. I make my exit from the stage and out the stage door and into the alley. Peter is waiting. He is pale and wears a shattered look of disbelief. Now, his ashen face turns red. For the first time, he raises his voice to me. He says that the producer and the casting director will probably not ever see any of his clients again. He storms off.

That was Friday. Today is Monday. Peter calls and says that the producer, apparently has taken what I had to say "under advisement," and has cancelled the production.

That's fun every time I go there. That deafening silence... oh, God. Seeing Peter's pale face. His new assistant was terribly confused. Had I done a terrible thing? Yes. No. Yes. No.

Another agent I had was Bruce Savan. He signed me after seeing me in the musical revue, *Put it in Writing*, for which I had won the Theatre World Award. He was very excited. He said that I should call him every morning. "Every morning?" OK. I called him every morning. He would say, "Nothing today, Brandon." This went on for weeks. Finally, one morning I called and Bruce said that I didn't have to call that if there was anything he would call me. I did find out about a national tour of *Luv* coming up. I called. Bruce said that he had already submitted me and that they were not interested. I got a direct call from the company manager of *Luv* with whom I had worked before. He wanted me to come in and read for the National tour. I said, "Thanks a lot, Bob. Bruce Savan has been trying to get me in there for weeks."

Bob said, "Brandon, he never called this office."

I called Savan: "Are you sure you can't get me an audition for *Luv*?"

"Brandon, I told you... I tried. They don't want to see you."

"I have a reading for *Luv* tomorrow. You never called that office about me."

There was a silence on the other end of the phone. I left that agency.

So, finally, I did get to audition for the role. I was not cast. I believe the part went to the actor known as Gene Wilder.

Sometimes, after auditioning and getting the job, the auditioning is not over. There might be auditions for backers... Investors. The show has to be financed. Ideally, this should be done before the auditions for actors begins.

A few years after *New Faces of '68* closed, Leonard Sillman, Arthur Siegel and I toured the country and the high seas (on the QE2) as we sought backing for our projected *The Best of New Faces*. We had access to the best songs and sketches from thirteen editions from which to choose. Leonard did the "shilling" while Arthur and I did the heavy work. We hit millionaire's homes in New York, Dallas, Oklahoma City and Los Angeles.

Here, we're at Mr. Blackwell's (famous for his The Year's Worst Dressed List) estate in Hollywood, with Leonard shilling, Arthur Siegel at the piano, and Himself performing at a gathering which included some New Faces alums, going back to 1934. I even sang "Boston Beguine," that Alice Ghostly had made famous. And, here, I am doing Ronny Graham's "The Unrequited Lover's March," in front of Ronny. That's Ronny and Inga Swenson in the front row, along with Eartha Kitt's knees. Standing Is Teddy Lynch Getty Gaston. Beautiful, still.

Front row: Ronny Graham, Leonard Sillman, Billie Haywood, and Inga Swenson. Second row: Alice Ghostly and two (DKs). Third row: Gus Schumer, (DK), Teddy, and (DK). Third row: Dodi Goodman, Jane Connell, and Billie Hayes. The top group of six, clockwise: Paul Lynde, R.G. Brown, Arthur Siegel, Bernie West, Himself, Eve Arden, and Eartha Kitt.

Charlie Walters was a dancer in one of Leonard's shows. One of Charlie's dance partners was also there... for a brief moment. As a matter of fact, Walters, also, was only there for a brief moment. When he made his entrance into Blackwell's home, he spied his old dance partner. With a flourish, he said, "Oh, my darling," and took her into his arms. They made an effort to do one of the Fred Astaire and Ginger Rodgers spins and turns into a dip. They fell against the glass front of a display cabinet and onto the floor... An ambulance came... And, off they went to a hospital for observation. He was there for less than a minute. He and his dance partner did not make the show or the group photo.

Charles Walters had directed many of the great Hollywood musicals of the forties with Judy Garland (*Easter Parade*). Fred Astaire and Ginger Rodgers (*The Barkley's of Broadway*) and Leslie Caron in *Lili*. He also staged Judy Garland's famous run at The Palace Theater in New York. I do not believe that Blackwell invested in our show.

Teddy Lynch married J. Paul Getty (one of the richest men in the world) then married a rich man named Gaston. She was a fine singer back in the thirties. Now, in her nineties, she is an author and has written several books. Teddy and her daughter Gigi Gaston introduced little Fiona and Maude Amber to the equestrian world. Fiona kept it up for several years at the Claremont Stables, riding in New York's Central Park.

In the spirit of a postmortem let's go back to how *New Faces of 1968* began:

The Spring of 1968 and New Faces

This is a very happy and thrilling time; albeit, a short time. Leonard Sillman has gotten Jack Rollins to produce and has finally secured the money to put *New Faces of 1968* on Broadway at the Booth theatre on the corner of Shubert Alley! Yowzah! Finally, finally, finally, we're to be on Broadway! But, there also comes the two tragic and gut-wrenching assassinations.

For the time being, "happy" is put on hold. During the first week of rehearsal, Dr. King is assassinated. There is a huge sadness over the whole country. I had just been asked in an interview, a few days earlier, what living person did I most admire. I had said, "Dr. King."

We begin previews at The Booth on April 18th. During the "Gypsy Run Through" (a special matinee performance for members of other shows currently playing on Broadway), the audience reaction during my first number, "By the C," by Clark Gesner, is so loud that, sometimes, I can't hear the orchestra. We think we have a sure fire hit. I also had two more of Gesner's songs of that ilk: "U R the 1 I'm 4." And "There's none more beautiful than U, R." Loved doing those three numbers.

BEHIND THESE EYES SUCH SWEET MADNESS LIES

"There's none more beautiful than, 'U R."

THE SPRING OF 1968 AND NEW FACES

But, hold on; *HAIR*, a new kind of Broadway musical opens at the Biltmore on April 29th. *HAIR* is a big hit. We open May 2nd. The opening night audience in the Booth is nothing like the preview audiences had been. Other than the critics, most of the rest of the audience is made up of friends, family members, and the many nervous backers who have already seen the show several times. There is no fun in the air... Only scattered, forced backer-laughs. Zounds! Crusher! Like auditioning for the Shuberts again.

On June 5th, Robert Kennedy is assassinated. The sadness, once again, is palpable. *New Faces of 1968* closes on June 15th, 1968. New York and the Nation will remain stunned and saddened for quite some time after these assassinations. In the scheme of things, the opening and closing of a little Broadway show does not matter much; except to us and a number of our investors.

So, revisiting that spring in 1968 has a very, very, wide range of ups and downs in the spectrum of the light and the dark.

Focusing on the lighter side; tonight, from my *travel chair*, I'll be performing the short comic opera, a la Mozart, "Die Zusammenfugung," about missing marijuana, found at last, in the soup... "The soup is in the pot... and the pot is in the soup!" written by Sam Pottle and David Axlerod... Performed with Ronny Graham, Marian Mercer and Himself, in a summer pre-Broadway tour of *New Faces of 1966.* This summer tour was basically a backer's audition.

Two years later is when I did the number with Robert Klein and Madelyn Kahn on Broadway, at the Booth Theatre. I had wonderful material, and I loved doing that show. I came to the theatre every night excited to get on stage. Robert Klein and I shared a dressing room. Bob hated or seemed to hate, doing the show… didn't want to be there… moaned and groaned about it until I said "Please, Bob, don't spoil it for me. I love being on Broadway… and doing this show. You're bringing me down! I'm happy… I feel privileged to be here!" He looked at me like I was crazy. But, he understood… and respected my wishes.

Ronny directed the show… for a while. Ronny was wrestling with some of his demons. Then, Frank Wagoner. Then, Leonard took over as Leonard was prone to do. And, Leonard became one of the Godfathers to my son Garett… the other being Jim Catusi, my partner on *Sesame Street*. And his Godmother was Marian Mercer. When Garett was born, Leonard sent over a signed contract acquiring Garett's services for "A FUTURE PRODUCTION TO BE NAMED." About thirty years later, I appeared as a guest star on Garett's television series, *The Sentinel. The Sentinel* ran for five years.

THE SPRING OF 1968 AND NEW FACES

Garett Maggart and Himself

Leonard loved "theatre" more than anyone I'd ever known. He was, in his own words, "extremely stage-struck." And, he was a wonderful storyteller. One afternoon, I sat quietly while Leonard and Sir Noel Coward swapped elegant and bawdy tales about shows, show folk, and folk on the periphery. I felt a little like George Gobel when he said he felt like the "world was a tuxedo, and he was a pair of brown shoes." When I was in college, I never missed his TV show... talking about "Spooky old Alice."

Leonard's home was a beautiful townhouse on East 79th Street, now owned by the former Mayor of New York, Michael Bloomberg. I performed sixty-five backers' auditions, over a period of four years, in that house. I guess I could do one more just to eat Ruth Dove's cooking. We were raising money for our next show that we hoped to get to Broadway. We had plans to do *The Best of New Faces.* We would be using the best material from the thirteen editions of *New Faces* that Leonard had produced since 1933. We eventually got it on, with me directing, at a small club called The Ball Room, in New York's Greenwich Village. It went by fairly unnoticed. But, as always, we had a good time. Leonard passed away before we could get it to Broadway. But he went down swinging.

During the run at The Ballroom, on a Saturday night between shows, Leonard clutched his fist over his heart, and said it was his angina, and he needed his heart medication, which he had left on the bathroom sink at home. I suggested that we cancel the second show, due in an hour, and take him home. He was in quite some pain. Leonard refused... saying that we were to have a full house for the second show. Then, our only course of action was to jump a taxi and head uptown... over a hundred blocks away..., with Saturday night traffic through midtown's theatre district. (Slim chance) I would hold the cab while Leonard would fetch his medication, and we would speed back downtown and do the second show. On the way uptown, Leonard's pain increased... moaning and saying he was going to die. I told the cab driver that we absolutely had to get to East 79th Street as soon as possible. The cab driver seemed to come unnerved, weaving in and out of traffic, with Leonard, continuing to moan, "I'm dying, Bud. I'm dying!" Just as we arrived in front of his home on 79th Street, Leonard shrieked...

THE SPRING OF 1968 AND NEW FACES

"My house keys!!! They're back in the dressing room at The Ballroom in my coat pocket!!! Oh, my God!!! Driver, take us to Lenox Hill Hospital on 77th Street... Hurry!"

By this time, the driver is out of his mind..., and so are we. We get there and rush into the ER. Leonard is pleading... then demanding... "Nitroglycerin pills... Now!!!" The ER, of course, can't give him medication without first examining the patient. Leonard yells...

"I don't have time to be examined! I have a show to do downtown in fifteen minutes!!!"

The ER staff is now, gathered around. Leonard is given a one dose amount of nitroglycerin, only after signing a release, stating that he would not hold the hospital responsible. He did, and we left. Our cab driver was waiting as requested. We sped back downtown. By this time, Leonard is laughing so much that I was afraid he would bring on another attack. I'm laughing too, but not nearly as robustly as Leonard. Our driver is laughing, only he has no idea why he's laughing. I tried to explain, but it was useless. We would stop laughing... for a minute; then, we would start up again. We were about ten minutes late for a very forgiving and happy audience. Leonard said, "The show must go on... especially, for a full house!"

What a night!

Leonard put on the front of being a wealthy producer; he had, indeed, produced many shows on Broadway. But, his finances were always in shambles. He always had to be on the trail of wealthy East Side widows, and bejeweled Texans, among others, to finance these shows. Many of the "older ladies" that Leonard pursued were said to be from European Royalty. Some of them knew about Leonard's financial condition, and when their husbands died, if the old boys were anywhere near Leonard's size, the widows would pass along their deceased husband's suits to Leonard. Before one of our backer's auditions… Leonard, looking spiffy, asked, "How do you like my new dead man's suit?"

One day I got a call from Leonard. When I answered, I heard Leonard all but scream, "Bud! Bud!" I answered back mocking Leonard's high pitched raspy voice: "Leonard! Leonard!" We did this again, and again, until he finally got out the words, "I've lost my finger!" He had climbed atop a chair to open a fuse box and got off balance and fell leaving the tip of his pinky finger in the little circular ring on the door. He was on the floor looking up at his pinky still in the ring. "You've got to get me to the hospital!" I lived across town on the upper west side, and he lived on East 79th Street. He took a cab.

(On the next page stands Leonard in his "dead man's suit.")

THE SPRING OF 1968 AND NEW FACES

There were rumors that Mel Brooks had modeled the Zero Mostel role, in *The Producers*, on Leonard. I have no idea..., although, there were surely some similarities. Mel had written material for Leonard, in the past, along with Ronny Graham, for *New Faces of 1952*, which was Leonard's most successful show. Many people didn't take to Leonard, but I loved the old fart. He was at his best and happiest when he was in his home, surrounded by show folk, and regaling them with some of his wonderful stories. I might go there sometime next week.

Leonard Sillman and Joey Faye: I believe that two of the happiest faces I ever saw were Leonard Sillman..., his face fairly exploding with joy while telling one of his own stories of the theatre..., and Joey Faye, the old vaudeville and burlesque comic, singing an impromptu ditty in a bar, in Baltimore..., after drinking about a half glass of beer. He wasn't much of a drinker. Joey was funny just walking down the street. Legendary director, George Abbott, once criticized Joey in front of a whole cast:

"Mr. Faye; don't try to be funny by walking in an unnatural way. Walk in your normal way."

The next day, in front of the whole cast, Mr. Abbott apologized to Joey.

"I must apologize to Mr. Faye. After rehearsal yesterday, I was gazing out the window, down to the street below... and Mr. Faye does, indeed, walk that way."

I worked, briefly, with Mr. Abbott, when he was ninety-nine years old. He was sharp as a tack, loved ballroom dancing with the ladies and lived to be a hundred and seven.

It was dangerous to see a show with Leonard. While we were working on *The Best of New Faces*, Leonard would often be given tickets to currently running Broadway shows. During the intermission, and immediately after a performance, he would mouth off his opinion about the show. Many times, his opinions were loud, in bad taste, and, of course, negative. I said, "Leonard, you shouldn't do that... what if the playwright's mother or Grandmother happened to hear you." He persisted. So, I made him leave our seats a few minutes before or after I would exit. In fact, the first time I ever heard Leonard sounding off like that was after one of my preview performances in *Put It in Writing*. He had just seen the show. At that time, I didn't know him, and I'm sure he didn't know that I was walking directly behind him as he and his entourage were leaving the theatre. What I heard was: "That was the biggest piece of shit I've ever seen."

So, Leonard's beautiful home on East 79st Street, where I spent many a happy afternoon and evening, dining and hobnobbing with the cognoscenti and literati, is now owned by Mayor Bloomberg. A few years earlier, I had played popular New York Mayor, Ed Koch, in a show called *Potholes*, at the Cherry Lane Theater. Opening night, the audience was filled with ex-mayors, ex-governors, senators, and other political types, both past and present. I entered down the aisle singing Koch's favorite query, "How'm I Doin'?" written by Elinor Guggenheimer and Ted Simmons. The audience ate it up. I loved that little show; in that little theatre. I'll be doing that again soon..., especially, that opening night. Of course, it didn't run very long either. But, again, it was fun. There's a pattern here. Was somebody putting a hex on me, or was it I that was putting a hex on my shows?

Leonard wrote a very funny and informative book called, *Here Lies Leonard Sillman, Straightened Out at Last.* If you can find it, it's a must-read for those of us who are *stage struck*. A quote on the book jacket: "Leonard Sillman is stage-struck. To understand that is to forgive everything."

--Moss Hart

At the same time, I was performing in *Applause* at the Palace Theatre; I assisted Leonard in producing Sir Noel Coward's *Hay Fever*, starring Shirley Booth, at the Helen Hayes Theatre. It ran for a swift twenty-four performances.

Timing

Today, on my stage, I'll do a little *traveling*. I'll do the classic "Pantomime Wine" sketch with Sherry Britton. We'll play to a packed house and wallow in the pounding waves of laughter. Sherry was recently called the most iconic burlesque dancer in New York Magazine's "Greatest New York Ever' 400 hundred year history."

The full-blown joy of working in burlesque; being bathed in laughter, and learning how to make that happen every night is great fun…, and addictive. Keeping that laughter ball bouncing back and forth between the stage and the audience is somewhat like tennis, and music; with its varied tempi and expressive rhythms. Keeping the laughter ball going as in a farce with two or three acts, requires precise timing and great stamina; somewhat like the best tennis finals at Wimbledon and Forrest Hills: keeping the ball in the air and between the lines.

Michael Frayn's farce, *Noises Off*, is a perfect example. It's said that Frayn got the idea for *Noises Off* while watching the backstage chaos (noises off stage) from the wings of one of his earlier farces, written for, and starring Lynn Redgrave. Lynn Rachel told me the story when she was playing *Noises Off* at the Piccadilly in London; while I was visiting her there. I saw the show several times from the audience, which was great fun. But, I paid notice to the precisely orchestrated rhythms of laughter from Lynn's dressing room, over the intercom. While lying on my back on her dressing room floor, I would close out the world except for the sounds. Amazing. Without clearly hearing the dialogue and seeing the actors; I heard only the pacing, the rhythms, the door slams, the screams, and the robust and punctuating laughter. Although, a most enjoyable experience for Lynn Rachel, it required enormous energy to play. Lynn Rachel, upon leaving her dressing room and heading for the stage, would take a deep breath and say "I'm off to climb 'Comedy Mountain."

I remembered, years ago, when I was doing burlesque with Sherry Britton... I had my agent make an audio recording (There were no video cameras back then) of our show while we were playing the Oakdale Theatre, in Wallingford Connecticut. The theatre was actually a large tent as were most of the big theatres on the summer circuit. I think that particular Saturday night was possibly our best audience all tour long... Ergo; it would be the best show to have recorded.

After the tour, and on into the fall, when I was having the usual down-time, I was back to being a waiter. I came home late one night and remembered that tape. I hadn't yet heard it. I dug it out of the closet... Poured myself a nice scotch and sat back to listen to my glory days with all that audience adoration. But, "Oh, no... no... no..." My agent, Peter Cereghetti had recorded only the audience sounds... With the dialogue barely heard in the background. If I didn't know the show, I would not have any idea of what was going on. Of course, I finished my scotch... And had another, while I listened and enjoyed the sounds from the audience. The rhythms, laughs, and applause were soothing balm for an out of work actor. Nice.

Pain Management and Sad Songs

Last night, I watched *Carousel* again on TMC. I'd seen it with John Raiit years ago on stage at the Wallingford Music Tent in Connecticut... The film is with Gordon MacRae and Shirley Jones. In both cases, I shed a tear at the final scene when Billy Bigelow, after his death, is allowed to have one look down on earth to see his daughter's graduation. The Starkeeper, in the person of the town's leading citizen, Dr. Seldon, in making his graduation speech, is telling the young students, mainly Louise, not to think about their parent's successes or failures, but to live their own lives. And, of course, then, we get hit by Rodger's and Hammerstein's great inspirational, "You'll Never Walk Alone." To me, that is one very emotional scene... The worst. Impossible for me not to tear up. I'm a father with daughters... and, sons.

But, some sad songs can make you feel better, if done in a way that lets you laugh at yourself. By going overboard with the tragedy, it can become quite funny. Today, I will continue with a short scene and a song or two that I have been working on for a month or more... Trying to get things right, if possible. I strive for melancholy, in the hopes that it will be somewhat "smile-able," if not funny.

Yep, pain management with sad songs. The first sad song was born in the cave with:

I kept her in my cave. She was proud to be my slave

But, she run away. Yes! She run away

I bring home fruits and meats, then I tell her: "Wash my feets!"

But, she run away. Yes! She run away

Ooga! Oh, my Ooga, Ooga. How I miss my little Ooga

Ooga does the Frooga-Looga at the Motel Chattanooga

The caveman, then, sits in his cave, forlorn, while continually honking his plaintive horn:

Ooga-ooga… Ooga-ooga… Ooga-ooga… Ooga……Ooga…… Oooga…

After three days, the caveman goes out and humps a pretty dinosaur. The male dinosaurs find out about this, and they capture the caveman and eat him. The dinosaurs then sit around a fire, picking their teeth with the caveman's ribs. The pretty dinosaur paramour is distraught. She wanders off into the woods, crying her pretty eyes out because she had feelings for the caveman. She hears the male dinosaurs laughing. She runs through the trees and over rocks until she jumps from a "lover's leap" and falls to her death on the rocks below. Not knowing this, the boisterous male dinosaurs continue laughing and singing songs of victory and good-times.

Now, flash forward to the more recent past when Country Songs became popular:

A Really Sad Song:

My heart is broken. It's been a bad season. "Cupid" and "Stupid" do rhyme for a reason. I'm running on empty. I'm flat on my back. But, a really sad song gets me back on the track. A really sad song is what I like to hear. A really sad song, with some peanuts and beer. So sad that I cry in my beer as I moan, "I'm all set to die now, please, Gov'ner, don't phone."

And, tonight I need a sad song. Oh, I really need a sad song

A git down so bad song… Like a, "They shot my Dad" song

    Really go, really down, "The bottom looks up song"

    "Down to Hell," might as well, drink and throw up song

I feel like a louse and my life's on the skids

My spouse took the house and the car and the kids

My hound dog's so slow, he can't pick up the scent

My pickup won't go and my wife up and went

BEHIND THESE EYES SUCH SWEET MADNESS LIES

Now, there's a really sad song… a really, really sad song

One of them "I know I've been had songs" that makes a good sad song

    Really go, really down, "Stepped Right in the Poop" song

    "Lost My Pal," "Root Canal" "Big Green Fly in My Soup" song

Just gimme sad tunes and some crumbs in my bed

Salt on my wounds when I'm "Shot Full of Lead"

One final sad song for my ride in the hearse

When everything's wrong, so it can't git no worse

    Dah Deedaddle Deedow, Dah Deedaddle Dedoo

    Dah Deedaddle, that's how, I have me a "Boohoo"

    A "Boohoo" that can do what "Boohoos" are meant to

    A beer and a "Boohoo" and a peanut or two

    Dah Deedaddle Deedow, Dah Deedaddle DeeDoooo

    What a beer and a sad song and a peanut can do

    Doo Deedoop, Doo Deedoop, Doodee Doo Doo

I'll let these tragedies simmer overnight, and continue polishing the amusing melancholia tomorrow. Maybe, the female dinosaur is pregnant with the caveman's child. Too much?

Tonight, I will spend a quiet evening at home with Vivien. I'll read to her what I have written concerning sad songs. She will say nothing. Then, she will smile and pull me back onto the bed. In the morning... I awake... Vivien is gone. There is a rose. And with it, a note:

'Neath the proscenium arch of your brow, behind your eyes, and under the flies, there the stage with your sweet madness lies.

Love,

    Vivien

Vivien knows the difference between "sweet madness" and the "not so sweet madness."

This morning, I pick up where I left off yesterday:

I continue with an unrequited love song. This song came about by watching a fellow of some girth, who came into the same diner that I frequent. He always sat at the same table. It was obvious that the poor fool had fallen (heavy) for the very attractive and vivacious, blonde waitress who works the evening shift.

I'll have him thinking: "My Waitress from Heaven."

"This is a song for the girl with the long legs that go from here to there

She moves with a motion that rivals the ocean in rhythmic and cool solitaire

She knows I exist 'cause I always insist on my table for one by the door

I order her cheesecake then boy do my knees shake when cheesecake starts walking the floor

"Her cheesecake's to die for and that is just why for I'm starting to put on some weight

She walks in a fashion that stirs up my passion for her as my "Special Blue Plate"

My waitress from Heaven from six to eleven, my table for one by the door

I'm fond of her fondue, my long legged blonde who keeps me coming back for more

"I know I can't take this, this actress slash waitress is driving me out of my mind

You'd think some producer would try to seduce her, but Hollywood sometimes is blind

If they'd take a minute, get out and come in it to see what a star they could cast

I'm sure they'd discover this fantasy lover who stars at my nightly repast

"I know I should end this… how can I defend this, this spellbinding force-feed of mine

Though it's self-defeating, I still keep on eating, 'cause up front I love her behind

My waitress from Heaven from six to eleven, my table for one by the door

She is my addiction and here's my prediction- I'll keep coming, keep coming, keep coming, keep coming, and keep coming back for more"

This should be very sad and even tragic because the "Marty" type fellow wants what's best for the girl, which would necessarily exclude any fantasy that he might have about ending up with the girl, himself. Maybe, tomorrow, I'll come upon a way for the waitress to not only acknowledge "Marty," but also to even express her fondness for him. The extended tragedy comes when she wants to introduce him to a "friend." Too much?

I'll have to think about it. I'll work on this until, or if, I get enough material to "workshop" it for some of my friends who attend my soirees... Ronny Graham and Marshall Barer could give me some excellent notes. Both were dear friends for many years. I miss them, but I do get to see them at my soirees: patterned after Marshall's own soirees.

Ronny wrote and performed a funny-sad song entitled,

"The Unrequited Lover's March," which I performed many times.

Different Laughter

It's fascinating to me how some people, as a group, laugh better than other people. You might very well call this stereotyping, but African Americans do laugh better than anybody else, case closed... Unless they went to Harvard or Princeton. Then, they won't give it up quite so easily. But, at the top of the form; say you've got a really good comic (preferably black) working a predominately black audience, and he or she is really *cookin'*... It's like there's a quilt of "funny spiders" all over the audience, and they're trying to shake the spiders off. Arms and legs flying. And beautiful white teeth twinkling like stars in a night sky. When they finally shake this "funny quilt of spiders" off, and it hits the floor, they stomp on it. Like stomping out a grass fire. This looks wonderful..., and, may I say, quite contagious. But, most other folk should not even think about trying it... Like Pat Boone trying to sing Little Richard.

Sometimes, it's like that at funerals, too. White folks tend to pack their emotions inside. African American's open the flood gates and let it go.

Gay guys are usually good laughers. From what I've seen, lesbians are reluctant to give it up. Why is that? "Lipstick" lesbians laugh a little if it's okay with their partner in the heavy footwear.

Might be because they're not too crazy about some of the straight-guy material. I can see that.

Stereotypes are good for jokes. But you can piss people off, too. You've got to be careful. But this being "politically correct" can really fuck up a good joke. Athena tries to guide me. Damage control. But it's really hard to tell a good Polish joke without saying, "Polish." Athena says to use animals instead of people.

"Okay, this dumb Polish bear walks in... Says, 'Hello' to this exceedingly tall dike giraffe..." Maybe, not. Too much?

Uncle Gravy was right; Democrats do laugh better than Republicans. Conservatives don't want to give it up. They want to keep everything. That's why lots of them are constipated.

Sometimes there can be a painful dilemma, when someone tells a joke that would be considered sexist, racist, or just in bad taste, but it's funny... But, to whom? It's funny, or it's not funny. Do you laugh? Sometimes you might laugh and chase it with an obligatory groan... attempting to apologize for laughing and condemning the bad taste.

I was in a play at the Ambassador Theater back in 1975, called *We Interrupt This Program*. Holland Taylor and I were starring in a Neil Simon type comedy that is going along nicely, until we get interrupted by an armed gang that bursts through the doors in the back of the house and from the wings, shouting and firing automatic weapons, and hijacks the theater. The gang, headed by the wonderfully imposing Dick Anthony Williams, holds the theater, including the audience, hostage; demanding the release of someone being held by the police. It will take some time for the mayor and police to arrive at the theater to negotiate, so there's time to kill. The gang calls audience members (not really audience members) onstage, demanding entertainment. This doesn't go very well, so one of the gang, played by the personable Taurean Blacque, begins to entertain from the piano that happens to be onstage. As I recall, the gang was composed of mostly if not all, African American members.

Here comes an awkward moment: Taurean Blacque tells a joke: "Two white guys were in a bar talking, and one asks the other if he had ever fucked himself a nigger woman. The other white guy says, 'Well, I thought I had, until I saw a nigger fuck a nigger woman.'" Who laughed? As I recall, I don't recall. It was funny but squirmy funny. But, had Richard Pryor told the same joke in one of his concerts, both black and white audience members would have laughed. The play was not well received and ran but one week, following two weeks of previews. The author said, "I'm going to write a play just for you." I never heard from him again.

Here's something interesting, at least to me; I don't remember how the play ended. But, I remember the awkward moment when Taurean Blacque told that joke. And, of course, the shocking moment when the gang entered the theater, yelling out curses and firing their weapons. One piece from the proscenium was rigged to look as if it were being hit by a burst of gunfire. I was afraid that some of the real audience might have heart attacks. 1975 was still a troubled time. It took some of the audience a few minutes to realize that it was all a part of the play. I imagined that there were mixed feelings of relief, even some disappointment, and finally some resentment in the audience.

My mother was a good laugher. She was, of course, a Democrat. But, she had that troublesome side effect of occasionally peeing at the same time. My dad laughed pretty good, for a Republican. I remember him laughing along with everyone else when they played bridge on Saturday nights. Most Saturday nights there were one or two tables of bridge played in our living room. It was musical in the sense that there was a rhythm. A tension and a release. Some oohs and aahs and a crescendo! Five years old... Falling asleep listening to those sounds of life... Not bad.

Sometimes, when laughter is inappropriate, it can be almost impossible to stop. My first play in New York was called, *Like Other People*. It was way downtown at the Van Dam Theater. At the "actor's run-through" before the opening, I had just exited the stage when another actor entered and began a tense scene with the remaining actor. The actor entering said his first line, and the way he said it got an unintentional laugh. The scene became a house of cards. This was a serious scene in a serious play. But, once that first laugh came, the scene snow-balled into a laugh bigger than the previous laugh. And, it got worse. The actor that had remained when I left the stage, took off his shoe and began to pound the table..., a la Khrushchev. This made it even worse. A cascade. An avalanche. A runaway train.

Remember; this was an audience full of other actors. A friend of mine, the actress Jane Hoffman came backstage after the performance and apologized for herself and the audience as a whole: "I'm so sorry, but we simply could not stop laughing. I know everyone felt terrible, but once it started, there was no stopping. It was awful. And, it was … It was wonderful."

I was playing the role of Berenger in *The Killer*, by Eugene Ionesco, at The Cherry Lane Theater back in 1962, when a similar thing happened; not onstage, but in my dressing room. The role of Berenger was the nearest thing I will ever do that in any way might compare to the stamina needed to play *King Lear*, but it was just as exhausting for me. The role took everything I had. I lost fifteen pounds during that brief run. It was in repertory there under the auspices of Richard Barr's *Theater of the Absurd*. Barr directed.

After a Saturday matinee and evening performance, I made my way up to the dressing room that I shared with Arthur Anderson. When the Cherry Lane was built, it must have been designed for short actors. I am only 5-10, and I had to stoop to enter my small dressing room. I sat at my dressing table and gazed at one exhausted but completely fulfilled actor. I was in heaven, sitting there and sharing a few words with Arthur, who looked past me to a small gray haired gentleman standing in our wee doorway. Arthur, immediately stood (or stooped) and welcomed the gentleman. He seemed to be impressed with the fellow.

The man introduced himself to me and proceeded to reel off a tumble of words that I found difficult to follow. It seemed that he had written a play he wanted me to consider. His determination in expressing himself was considerable. According to him, I would be perfect to play his lead character. "It's about a man who wants to become a fawn," he said. And, he went on from there… Nonstop.

His single-minded determination to convince me was relentless. I stifled a laugh, but the gates were open. And, the more I laughed, the more determined he became. With eyes ablaze, he forged ahead. I tried hard to apologize through my laughter, but by this time it had a life of its own. As I tried, he continued. I looked at Arthur, who looked back at me as though I should be shot. The man finally tapered off and made his exit..., without leaving his script. I never heard from him again.

Arthur told me that the gentleman was Charles Bruce Millholland, the actor and playwright, who had been the inspiration for Ben Hecht and Charles MacArthur's film, *Twentieth Century*.

Had he been Abraham Lincoln, under the same circumstances, I venture that I would still have embarrassed myself and insulted our great President. I had absolutely no control over my actions. I went over the cliff and could not stop my fall.

In a supermarket, while in college: the same thing. I was in a mad rush to get home with some hamburger meat from the butcher when a lady, representing some brand of frankfurters had a spiel that she had memorized and was rattling off to me. She had a wiener on a toothpick and was offering it to me. She was bound to complete her spiel as written. So, same thing: I apologized and laughed uncontrollably. Same cliff. Same fall. I felt terrible. She seemed to be unfazed.

On the *Mary Tyler Moore Show*, Mary had a similar problem at a funeral. Same cliff...

The Foraging Wino and the Chow Chow in Drag

On a warm summer night, about fifty years ago, I was walking along 6th Avenue, in New York's Greenwich Village, with a friend who was struggling through a bout of depression. Among other things, she was about to turn thirty! Go figure. It was quite late, but I was reluctant to leave her to her own devices. At 4th Street and 6th Avenue, there was an Italian restaurant, O'Henry's, on the corner. Fourth Street was deserted... Just us..., and a man who might loosely be described as a "wino." He seemed to be alone in his own world as he rummaged, head-first, through the restaurant's garbage cans. He didn't notice us; even when we got almost even with him. He stood... Quit the garbage cans in disgust, and muttered: "Every fuckin' day... spaghetti." And, my friend laughed, off and on, for about ten minutes. Laughing is good. Laughing is healing. Laughter is fascinating. My friend, Mary Louise Wilson, has had a long and successful career on Broadway, mostly, by making other people laugh.

Back when I was doing *Brothers* and then *Chicken Soup*, our family and friends usually gathered at my house for "Fight-nights" when an interesting bill came along. I don't remember the specific fight... It might have been the second Tommy Hearns and

Sugar Ray Leonard fight. Maybe fifteen or twenty guests and five or six dogs were there. My dog, Lou, an old, white cockapoo, was blind, but hip to any gathering. A married couple, John Schwartz and his wife Joan Alperin-Schwartz came with their newly bathed and coiffed young male chow-chow named, Jaxon. Jaxon, although male, was much too pretty to be other than female. Possibly, a male chow-chow in drag. This little teaser walked around like our star stripper for the night. The other dogs took note and gathered around. Then the five or six dogs encircled the attractive little, Jaxon and began to hump the poor thing... right there in the middle of my living room floor. It was a frenzied hump-scene. All the dogs were humping on poor Jaxson.

John yelled out for all dog owners to help stop the abuse.

Joan insisted: "No. Don't stop them. This is good. It's like prison."

Jaxon managed to exit the living room, but the horn-dogs were in hot pursuit... except for poor, blind and horny Lou, who was left standing on his hind legs frantically humping thin air. Lou was going at it. It was quite pathetic and quite funny.

"Go Lou! Get it, Lou!" Then, "Poor Lou. Oh, poor old Lou."

Finally, when John and Joan left with their precious little Jaxon looking half his original size, the poor thing had lost his beautiful coiffure and left fight-night as a matted wet mess. Sad. And funny. And sad. And funny.

If it was the second Leonard-Hearns fight, Leonard won a controversial decision.

But, Lou and Jaxon won the night.

Sometimes it helps

The death of my daughter, Justine Marie, in 1985, at the age of twenty-five, in a car crash on the Merritt Parkway in Connecticut, left me in the depths of a very dark and dismal limbo..., with enervating emotional and visceral pain. Even today, twenty-nine years later, it's difficult to look at her pictures, watch videos, or even to think about her, without feeling a hard punch to my gut.

Photo by Jennifer Maggart

The terrible news came in the middle of the night …

Maybe, Justine had just gotten spun around by life, and she needed to start over. However, she had written a letter to me, yet to be mailed. It was still on her desk at work. One of her friends picked it up and gave it to Jennifer, who sent it to me. Justine had written that she was very excited about coming to California in just a few weeks. I thought maybe that Justine might even consider staying and living here. But then, I realized that she would never want to live so far from Jennifer, who was married and living in Connecticut. I got the call from Jennifer. Justine was gone. I asked if she was sure...

"Yes."

I had always heard that only the parents who have lost a child have any idea of the anguish. I retract that. Jennifer, being so very close to her, was equally hurt, as well. Also, Bran. Alone, in the middle of the night, I heard myself wailing and growling like an angry dog until finally I was numb and fell asleep for a couple of hours.

On the plane ride to New York, exhausted and half asleep, I wondered if Justine was okay now. After her car hit that big tree just off the Merritt Parkway, did she walk into a beautiful white light? A well intentioned male flight attendant cheerfully offered: "You're not looking too happy this morning, sir."

We, all of us, have walked around with holes in our hearts ever since Justine flew away. I suspect that she might have visited us from time to time. There certainly have been comforting echoes in my nocturnal attic. I see her smiling face. So, I guess she's good.

I was fortunate in that I had been doing a television series at the time, and being able to go back to work was helpful to some degree. Being focused on something so far removed gave me some respite. Performing those shows in front of a live audience and hearing that laughter gave me some space to heal. I began to think of things that had made me laugh when I was a child. I remembered how laughing was contagious. I thought of my Mother and Dad laughing so hard that I, myself, began to laugh, even without knowing exactly why we were laughing. Laughter or even a smile can be a touch of balm for a broken heart.

The very first joke that I could remember was told to me by my mother, and I put it on canvas. This evolved into painting the essences of other stories, or jokes, onto their own single canvas…, or storyboard. Soon there were dozens and dozens of sketches and paintings. I began to incorporate the paintings into a never ending "Papa's Quirky Quilt of Humor" that covers most of my three story wall space…, not to mention the ones stored in my closets and garage.

Friends began to take some fun in looking at the paintings and sometimes recalling the story (sometimes, even the storyteller) from fifty or more years ago. Sometimes a hint, a word or two, or a punch line, might evoke a memory… a time… a place. I used what my Dad, my Uncle Oscar, and my Angel had said. I began to use my sense of humor, and started throwing some "jokes" to "ease my mind and to let it be."

Photo by Annabel Clark

"Laughter be my opiate... Free my mind... Let me be"

This inserted: 8/1/2014

It's now the first day of August, 2014. The time is early morning. I just awoke from the worst nightmare of my life. The end was so devastating that I shot up in bed and, painfully, began to relive it... trying to make sense of it as best as I could.

It was sunny. We, the family, were at a summer house. A white, wooden, two-story frame with a balcony. LuJan was there. Three of my young children were outside playing near her. As I was watching them, when Julienne ran across a flat fence railing and jumped onto my back. She was hugging me. And, she whispered into my ear, "Did you pick me out?" as if it would be a secret between us.

I said, "Yes."

We went upstairs, with Julienne riding my shoulders as she liked to do. I was with her and watching her play in a sunlit room. I watched as she was enrapt in some coloring, or reading. She seemed happy. I went out of the room to do something... I don't know what. I went back downstairs where LuJan was, and the other children were still playing. Jan said, "You're in trouble. She's crying. You left her."

I said, "Don't worry. I take care of it," and went back upstairs onto a balcony of some kind. It wasn't Julienne. It was Justine that came out through a window and onto the balcony. She was upset. She had been crying. Though, she said nothing. She seemed to be about five or six.

She, then, looked at me and said, "You left me."

She was standing on a ledge. She began to lose her balance. I couldn't reach her in time. I watched her fall. I saw her hit a picket fence and then to the ground. I saw blood coming from her head and onto the ground. LuJan screamed. A dark feeling of hell was crushing my chest. The sickening feeling of it jolted me awake. That terrible, unbearable, gut-wrenching, pain, I knew. I recognized it. I recognized that awful shock and pain I had felt, twenty-nine years ago, when I was here in California, and Jennifer had called from Connecticut saying to me, "Justine is dead."

"Are you sure?"

"Yes."

It was my fault. I had left my post. Justine was gone. I was late with my reach. Justine was gone.

For all seven of my children, I have told myself that I was always with them. I have done my best to let them know that I am always there. But, in fact, I was missing at some very crucial times as they were growing up. I had left my post. I cannot ever, ever, ever, un-ring that bell.

At present, I can think of nothing that is funny.

Sherry Britton and Burlesque

After seeing me in *New Faces,* is when Sherry Britton *cast* me in her *Best of Burlesque* show. It was a much-needed time for laughs... Belly laughs! Sherry said that I was born too late; that I could have been a huge burlesque star. I said, "Maybe so, but I'm pretty sure I'd be dead by now." Walter Kerr had indeed likened me to Jimmy Savo, from those earlier times.

First... Sherry invited me to come see one of her performances. Her "Banana," at the time, was an older bona fide burlesque comic, named Irv Harmon. Irv had been with her for years. And, he was amazing, and I was in awe. How could I ever do that? He was a fluid stream of timing with exploding punctuations of laughter... Smooth as silk... And, effortless. He wasn't spontaneous. He didn't need to be. His performance was orchestrated down to a split second as if performing a Mozart piano concerto. He timed every laugh to perfection... Precise... Like stepping on stones while crossing a stream. At his age, Irv didn't want to continue. He could not learn new material. Sherry's new show would be within the same framework, and would keep some of the classic bits and sketches, but would be infused with new material: Songs and sketches written by Fred Tobias and Stan Lebowsky.

Most classic burlesque sketches were not written down. They were passed along. But, Sherry remembered them down to the last detail. Sherry had seen something in me that gave her confidence. From the very first performance, I knew I was in my element. We kept the best of the old and added some really good stuff. I fell in love at first laugh with being Top Banana in this well-honed burlesque show. I was one lucky guy. As they say, "Most fun I ever had with my baggy pants on."

Sherry Britton and Himself

We worked with a straight man, two second bananas, talking girls, ponies, (young dancing girls) specialty acts (Usually, a belly dancer). Oh, and the "candy butcher." (A guy who hawks things during intermission.)

This was our "talking girl's" first professional show. Sherry had another good eye for casting. Her name was Landy Sten. Landy was a blonde Lucille Ball. Great in sketches... Very attractive... Natural timing... Great attitude... Everything you could ask for. I felt sure that she would be successful in television or on Broadway. Landy worked on our first tour and retired. She got married and had children.

As stated before: Sherry was recently called the most iconic burlesque dancer in New York's *"Greatest New York Ever' 400 hundred year history."* In *New York Magazine*! Liz Goldwyn wrote: "Sherry had this air of dignity and grace: She was a star, and she had the attitude of a STAR... She was a diva. She behaved as though she were too good for burlesque, and that created a fantasy: that Sherry was a princess who just happened to be traipsing across the boards at the Bowery." Yowzah!

BEHIND THESE EYES SUCH SWEET MADNESS LIES

Yes, that's Sherry's hair... And her eighteen inch waist, too. Sherry began in burlesque at the age of fifteen... When we recorded our live television version, she was sixty-three... And looked much like this picture. Not, still with her eighteen inch waist, but, with her twenty-four inch waist. Still, phenomenal. At the end of our show, (Her eleven-o'clock-number) Sherry did her original Warsaw Concerto striptease as she had done it all those years ago. Except this time, mid-dance, she would invite some innocent looking gentleman from the audience to join her onstage. He would then be seated in a chair... Center stage... And, was told to sit there while she finished her number. This part bordered on being what is now called a "lap dance." It was always very sexy, but funnier than sexy. At the end of the number, Sherry would end up sitting on the fellow's lap. She would take a moment to let the audience drink in that picture, and then, she would stand beside the poor fellow... while telling him that she was going to count to three and that he should stand up...

"One... Two... Three!"

The blushing man would stand.

"Where is your wife?"

"There, in the second row."

"What's her name?"

"Sadie."

"Sadie, you can take him home now... He's ready."

Big laugh as the man stumbles back to his seat.

At the closing night party, little Maude Amber did her version of Sherry's dance. I had no idea that she had paid such close attention to that part of the show.

Touring the summer circuits and playing The World Famous Lou Walter's Latin Quarter in New York with Sherry Britton was about all this stage-struck comic actor could have asked for. I was Sherry's Banana, off and on, for over ten years. Great fun and treasured times. And, I did feel "at home," doing burlesque. And, yep, I rode that fine horse to the barn every night.

On March 1st, 1942, Mayor Fiorello La Guardia closed the doors of burlesque forever. A huge number of dancers, comics, stagehands, and others were put on the street. But, during the war, Sherry performed a slightly different act at Leon and Eddie's club on 52nd Street for seven years. From there, and elsewhere, she entertained our country's servicemen.

President Roosevelt made Sherry an "Honorary General" for what she did for the soldiers during the war. Her picture adorned the nose of one of our bombers.

Sherry had been engaged to at least fifteen prominent gentlemen until marrying businessman, Robert Gross. They were happily married for thirty years until Robert preceded Sherry in death. They were a great couple.

I found Robert's business niche to be fascinating. He had a large file cabinet…, filled with three by five cards. On these cards, he had lists of airplane parts held by numerous aircraft companies, airfields, and private owners, around the world. This, of course, was before computers. If someone needed a certain part for an older plane, he could go to Robert, and Robert would broker a deal.

Sherry and I were one of the last acts to "headline" at the "World Famous Latin Quarter" in New York… During that engagement, after the show, I danced with my daughter, Jennifer, on her twelfth birthday. I think I was happier about that than was Jennifer. This was the same The Latin Quarter I went to with my family when I was a teenager. Straight from having my name on the marquee of The Latin Quarter, I was back to, "May I take your order?" At least, I had a job… And the rent must be paid.

Casting

In productions, here on my attic stage, I perform with different players of my own choosing... Never mind not having played with them before... And, in quite a few instances, they may have been long deceased. However, sometimes, I've found that to be treacherous. I sang *"Indian Love Call"* with Jeanette MacDonald. I loved her, even though she didn't respond to my overtures. She said that I moved around too much... And, even accused me of "mugging":

"Nelson always stands perfectly still, without facial expression... You should sing with Judy Canova."

Recently, I made an extremely unwise casting. I did a scene from Ibsen's *A Doll's House* with the great Polish actress, Helena Modjeska. I became so mesmerized by her performance that I faded meekly into the background as she blew me off the stage. She suggested that I should seek work elsewhere:

"You might do fairly well in the circus; as a clown*!"*

I will soon be going into the deepest of waters. I'm working my way into performing *Rigoletto* with Maria Callas and Jan Pierce. To prepare vocally, I will call upon the voice of Leonard Warren.

To be more precise, I will be using the voice of Leonard Warren, but not the body of Leonard Warren. I plan to sit in the first-row mezzanine and watch my magnificent performance with Callas. I tried using my own voice in a recent rehearsal with Callas, and she demanded that I use either Warren's voice or Tito Gobbi's voice. The final scene when Callas as Rigoletto's daughter, Gilda, is dying… and Rigoletto understands that this is his fault… This is difficult for me even to watch, much less to play. I wish me luck. As I hold her and sing, "Mia Gilda…" God, forbid that I should rain down tears onto the face of Maria Callas. I wonder what her reaction might be.

Lately, I have been able to dance both roles in a *pas de deuce,* or if you prefer, the *"pas de deux."* I am both, Ahab and Moby Dick, dancing as one. As Ahab, I am much the skilful toreador; while Moby Dick is the befuddled, but dangerous bovine; or fish out of water if you will. They are in my perception, two sides to the same coin. One can only guess the significance of what a dark Ahab and a white Moby Dick would be doing while swimming around in Melville's head. Nevertheless, I can do that. I tend to stress the humor and the irony of the two combatants being in the same orbit. Getting those laughs and applause can perk up any otherwise dreary afternoon. I came upon this concept while rummaging through an old family trunk. Just a few notes, but they were quite useful.

Even though, most of my best and dearest partners have "passed over"… I resurrect them with all their beauty and talent for each and every affair. Sometimes, the best evenings are spent just being together and listening to Gershwin or Puccini... Or, Jo Stafford... Or, Sinatra... Then, followed by Chopin nocturnes and an easy trip to the Land of Nod.

More recently, I've enjoyed sitting in my *travel chair* and seeing my son, Garett, on stage. Or, sitting in the audience at performances by my two youngest daughters: Maude, or Fiona. Actually, I recently saw them, on stage, at *Largo*, singing together. I'm still smiling. I, especially, enjoy occasional *out of body* observations of all my children and grandchildren as they go about their daily lives. I have watched my Jennifer tend to children in the pediatric clinic where she works. Jennifer was an RN, living and working in Connecticut. (Now in California with the rest of our family, including her two daughters, Loren and Lindsey... And, back to school for a career change.) She has my love and admiration. And, I see Julienne constantly dancing and manuevering her way through one crisis after another while laughing, albeit with an occasional escaping tear. Wisely, she turns up the volume and dances away her troubles. She, too, has my love and admiration. And, to see Bran remaining the cornerstone of us all. Bran is truly a unique character. While being a writer, I'm sure he's gathering tons of material while managing Fiona's tours. Bran shouldered the responsibilities of being the man of the family during my absences, and did it very well. And, to have witnessed Garett's and Cindy's wedding... Childhood sweethearts finally getting back together... Maude and David, with their artistry and sharp wit, singing and laughing together... And, my Fiona, demanding that she be able to fight her own battles and to love her own loves and to make her own music.

That takes courage and self-conviction, of which she seems to have an abundance.

It is a great blessing to still be breathing and to be able to watch my children and grandchildren as they make their way through life. Fascinating. But, I do so very much miss my Justine.

Buddy and Jim on Sesame Street

In 1969, while Jimmy Catusi and I were holding forth in a revue at The Upstairs at the Downstairs, called *Free Fall,* by Bill Weeden and David Finkle, (Yes, the well-respected New York theatre critic, David Finkle). I got a call from Jon Stone (the heart and soul producer of Sesame Street) asking me if I would do some sketches for a children's television project for him... And, I would need a partner... Who would I like to work with? I said, "Jimmy." And, we did a few sketches on tape that were great fun. I, more or less, used a spinoff of my character in burlesque, but with a lesser IQ... Even using the same hat and tie. Jimmy was perfect for the team. And, we used our own names, Buddy and Jim, since the scripts we were given still had the character's names of Fred and Al (Fred Gwynn and Al Lewis) who, apparently, had dropped out at the last minute.

We forgot about Jon's children's show and carried on at The Upstairs at the Downstairs. Several months later we got invited to a screening, at the Plaza Hotel, of a children's television show called *Sesame Street.* This was Jon's show!?! We arrived and could see that this was some big-time event! We, along with tons of press and television folk watched... And, soon, there we were on a large screen, "Buddy and Jim" getting huge laughs! We had no idea... Sesame Street was and is a gift to all children, from PBS and Children's Television Workshop. Many of these old sketches can now be seen on Utube as "Sesame Street – Buddy and Jim." We were told that many children while watching Sesame Street, were told to call the parents when our sketches began.

Joe Raposo was the musical director for the show. Joe also wrote most of the songs, including… "It's not easy Bein' Green." My first musical in New York called *Sing Muse*, was written by Joe and Erich Segal. I knew Joe from when, as a teenager in short pants, he conducted the matinees at the Framingham Music Theater... near Boston. Also, making her New York debut in *Sing Muse* was Karen Morrow. In my opinion, Karen Morrow is the best belter of all the big belters ever to play on Broadway, including Merman.

We, "Buddy and Jim," were a big hit in the show, and the show was getting lots of promotion and praise in the press. But, there was a problem… They had already inserted our sketches into the shows without ever having given us a contract. I guess in all the rush; they had overlooked this. No problem; we would gladly work for AFTRA scale… And we continued doing more sketches… About twenty-five in all. Finally, a shocker! They presented us with contracts that were completely prohibitive for anyone having to make a living for a wife and five children, in New York. What's more: The "suits" at *Sesame Street* demanded that they would have approval over any commercials, movies, and other TV shows that might be offered to us? What???

On my own, I had already turned down the starring role in a film because I didn't think it would be appropriate for me to do at that time. Plus, I must say, I didn't like the script. Here's the thing; producers of TV commercials can't wait for such approvals from a third party. They cast and shoot almost immediately. This made it impossible for me. I had to make a living. I had to do shows and commercials at the same time just to make the month for my large family. This was sad... Heartbreaking... Especially, for Jimmy. Also, I was about to be cast as Buzz Richards (playwright) in the Broadway musical, *Applause*, starring Lauren Bacall.

Jimmy and I continued making trips to hospitals, two schools on the upper west side, and even private homes for children that were in need of some brief entertainment. On request, we were privileged to visit Pulitzer Prize-winning journalist Murray Kempton's home, and spent time with his young son. It was our privilege. I was doing *Applause*, so Jimmy dealt with all the requests. I think that Jimmy felt his calling was about bringing some laughter to children who needed to have some laughter. And, he was devastated that we couldn't continue. I don't think he ever got over it... Although; he was a regular on the *David Frost Show* after that, and toured with Lily Tomlin. Jimmy passed away this past year... A great friend and a very funny man.

But, with my "traveling without leaving," I can always throw in one of those sketches that Jimmy and I did as "Buddy and Jim" on *Sesame Street*. I think my favorites were... Getting an ironing board through a too narrow doorway... Locking my piggy bank key in my piggy bank for safe keeping… And the one about making a peanut butter and jelly sandwich, which, of course, was not practical to do in hospitals, schools, and private homes… Too messy… But, a favorite with the children.

About three years later, while I was doing my eight shows a week in *Lorelei* at the Palace, Jimmy and I were asked to do a children's theater show, called *The Man Who Hated Spring*, with music by my friend, Shelly Markham, at Town Hall in New York. As I recall, due to my schedule, at the Palace, just blocks away, we only did Saturday morning and Sunday afternoon performances for two weekends. The NY Times reviewed the show saying, "I think I may have just seen the best children's show I have ever seen in my life." We used a version of the "Seesaw" sketch we had done on *Sesame Street*. Of course, the children went crazy over what they had seen us do on *Sesame Street*. However, this was done without getting permission, by our "Theatreworks" producer. I'm told that the Sesame Street suits were not thrilled… And justly so. A husband and wife team wrote most of the sketches. I'm sorry, but I can't recall their names… My sincere apologies to them. The show would not have been nearly so good without their *"Seesaw"* sketch. They were complicit in making a lot of children laugh and have a good time.

The Theatre World Award

I was thrilled and proud to have won that Theatre World Award for my performance in the musical revue *Put it in Writing*, performed at the Theatre de Lys… Now, the Lucille Lortel Theatre. The Theatre World Award is given to the "Most Promising" new actors and actresses for performances during the year's theatrical season. I called my mother, back in Carthage, Tennessee, and told her that I had won the Theatre World Award.

"Now, what is that, Buddy?"

I explained the significance of the award, reeling off some of the major stars that had won the award in past years. Mama recognized the ones who later became movie stars.

There was quite a talented list of winners in 1962-63: Front row... Alan Arkin, Julienne Marie, Carol Channing (who was the award presenter), and Melinda Dillon. Second row... Stuart Damon, Dorothy Loudon, Daniel Blum (Publisher of *Theatre World* and the man doing the choosing), Diana Sands, and Liza Minnelli. Top row... Himself, Robert Drivas, Swen Swenson, and Bob Gentry. My friend, Estelle Parsons missed the awards ceremony.

I think she was impressed... Very impressed. I received my hometown paper, *The Carthage Courier*, about a week or two later. As usual, I always read my Uncle Vernon's "Maggart Community" column first. Uncle Vernon wrote this weekly column for over sixty years. On the front page of the Courier, I think there was a picture of a very large hog. Near the back page, there appeared as usual, "The Party Line," identified by a line drawing of a young girl on her telephone. The column was devoted to brief local news items that had occurred during the past week. As I read about a family reunion in Pleasant Shade, I came upon something that made my eyeballs bulge... Like in a cartoon. Keeping in mind that my mother was prone to having a few glasses of wine in the afternoon, I imagined a phone call having been placed from my mother to the editor... I believe to be Andy Reid, at the time. How Andy must have weighed the call, was reflected in how the item was hidden... Deep... In "The Party Line":

"Brandon Maggart, son of Agnes Maggart, of Main Street, has recently won an award for being 'The Best Actor in the World."

"THE BEST ACTOR IN THE WORLD!!!" And, not on the front page. Andy was having a little fun. Indeed, I have put that story to good use for many years. It never gets old.

After that brief recognition, as a "most promising actor," I had to go back to, "May I take your order?" What a shame that my customers were not aware that their waiter was the best actor in the world.

But, doing shows, commercials, and waiting tables had, thankfully, sustained us until finally I landed a hit... A big hit... With great reviews!!! I, finally, hooked the big one with *"Applause."* Lauren Bacall was our star.

Applause

With unanimous rave notices, my *Tony* nomination, and a projected two-year run at the Palace Theatre, I was in hog heaven. It was a heady time. Now, I would make-the-month for at least twenty-four months ahead. This was unbelievably reassuring. Following each performance, luminaries from stage, screen, and politics came backstage for brief visits with Bacall. When lots of men in business suits with short haircuts were backstage and in the wings, we knew there must be a high-ranking member of the government, such as George Bush Sr., at the performance. Also, at the same time, I was still appearing on *Sesame Street*.

For the first time in my career, I could see, financially, beyond the current month! I didn't know it at the time, but... No more would I ask, "May I take your order?"

I can't possibly write about *Applause* without mentioning Diane McAfee. I had admired Diane in the role of Eve Harrington when we were in rehearsals in New York and later in Baltimore at the beginning of our out-of-town tryouts with *Applause*. She was very attractive and smart, with a somewhat contagious positive attitude.

Our opening in Baltimore was chaotic. The show ran over an hour too long, due to sets continually crashing into each other. The sets were made to move along tracks in the deck. The tracks had not yet been reinforced with metal runners. Crash... Crash... And crash as the sets crashed through the wooden deck. Every time that happened, if you were in your dressing room, you would hear the same filler music. "Oops... Not again."

Also, Eve was supposed to be given choreography for her big "Halloween" number. After the final run-through, Diane had still not been given the choreography. She approached Ron Field the director concerned about what to do in that important spot. "Improvise something," he said.

Over a two-year search, the producers had auditioned the finest actress/singers in New York, Los Angeles, and under any rock they could find, to play the role opposite Lauren Bacall. Diane had, at that time, been an ensemble singer in several Broadway musicals. And, she had come to audition for the chorus of *Applause*. She had overslept past the time for the Actors Equity audition, so she came to the later, non-union call. And, a "Broadway Cinderella" was discovered, a la *42nd Street*. Diane was cast as Eve Harrington.

Bacall and Diane at first rehearsal.

Her story was well-publicized in the New York Press. With her family's show business background, it made for great publicity. Both her mother and father had been singers. Her father, Johnny McAfee, played reeds and sang with the Harry James Band, and her mother, Millicent Green (living to be one hundred years old), had been a singer in the Johnny Hamp Band... Plus, she had been in most all of the *George White Scandals* on Broadway, beginning in 1926, when she was fifteen years old. Her father brought her, back and forth, on the train, from Rockville Center, L.I. for each show. In the *1928 Scandals*, she sang and danced with Nick Long Jr, introducing the song, "I May Be Wrong But, I Think you're Wonderful."

During her time on Broadway, Millicent had double-dated with a handsome young actor that she liked named Archie Leach, who later changed his name to Cary Grant.

When we were in Baltimore, another version of that *Cinderella* story emerged; the pumpkin made its appearance. I remembered how good I thought she was in the plum role of Eve Harrington... But, as often happens in show business, she was given her "notice" and was told she would be replaced at the end of our first week in Baltimore. I was assigned to break the bad news to Diane. I was told that Bacall wanted to tell Diane how much she liked her, but Bacall was away that weekend, and it had to be done right away.

I was told that the producers thought Diane's youth and light soprano voice weren't competition enough for Bacall's stronger, bigger than life, Margot Channing. I couldn't see the logic in that. There was a scene in the show, when the scheming Eve auditions to be Margot Channing's understudy. I adjusted the scene a bit and presented it, with Diane, to Ron Field, the director. Ron was impressed enough to suggest a meeting.

It was my opinion that with Margot, playing the broader theatrical style that just the opposite of that would be the best competition; with a smart, attractive, youthful, more accessible, Eve. The audition would be with the stage manager as in the script, but without holding scripts. The stage manager only had two lines, and Eve knew her lines. At this point, the audience, as I saw it, should not know that this was an audition. The way that it was currently played, it was obvious that it was an audition for the job. Here, in my opinion, it should be seen as a realistic backstage spat; and not an audition. The audience should know that it was an audition only when the producer and writer (with Karen) come onstage, applauding.

With Ron's blessing, we presented the scene to the producers, including the writers, Betty Comden and Adolph Green. They were kindly receptive, but not sufficiently moved. Under a ton of pressure, Diane reverted back to what she had been doing each performance. I was disappointed, to say the least. Everyone had gathered to see nothing really different. It was a long, long shot, since Penny Fuller had already been signed.

Betty and Adolph approached me. They had every right to dismiss me; me, with such effrontery. But, they thanked me for letting them think about the scene in a slightly different way. They gave me a pass. Whew!

Diane posted a note on the callboard stating that she did not wish to discuss the matter and that she would appreciate it if the cast would not approach her with their well-intentioned support. She had yet a week to play her role as Eve Harrington. At her final performance in Baltimore, during the curtain call, there were many tears, especially from the singers and dancers. Diane's mother did get to see her perform the show during that final week. Ron Field, subsequently hired Diane to play the role in a touring version, with opera star, Patrice Munsel; figuring that would be a better match. She also, later, played the role with Arlene Dahl… Then, with Alexis Smith.

Penny Fuller came into the show, on short notice, and did a terrific job. I had known and liked Penny from when I played her new husband on an episode of *Route 66*... called, appropriately, "The Wedding." After we finished our run in Baltimore, we played Detroit and came directly into the Palace Theatre, in New York, for three previews before opening to rave notices across the board... And, just in time for lots of Tony nominations, including Penny Fuller, Bacall, Len Cariou, Bonnie Franklin, and me. Both Bacall and the show won Tonys. An interesting side note; after a year, Anne Baxter came on to play Margot Channing. In the original film version, Anne Baxter had played Eve Harrington.

This was quite an event. On her opening night, the "roof blew off"... Partly because every gay man in America was there and loving it.

(On the following page: Anne Baxter with Himself)

Unfortunately, after about the end of her first week, the attendance dropped considerably. After such a wonderful opening, it was a big let-down for Anne. As Anne and Gwyda DonHowe (replacing Ann Williams in the role of Karen), and I were awaiting our entrance to begin Act Two, Anne muttered, "What a dish of crow." But, she soldiered on and always gave her very best.

(A tidbit: Anne's Grandfather was the famous architect Frank Lloyd Wright.)

The lovely Arlene Dahl, eventually, replaced Anne Baxter. Arlene seemed to take it as a lark. However, on her opening night, I was standing in the wings watching as she was about to answer the phone from Bill, who was calling from Italy. She picked up the phone and said, "Hello," before she got the phone anywhere near to her face. But, she looked good doing it. Years later, while doing an episode of *Ellen,* the director told me that he had been there that same night, and remembered the lovely Arlene Dahl saying "Hello" before the phone was near her beautiful face.

Diane, the fiery and very capable mother of, Maude Amber Maggart and Fiona Apple Maggart, was a very dedicated member of La Leche League… Sometimes nursing both daughters at the same time. I walked into the apartment one afternoon and found six or eight young mothers chatting away while serving up fresh mammary lunches to their offspring.

(As you can well surmise, LuJan and I were divorced by now. And, Diane and I were not doing too well either.)

I was sleeping in the spare room down the hall during that period. I was in *Musical Chairs*, my last Broadway show before moving to Hollywood. And, when I got home one night, after the show, Diane informed me that the police had been there. She had been awakened from her loft bed, where she slept with our two little girls. She heard a noise and thought she saw me in the front room going through her sewing basket... "Brandon?" Someone ran down the hallway and out the front door. She called the police. The police came and discovered the burglar had come in through the back window from the fire escape by bending one window bar just enough for a slim fellow to squeeze through. The police checked all seven rooms to make sure that he had not left an accomplice behind.

According to Diane, when one policeman came out of my little room with half-bath, he said, "Jesus, he really ransacked that room." Diane informed the policeman that the interloper had probably not gone into the room, and that was the usual condition behind those doors..., with dog-eared books and magazines spread all over the bed and opened to specific underlined pages. That small space, usually, with a can of beer and a pint of vodka, was where I did my research on the big mysteries of life. The "keys to the universe" were beyond my grasp, but that didn't stop my pursuit... Especially, late at night and into the early morning hours when the world was quiet around me. In this solitary cocoon, I did ponder... And write... And drink... And drink.

So, I pondered, is there a "God" or a "Higher Power?" (Hasn't everyone?) Is my God an energy source operating by means of trial and error as do we; one step forward... Half a step back... Closer to perfection... Closer to exacting Pi... Attempting to square the circle... Closer to the "God Particle"... And then what? What's on the other side of that? I predict: More. Much more. Endless... and circular.

Did my Maker leave His footprints, time and time again, in this little room, on these pages, and in my mind, for me to immerse myself in the wonderments of this world? If so..., well done! Among this concatenation of footprints are gravity, electricity, geometry, Fibonacci numbers, the Golden Mean, music, harmony, all the sciences, the infinitely complicated blueprints within each of our cells, human and animal friendships, the colors and sounds of the human voice, the miracles of evolution, the complicated workings of the vertebrate eye, the magnificence and scope of our brains, sounds, rhythms, ratios, algorithms, the joy of accomplishing a difficult task, to love and be loved, songs about the highs and lows of love, an ability to laugh at our own missteps, having available a few expletives to defuse our many frustrations, the responsibility of raising our children, the personal rewards of doing something altruistically, the ability to forgive ourselves for unfortunate blunders, observing our children as they take a win or a loss with grace, the power of laughter, the popular act of making physical love, combining traits of two of us to make a third individual (absolutely amazing), crossword puzzles, skateboards, the thrill of grasping a new idea, the various arts as a better way to communicate. These are fascinating footprints made by accident; or are these footprints made by a higher power? I wonder.

All this has been and remains fascinating. And, the gift of being able to be fascinated and entertained is paramount. It's been years since I can remember being bored. At times, I feel I might explode with happiness... Or pain... But, more often with happiness. On some such occasions, I have a spiritual experience of focus and calm... In touch with and in communion with the whole beauty of existence... Warts and all... One wart that night being: my Grandfather's gold watch was missing from my little cocoon. I imagined a very optimistic burglar assessing my room full of all the chaos and thinking... "There's got to be a gold watch in here somewhere!"

(This added on 8/12/2014)

Just a few minutes ago, I received an email that Lauren Bacall had passed. She was eighty-nine. Not a bad life. Just a few minutes before that email, I was making edits in the *Applause* chapter of this very book. Bizarre. Even more bizarre; Diane McAfee is here visiting our daughters, Maude Amber and Fiona, and I was checking with her about the note she had written and placed on the callboard in Baltimore after she had been "let go."

Yesterday, Robin Williams was found dead in his home in Tiburon, near San Francisco. I had begun my thirty-three years of sobriety while filming *The World According to Garp* with that master of the comic mind. Robin was sixty-three. And, Robin had lived with both laughter and demons.

In both cases, those were two very important times in my life.

As I sit here, I am wondering if there is another shoe teetering on the edge.

(This added the following day)

Yesterday was not real. We were watching a sad and unsettling film, starring Lauren Bacall and Robin Williams. Today: Yesterday was not a film.

Lorelei and Carol Channing

The following is the true packed-to-the-rim, typical in many ways of storied Broadway lore, show business account of two years in one show. First, a year on a national pre-Broadway tour ending up at The Palace Theatre on Broadway for a second-year odyssey.

Lorelei, with Carol Channing, was essentially a continuation of the Anita Loos' *Lorelei Lee* story from her book, *Gentlemen Prefer Blondes* that became the Jule Styne musical of the same name. Carol had become a huge star, playing the role of Lorelei Lee; so, why not revisit a bit of that success? She had been on the covers of both Life magazine and Time magazine. And, that's a big star, folks.

This past year, I, along with throngs of others, signed a petition that Carol Channing should be given a Kennedy Center Honor. In my opinion, she deserves it. (Alas, this did not come to pass.)

Carol, truly an icon in the annals of American Musical Theatre, and her then husband, Charles Lowe, seemed like the right and the left hands of a show business dynamo. Carol did the performing, plus every promotional opportunity that Charles lined up for her. And Charles saw to it that they were properly rewarded financially for their successes.

With my professional life moving along nicely, my personal life, at the time, was in disarray. So, I looked forward to getting out of town with a nice, fun, pre-Broadway national tour to clear my head... Send home some decent bucks for LuJan and the kids... And, maybe get a different perspective on my life and what I was doing with it. We would tour a year before opening on Broadway in 1974..., again, at the Palace Theatre... Yowzah!

Photo by Swope.

We opened in Oklahoma City. We were not a big hit. And, we were very long. My duet with Carol was cut in the first week. As I exited the stage for the last time with that number, the director, Joe Layton, said that he was sorry. Although, I was "very good in the number," it had worked better for me than for Carol. (Remember that for later... A harbinger of things to come.)

From time to time, along this extensive tour, we would have new creative people... New directors, choreographers, and writers coming in, hopefully, with improvements before facing the New York critics. When new creative people came in, we were constantly in rehearsal... Doing the old material at night and learning new material and new dances the next morning. This is common with pre-Broadway tryouts, usually lasting four to six weeks. But, the *Lorelei* Company did this for a year.

I haven't the faintest idea how Carol kept going at that pace. She began her day, before rehearsals, by doing radio, TV, and newspaper publicity. I remember thinking, "That girl is a slave." Still, I admired how Charles managed his job, and Carol, and I told him so. He seemed to be with her every single minute. Charles and I, also, seemed to be getting off to a great start, especially since Charles would drop off his *Sunday New York Times Crossword* for me each week.

Carol's stamina was unparalleled. She did it all. In the show, I was the "Zipper King"..., a character based on a Bernarr Macfadden-like health nut. At one point, early on, when we were without a director for a time, I told Carol that I could get a big laugh incorporating the zipper on the side of her dress. Carol said, "Go on Brandon... If you can get a laugh there... Do it..., by all means." I did..., and got a big laugh there every night. Things were going along just fine. I was exploding into my character. Well, maybe not exploding..., but I was having a great time polishing my character's exuberances.

Tamara Long, who played second fiddle to Carol's Lorelei, happened to be a dedicated health freak; and, she might possibly have saved my life. We became close, and Tamara persuaded me to stop drinking..., and to begin a healthy diet, which enhanced my life, as well as my performances. Things were going well.

After our troubled opening in Oklahoma City, we played Huston and Indianapolis, before opening at the Fisher Theater in Detroit for a four-week run. When we opened, producer, Lee Guber, along with Betty Comden and Adolph Green and others, came out for our gala opening. There was a party in Carol's dressing room celebrating what had been a very good opening night performance. At the party, producer Lee Guber approached me, with a smile, and said:

"Brandon, the last time I saw this show, it was about a Blonde from Little Rock, and now it's about a health nut Zipper King."

"Lee... not so loud... You'll have me on a bus to New York by morning!"

Charles was standing close by... Almost as if to be eavesdropping... Or, over-lording. Hmmm... For some reason, my New York Times crossword puzzles stopped arriving.

Six weeks later, when we opened in Washington, all five of my children, Jennifer, Justine, Brandon, Julienne and Garett, ranging in ages from eighteen down to five, took the train from Darien down to Washington for a week's visit. Wonderful! And, I would get them on their train ride back home to Darien on Saturday morning, early enough, with time to spare, for me to get over to the National Theatre for my matinee. For many years, I have had terrible nightmares about missing my call for, "Places... Places please... Your call is places." So, I always arrive a bit early for any and all engagements... Especially for the theatre. I'm always at the theatre before the "half hour" is called. My nightmare was about to come true.

After their few days visit, I got the children on the train with plenty of time to spare. I boarded the train with them to see that all five could sit together. My ten-year-old daughter, Julienne, kept telling me that I should get off the train. She was very persistent. I told her not to worry that I had plenty of time. Without me heeding her warnings, the doors closed with me still on board. Whoops! Panic! Julienne began to cry..., because she had seen panic on a face that never panicked. A conductor came through the doors, separating the cars, "Tickets, please." I told him that I had to get off the train.

"Sorry sir, the train doors are controlled by computer... And, can't be opened until we get to Baltimore."

Oh, My God! Oh, my God!

"But I have to get off... This is an emergency! I can be sued for untold thousands of dollars (I didn't have thousands of dollars). I have to be at the National Theatre at one thirty!"

"There's nothing I can do, sir."

He did provide a phone for me to call Ben, our stage manager. I told Ben that I was on a train headed to Baltimore, and might not make it back to Washington in time for our matinee.

"Brandon..., you have to. You know we don't have an understudy for your role yet."

"Believe me, Ben; I'll do everything I can. I'll get the first train back from Baltimore... Whenever that is!"

Julienne is sobbing.

The conductor checked his schedule and found that there would be a train scheduled to leave Baltimore for Washington about five minutes before we get there. And, with it being Saturday, another train wasn't scheduled until one o'clock.

Oh, my God... What have I done!?!

Julienne kept crying. The conductor said it might be possible that if that Washington-bound train was late and still in the station that I could run across the platform and board it. But, chances were that the train would run on schedule. Except for Julienne crying, Jennifer, Justine, Brandon, and Garett, were stunned into silence. I'm pretty sure they saw tears welling up in my eyes. This was a disaster. I was right in the middle of my much-feared nightmare.

The train was there, and I ran across the platform and boarded it as the doors were closing. I looked across the platform and saw my children smiling and waving to me as their train pulled away... Going home to Darien. Whew!

I called Ben... "Ben, I'll be there!"

Ben's calm reply: "Good."

I was sitting in my dressing room, weak as a kitten, in costume and makeup, when Ben called:

"Half hour... Your call is half hour... Half hour, please."

Both Julienne and I recovered. But, both of us are always punctual.

Nevertheless, to this day, 11/2/2014, the same two nightmares visit my otherwise peaceful slumbers. The one last night involved the Schubert Theatre, here in LA. The Schubert (now gone) has been the home of several nocturnal panics. As usual, I couldn't find the stage door... Running late... After trying forever to get to my dressing room... No wardrobe... Wrong shoes... Hearing the overture... Donning whatever rags and shoes I could grab... Wrong elevator... The right elevator, but it goes to the wrong floor... Goes past stage-level... My cue is about to take place... Here, I usually wake up, but last night I didn't make it... There was no understudy... Opening night... But, it started without me. The cast ignored me... I felt like shit... I had destroyed the opening night. I bolted upright in bed. Whew!

The other, of the two nightmares, involves being a waiter and being "slammed" with too many crowded tables to cover. The bartender is too slow... The cook is too slow... I am panicked... Customers are leaving without paying their checks... I chase one down the street... I wake up. Oy.

Back to *Lorelei*: Four other cities, and now, Chicago! Jennifer, Justine, Bran, and Julienne flew out for the show and to splash in Lake Michigan. Garett was deemed too young for the trip. Tamara opined that Jennifer and Justine needed special diets, with enemas, for cleansing. Justine didn't react well and had to be taken to the hospital emergency room. Julienne's foot got infected and had to be taken to the same emergency room. One doctor wanted to amputate her toe... Another doctor said, "No", and saved her toe. Needless to say, their mother, LuJan, was not pleased with my supervision.

I got a call from the stage manager that I was to meet producer, Lee Guber, backstage at ten in the morning. Lee always seemed happy to see me... But, not so much this time. And, I was truly shocked at what he had to say. But, now, thinking back to Detroit, and Carol's dressing room, maybe not. Lee said that I was to change my character to a less ebullient, and more restrained performance... Take out the flying leaps from the wings... No zipper business... Everything... Gone. I'm stunned. I told him that a full cast rehearsal would be needed. Reactions would have to be cut by those in scenes with me... etc...

That afternoon, a special rehearsal was held to incorporate the changes. On the bus ride back to our hotel following the show that night, with Charles and Carol aboard, one of the young children, sitting up front with his dad, at the top of his voice, called out:

"Brandon, why did Carol make you stop being funny in the show?"

It got very quiet and remained so, on that bus ride back to the hotel. The next day, Jennifer, Justine, and Julienne flew back home, and Bran continued on with me for two more stops... St. Louis and Dallas.

Two more cities before opening in San Francisco for a four week run at the Curran Theatre. My mother, back in Tennessee, became very ill and went into a coma. I did have an understudy by that time, and it was Sunday, so I hopped a plane back home. When the doctor said she could, possibly, remain in that state for weeks, I immediately flew back to San Francisco and, after paying a cabbie twenty bucks extra, arrived Tuesday night at the Curran... Five minutes before curtain. My understudy was dressed and ready to go on. Carol saw me rush in. She told Ben that...

"Brandon will go on... No understudy!"

So, I didn't miss a single performance. The understudy was from San Francisco. His parents and others were in the audience expecting to see him in the role. I felt terrible. He could easily have performed the role. I wished he could have gone on.

The least I could do, I thought, was to pay for the six tickets. He accepted my offer. Drat!

Next stop... Los Angeles! We did one charity preview at the Schubert Theatre the night before opening. There were more diamonds in the audience than Carol Channing had rhinestones on her forty-pound dress. It was like playing Palm Beach. No laughs... silent... Like a bejeweled painting. I'm singing my big number "I'm Alive, I'm a Tingle, I'm a Glow," when I hear, just as loudly as I was singing, which was loud... Tamara Long vocalizing from her dressing room... And, it's going out over the speakers. The stage manager had forgotten to turn off her body mike. I loved it. I kept in character while acknowledging an eerie voice from above. That was about the only excitement for the evening.

We opened the next night, and thankfully; it was much better than the night before. I got the morning *LA Times* and read Sylvia Drake's review... She said that I was good in the role..., but that I "needed another number."

So, then, I get a call to meet the producers, writers, and the conductor, my good friend, Milton Rosenstock, at a rehearsal studio. Here we go again. I must alter my performance even more, and they were cutting my big number. The LA Times thought I needed another number... They did them one better... They took away the one song I had left. That song, "I'm Alive, I'm a Tingle, I'm a Glow," is on the cast album, made while we were in Detroit, I believe. They did a new recording after opening in New York, but my number is included.

The song had worked much better when I had my freewheeling eccentric character going for me. The song, by itself, was without that character. Even though it was fun to do, it was gone.

I was to face Carol from the side, looking towards the wings, and I was to "speak without inflection."

"Just say the lines."

I must say; their point was valid. I was getting laughs. Not good. When we began, I was led to believe that I was "Second Banana'… Not the 'straight man." Now, I'm to play "straight" for Carol. The straight man's job is to set up the comic, especially, the comic star. George Burns, friend of Charles and Carol's, was in the audience, and I'm told he said that he would never have allowed me to be on stage with Gracie. And, George knew what he was talking about. George, himself, wasn't funny until he worked solo as God. I had been riding the wrong horse; now, the fine steed that I had brought, and was riding, was to be replaced by a more suitable nag for the occasion. I got it. I did it. I had to have my salary to send home.

Let's revisit the shows before Chicago, when we were working without a director, or writers. In Carol's "Diamonds are a Girl's Best Friend" number, Carol wore a Bob Mackie designed, rhinestone covered dress, weighing forty pounds. The famous dress is now in the Smithsonian's National Museum of American History. Carol had to, and did, make a one minute change, following the number. And she would rush right back onstage for the next scene. Suddenly, she couldn't make the change and get back onstage for the next dialogue. It had something to do with the rhinestone dress. Maybe Bob Mackie had added more rhinestones... I don't know. That didn't bother me.

We were supposedly on an ocean liner on our way to Europe. I was the Zipper King, and Peter Palmer was the Button King. We were in competition for Lorelei's attention and were waiting for Lorelei to return to our table. When we ran out of dialogue, to fill the gap, while, in character, I would improvise... Depending on how long she took to make the change. To be honest, it became my favorite part of the show. Among other impulses, I ambled over to the lip of the stage and curiously gazed down into the orchestra pit: "Holy bejeezus... There's a big hole over here, and, it's full of penguins with musical instruments." (Orchestra members wore tuxedos back then) I would continue until Carol made it back onstage. I looked forward to this spot.

At the first performance in New York, miracle of miracles, Carol made the change on time. Afterwards, I congratulated her: "Carol... You made the change!"

Carol said: "Why, Brandon, did you think the audience was interested in anything you had to say?"

Ouch! Perfect. I had heard that the problem was something to do with the sleeves. With that problem solved, she never missed that entrance again.

We opened to lukewarm reviews. But, we had Carol's name to sell tickets.

Couple of nuggets: I must say; Charles Lowe was always on the job. If an audience was not laughing very much, if at all, Charles would walk around to different parts of the balcony and laugh. Being the only laugh and being very distinctive, it was quite sad and desperate. Nevertheless, he tried. For a while, in New York, there would be a few people in the front row that stood, sometimes sparking a standing ovation for Carol's curtain call... The same people that stood the night before... And a couple of times last week... Same young two or three people. Suspect? Were they paid? Did they get free tickets? It worked, sometimes. If the first row stands... The second row feels obligated to stand... Charles was on the job. As the song says, "He works hard for the money."

A famous Hollywood producer told a member of my family that Charles Lowe had found out how to get in touch with the Neilsen Families. Supposedly, Charles was making an effort to raise the ratings for a two-hour-sketch-comedy-special that Carol was doing. Might it have been the one called, "I'm a Fan" that Alex Cohen produced, starring Carol and Dick Van Dyke? And, yep. I was in that one too.

Being on Stage with Tamara Long and Carol Channing

Being onstage with Tamara Long and Carol Channing at the same time was truly a unique experience. On tour, Tamara and I had been lovers, but we broke it off (so to speak) in Philadelphia, before getting to Broadway and The Palace Theater. Tamara was so displeased with me that she would not speak to me. Onstage, when required to speak to my character, she would not look at me. She looked slightly upstage of my upstage ear, giving the audience the impression that she was looking me in the eye. Carol, of course, would address me, "Why, Mr. Gage...," and, as usual, would complete the line or lines, out front over the audience. I was in no-man's-land... A unique theatrical experience, indeed. The devil in me, once or twice, made me drift upstage in the direction of Tamara's gaze. To keep from being "upstaged," she, unflinchingly, switched her focus to my downstage ear. This was unprofessional fun to be sure..., for me..., not so much for Tamara. I could see the smolder behind that bright smile of hers.

Here, I must own up to another guilty pleasure; undoubtedly, given to me by the same devil. I, usually, after the final curtain, would run up the stairs to my dressing room. But, after the second show, on a Saturday night, I saw Lee Roy in the elevator and decided to ride up with him. Once inside the elevator, I faced front and saw Tamara walking towards the same, one and only, small, antiquated elevator, installed a century earlier for the Great Sarah Bernhardt. (Bernhardt had only one leg) As Tamara approached her usual winged chariot, her tired brown eyes saw me. The expression on her face said that she was not about to get on the elevator…, with me inside. And, just as quickly, her expression said that she was exhausted. Contemplating being in that tiny elevator with me was an unexpected horror for her, I'm sure. After two shows of tap dancing, and at the end of a long week of the same, she had to make her decision. She chose to take the elevator.

Once she was inside, I said, in a pretend-formal manner, "Good evening Miss Long. How are you this evening? It's been a long week, hasn't it?"

Tamara took the required beat and in her measured Oklahoma accent said to Lee Roy: "Lee Roy, did you ever think you heard someone speak, and when you looked…, there was no one there?"

On cue, the elevator door opened on her floor and as she walked off, I gave her a little boot in the butt with the left side of my right foot. She turned… Eyes aflame…

I responded: "Wasn't me… I'm not here."

She had no reply. She wheeled about and exited the "elevator scene," into her dressing room.

I will never be able to explain just how extremely, insanely, delicious that was! We never spoke of it. And, she never spoke to me until years later.

By the way, Tamara had a voice that could penetrate a steel wall and a will to move mountains. Tamara was quite a gal. I was privileged to have known and loved her.

Oric Bovar

Oric Bovar was a popular astrologer who did life charts and told followers what to eat and, later on, whom to marry. He was popular with many well-known figures in the entertainment and artistic world. Opera stars, Broadway and television stars and others hung onto his every word. In some respects, he became like Sun Myung Moon, the Korean religious leader who paired thousands of unknowns to each other in marriage. Oric Bovar did some of the same but on a smaller and more exclusive scale.

Many people were "looking for something." There was Werner Erhard's EST that some of my friends swore by. Also, on a more lethal side, there was Jim Jones and his Jonestown... "Don't drink the Kool-aid." An increasing number of people had become disillusioned with the established religions... Looking for someone or something to make their decisions for them..., to tell them what to do. Sheep came to mind.

I had never heard of Tamara Long before we were cast in *Lorelei*, starring the luminous Carol Channing. Likewise, Tamara had never heard of me. This was a bit unusual since, back then, Broadway was a relatively small community. Tamara told me about Bovar while we were touring in *Lorelei*. She was in constant touch with him. On her recommendation, he did my astrological life chart. It made some, sort of, generic sense. And, at this time, I was, indeed, looking for "something." Being somewhat at sea with my life, I sought any reasonable and available port in my personal storm.

I had a drinking problem. I was not well. With Tamara's prescribed diet, I got healthy and stopped drinking. She might very well have saved my life. Although, it was only after going to Alcoholics Anonymous, those thirty-three years ago that I stopped drinking "for good." So, I was interested in and did, Bovar's meditations. The few meditations that I did, made some sense to me. I still, occasionally, use two of them for calming and centering; Preceded by the invocation: "From the point of light within the Mind of God, let light stream forth into the minds of men. Let light descend on Earth."

After our long national tour and an extremely torrid affair with Tamara, we ran for a year on Broadway at The Palace Theater. After the show closed and not hearing from Tamara for, I believe, two years; she called. Diane answered the phone. I don't think the two had ever spoken. Tamara told Diane that her call was urgent… She had, somehow, sensed that I had not been doing "the work," as it was called. Diane informed Tamara that I was more or less incapacitated due to excruciating neck pain from jumping speed-rope in the park. At that, Tamara was convinced that my pain was a symptom of my "not doing the work," (The meditations) and that it was not a coincidence that Oric Bovar was in New York, and available.

Tamara called Bovar, and then called us back with a phone number to call. I spoke with The Oric Bovar for the first time. He said that I was to come to him immediately. I said that I could not walk and that I could not possibly get into a taxi and ride to the given address. He said, "Yes, you can." And, I did. The brownstone was in the mid-sixties on the west side. Every bump and there were many that the taxi hit I suffered through. The apartment on the first floor was owned by someone associated with the Metropolitan Opera Company.

He met me at the door and motioned that I should come inside. I did. He was slight and almost ethereal (to me) and dressed in a white "something." He told me to sit in a chair. I did. He walked around me and behind me and asked where I felt the pain. I told him, and he placed his hands (or hand) on my neck and upper spine. After a brief moment, he asked if I knew what he was doing. I didn't know. He said that he was giving to me the "highest form of energy." I could feel his concentration and focus. He kept his hands there for a short time and removed them. He asked me how I felt. I said that the pain was about the same. He repeated the ritual.

"How do you feel now?"

"About the same."

As I recall, he did the same thing again, placing his hands on the same area that was still giving me the same amount of pain; with the same results.

Bovar, then said that I would be pain-free by tomorrow.

I was. The next morning I woke with considerable pain. I went to Tamara's chiropractor, who gave me an adjustment. I was good as new. Like Bovar had said, I was pain-free… But, with the help of Dr. Alan H. Pressman.

I began to struggle in my relationship with Oric Bovar. He had lived in Italy for some time, before moving to New York, where he lived in an apartment on West End Avenue. By the way, Bovar did his healings for free, and according to several followers, he was more often than not, successful. My feeling was that he was essentially a good and talented man (placebo or not) who, for various reasons, was beginning to run off the track.

A year before Tamara met Dr. Pressman, she had been on a downward spiral, and was trying to drink herself to death. She got two cases of vodka and she made the attempt, but, in her throes, she had a vision. The vision was an address. The next day she found that address. It was the address of Dr. Alan H. Pressman. Pressman was a chiropractor and a nutritionist, as well. She stayed with Pressman's office for a year, "studying, mostly, the B vitamins," she said. She became a sponge, soaking up Pressman's knowledge. A year well spent as she invested herself in nutrition and healthy living. (Having a vision? Seeing an address? The special doctor's office? I know… Sounds a little looney) However…

Then, she became a healthy recluse, staying in her dark apartment, opening the door and gazing at those who sought her out, in need of regaining their health. She said that she saw their auras, and from that, told them what minerals, vitamins and foods they should consume. Again: I know this sounds wacky, but I witnessed people who would seek out and find Tamara on the *Lorelei* tour and come backstage to thank her for saving their lives. I saw one young woman with tears and smiles while thanking her for saving her smiling, young son's life. One man had driven from Florida to Detroit to thank her. The young woman with her son was in Toronto. Another man came to Washington D.C. to thank her.

Some say, "Placebo." I don't know. But, they were happy and extremely thankful. Tamara worked her "stuff" for free, as did Oric. Oric would charge for charts but not for healing.

A few years later, I visited Oric in his apartment on West End Avenue. At six o'clock in the morning, there were already one or two people waiting in the hall to see him. Inside there were five or six more. Finally, I saw him, for only the second time. This time I had no physical pain. I was having a life pain. Reconciling my life with his current activities and positions was bothering me. As much as I wanted him to be the "real thing," I did not feel comfortable. Something was wrong. I, truly, believed that he did have certain insights and talents that had helped many people. But, I, also, had a feeling that I later found out was held by others that Bovar had become overwhelmed and enamored by his own perceived ascendance and assessment of his earthly powers. Allegedly, he had said that he was Jesus Christ.

At that last meeting with Oric Bovar, I told him that I had these problems, and I would no longer be in touch with him. On my leaving, he told me that I was making a disastrous (maybe not his exact word) mistake, and, that I would be condemning (also, possibly, not the exact word) my life. I told him that if I messed this one up, I would get it right the next go around and that I trusted my own feelings. I trusted that I had been given the rights to my own decisions... That those decisions had not been given to me to pass off to another party. He was not pleased.

He, Oric Bovar, then said that under no circumstances should I ever answer a phone call in the middle of the night... That a demon would be after me once the connection was made. That nailed it for sure. I was gone, and I left... Walking on air and feeling a little elevated myself... In charge of my own path.

The ancient proverb of, "When the student is ready, the teacher will appear," often holds true. But, maybe, sometimes, when the student is ready, a misguided teacher will appear.

Coincidence? One afternoon, I had been out to the local bodega for beer and eggs, and when I returned to our apartment, Diane met me at the door wearing a stunned, pale face. Diane had just gotten off the phone with the mother of a much-loved family that had lived next door to her in Rockville Center, L.I. when Diane was growing up there. The family later moved to California, but Diane had kept in touch.

At one time, Diane and the son, Dean, a talented and very funny musician, had been a couple. They parted ways but had remained friends, even to this day. When Diane asked the mother the usual, "How is everyone?" the mother said, "Oh, alright, except Dean has just married some actress named, Tamara Long." (What???)

"Tamara Long?"

"Yes. Some guru named: Oric Bovar had told them they had to get married."

The next time I heard anything about this man, Oric Bovar, was when he had jumped from his apartment window on West End Avenue, and shuffled off this mortal coil. He had elevated himself to an untenable height.

Apparently, he was to appear in court that day, due to a violation of the Health Code for not reporting a dead body. He and a few followers, for quite some time, had been chanting over the corpse of another of Bovar's followers. They had been attempting to resurrect the corpse. Their sincere and sustained endeavors did not work. Neighbors had complained about a terrible odor.

The confluence in the lives of Diane, Dean, Tamara, and me, with Oric Bovar being in the center of this quartet, was certainly an odd coincidence. Coincidence? Synchronicity? Anyone?

Wedding Band during Lorelei

Before *Lorelei*, I was in *Wedding Band* at the Public Theatre, starring Ruby Dee and Jimmy Broderick... A wonderful play by Alice Childress, directed by Joe Papp. What an experience that was! Especially, during previews, some African American audience members became quite vocal about their feelings when Jimmy and Ruby kissed and expressed their love for each other. This, remember, was still at a time when mixed race couples were not seen on stage kissing and whispering sweet-nothings such as, "...loving your sweet blackberry kisses." A few times, some in the audience became vocal in their displeasure.

There was quite a stir one night when Angela Davis was in the audience.

My character was called "The Bellman." A peddler of his wares, entering playing "Onward Christian Soldiers" (of all things) on an old beat-up cornet... Then delivering his spiel and dance loosely akin to what is now called rap. "I got anythang y'all might need...I got stockin's for box-ankles, big thighs, any kind of legs y'all got..." Also, he had one eye on Ruby's character for some afternoon pleasures... In his own lustful mind, he was a charmer, alas, to no avail. Then off to the next possibility with, "Onward Christian Soldiers."

Photo by Swope

Himself, Hilda Haynes, Ruby Dee, Vickie Geyer, and Calisse Dinwiddie

WEDDING BAND DURING LORELEI

This was an excellent production of a significant work, thanks to Joe Papp, Alice Childress, and The Public Theater of New York.

After several weeks of playing, I gave my notice and left for a nice salary on the Lorelei tour. Upon returning to New York from the tour, Joe Papp called and said he was doing *Wedding Band* as a TV Special on ABC, and again with Ruby Dee. Ruby had asked him if he might get me to resume my role for the TV production. According to their schedule, I would have to miss only one performance of Lorelei. I smelled trouble. I told Tom Porter, our stage manager that I needed to miss one performance, and gave him the date. Tom said he would have to run that by Charles and Carol. "No," was the answer. And that if I did miss the show in order to do Papp's TV special on ABC, I would be fired! Of course, Charles, the man I liked and admired at the beginning of the run, by this time, I knew was the dark side of everything. And, I knew they could have their choice of many competent actors that would be happy to work for much less than my salary.

I had already signed my contract for *Wedding Band* through my world famous agent, the dapper and gregarious Milton Goldman, who just happened to be vacationing in Mexico with Carol Channing's attorney, Arnold Weissberger. Milton and Arnold were life partners and were central figures in New York and London Theatre. What a plot! Milton had me booked to be in two places at the same time. I told Bernie Gersten, Papp's second in command, about my problem: "Sorry."

Joe Papp said he had me signed and would sue me if I didn't meet my obligation. He did have my previous understudy standing by, should I walk. Being on that train to Baltimore seemed like child's play compared to this.

I was on the set in the Brooklyn Studios in case some last minute solution might be found before I would have to leave for The Palace Theatre in Manhattan. My attorney, Mort Levy, had advised me that I should opt for my *Lorelei* salary since it would be coming in for at least six more months. My *Wedding Band* check would be a one-time-only infusion. I agreed, but it was breaking my heart.

I was standing with Ruby, when Bernie Gersten approached me and said:

"Brandon, you got lucky. We can't get to you until Monday."

I made it back from Brooklyn to Manhattan in time for half hour. Yowzah!

Unfortunately, some ABC stations did not air *Wedding Band*. Others delayed the airing to an 11:30 pm - 1:30 am time slot. One of my daughter Justine's teachers in Middle-school in Darien, CT expressed her dislike over the airing. Justine spoke up, saying that it was a "very good play" and "My Daddy was in it."

More on *Lorelei*:

Okay, this is a never ending tale... But true. I might as well finish it with its proper bang.

Later in the spring, my eldest daughter, Jennifer, was to graduate from Darien High School. I would definitely be there for her graduation. But, I would have to miss one show... Sound familiar? Here we go again.

But this time, I told the understudy, and the wardrobe mistress that I was planning on being sick the next night. I went to Jennifer's graduation. When I got back to the city, Carol and Charles had phoned and left word that they would be arriving after the show with her doctor in tow to see if I was really sick. They didn't follow through. But, they had me in their crosshairs.

Hold everything! Carol and Charles then brought me up on charges at Actor's Equity for "ruining the morale of the company," stating that I had missed a performance the previous year to attend my mother's funeral. They were right. Of course, I did attend my mother's funeral... And, I did miss one performance. I, then, flew back to Los Angeles and made it for "Places, Places, please. Your call is Places," the next night. Actor's Equity and our Equity Deputy, Peter Palmer, gave them no satisfaction on their charge. I got my paychecks until the show closed.

By the way, Carol and Charles warned the company that if anyone took their one-week vacation that, by Equity rule was due to them after playing in a show for one year that Carol would take her vacation and end the show's run. That's some muscle! No one took their due vacation. A paycheck is a paycheck on Broadway.

There is a happy ending to this story. A few years ago, I read that Carol had divorced Charles Lowe. Recently, Carol was quoted as saying that she and Charles had made love only twice, and that was "forty-one years ago." The happy ending here is that Carol finally found happiness. Carol married her childhood sweetheart. I saw them on some talk show, and they both looked and sounded very happy. I could see that this new man's gaze at Carol did not involve dollar signs. Good for Carol! And, at this writing, Carol is still performing. I believe she is ninety now... And, still beloved by many who love Broadway musicals.

Closing night of *Lorelei*, as I was leaving the Palace Theatre for the last time, Jule Styne was making his last exit as well. Jule waved as he walked away. Then, he stopped and came back to me:

"Brandon, I know... (He paused) I know that lots of things were done to you in this show. I'm sorry about that. But, I want you to know... I always enjoyed watching you." Thanks, Jule.

A Jule Styne nugget: Jule had a gambling problem. Over the years, he had lost a considerable amount of money. I asked him, with knowing what the end-result would usually be, why did he do it? Jule said, "It's not the winning or the losing. It's the action."

I wonder if he felt the same way about the next show we did together: *One Night Stand*, with book and lyrics by Herb Gardner. I admired both great men of the theatre, but theirs was not a perfect marriage. We closed in previews. There was plenty of "action," in a very short time. Of course, writing and putting the show together took quite a while... Yes, plenty of "action," with tempers and disagreements, and financing, and... Lots of foreplay, but the climax was a bummer.

The Theatre-Party-Ladies had reserved most of the seats for our scheduled three weeks of previews. The names of Jule Styne and Herb Gardner had been the attraction. With the support of the Theatre-Party-Ladies, we did not have to have out-of-town previews. During our first preview, the Ladies began to walk out in the middle of the first act. Word spread, and the Ladies cancelled their reservations for the remainder of the three weeks, forcing the producers to close the show. It wasn't the quality of the material. It was the unfortunate subject matter. Singing and dancing about cancer was not an enticing treat for them.

That was when my name was still up on two marquees at the same time... And, I was unemployed.

South Pacific with Howard Keel and Jane Powell

I spent nearly a year on a national tour, playing the wonderful comic role of Luther Billis in *South Pacific*. Howard keel and Jane Powell were the stars. What a wonderful show. The twin soliloquies with Howard Keel and Jane Powell singing was a thrill to hear eight times a week. Rodgers and Hammerstein ain't bad.

I do listen to Pinza's and Mary Martin's recording every once in a while, even now. Ezio Pinza owned that role. Howard was good, but it belonged to Pinza.

A Pinza nugget: I had a voice teacher named, Vera Covert, who loved to pass around show business gossip. She said that, reportedly, Pinza was a bull. And, that he was known to have assignations between acts at the Met... With, oftentimes, his third act being noticeably not as strong as his first and second acts.

Howard had befriended me following the first time we did South Pacific. That time, our Nellie Forbush was the wonderful Elizabeth Allen. Howard cast me in my first film, Armored

Command, shot in the Bavarian Alps, in Germany. That's where I met a charismatic young actor named Burt Reynolds… His first film too, I believe.

In *South Pacific*, Howard was strict with his supporting cast. He demanded a full out and disciplined performance eight times a week. God forbid that someone might miss a cue or even be slightly late on an entrance. We were playing The Pantages Theater in Los Angeles. It was the October that Reggie Jackson became "Mister October," by slamming three home runs in game six and winning the World Series at Dodger Stadium.

One of the two young actors playing Emil De Becque's Tonkinese children missed a cue. He was supposed to enter with his sister, but he was late. Afterwards, Howard ripped that young boy a new one. The boy was embarrassed and frightened and appropriately apologetic. I saw the boy, Jason, with tears in his eyes. He would never miss another cue.

Later in the week, a miracle happened. I was alone onstage following the Honey Bun number I did with Jane. I was doing my "shtick" with a hot cigarette lighter. (At a rehearsal in New York for the original South Pacific, Josh Logan, the director, noticed Myron McCormick, the original Luther Billis, standing around in his grass shirt and coconut shell bra for the "Honey Bun" number. He carried his cigarettes under one of the coconut shells and his cigarette lighter under the other. McCormick lifted one side, and his cigarettes fell into his hand. He lifted the other side, and his lighter fell into his hand. He lit his cigarette with the lighter and tucked the lighter back under its shell. He flinched a bit because the lighter was still warm, and had burned his masculine mammary. Of course, I incorporated that bit of business into my performance.) At the completion of that bit, and following the laugh, Emile De Becque (Howard Keel) is to join me on stage for a brief scene. Howard does not make the entrance. I glance into the wings and see Howard in conversation with an assistant stage manager. Oh, Heaven sent! I roam around the stage for just a few seconds and say to myself: "Where is that damn Emile De Becque?" Howard jumps out of his skin and enters, and we do the scene. After the show, I take Jason with me, and we stand in Howard's dressing room doorway. We have two big smiles plastered across our faces. Howard was not amused. Nor, did he apologize to me for missing his cue.

After a few too many drinks at a cast party that Howard threw, I told the story in front of the cast. Howard approached me and threw his drink into my face... And, made a dramatic exit. Now, that's Hollywood. Delicious. Howard remained icy for the remainder of the tour.

I liked Howard's wife and child... And, his three children by his first wife, as well. He was a good man. Both of his wives were quite attractive and extremely nice. Two of his first brood played the Tonkinese children in our earlier production.

I was having great fun playing Luther Billis, but in Denver, one night after the Honey Bun number with Jane, I had trouble catching my breath. This was unusual for me. Okay, it was in Mile-High-Denver, but I was in great physical shape. This was in the middle of the run there. Why hadn't it happened in the previous performances?

Fiona, nee Fiona Apple Maggart, was born during a two-week break in that tour. Being in September, naturally, proudly, holding her in my arms, my first words to Fiona were documented on video… "Fiona… say, 'Come on Yankees!'"

Later on, we had a four-week break in the run. We came back to New York and during that time, I was rehearsing one of Marshal Barer's, *Men's Sportswear Shows*, when during a lunch break I had a very rapid heart fibrillation episode. It felt like my heart was revving up for a race. (I had just entertained a beautiful female visitor.) After a few seconds (seemed longer), it regained the normal pulse. We had our first show the following morning: Our "breakfast show." And, between that show and the evening show, I had a doctor's appointment. The cardiologist said that I had a heart attack and that it was still evolving. He told me to get to Mount Sinai Hospital, "now." He would meet me there.

During the cab ride, I was thinking, I'm forty-four years old with seven children and I am having a heart attack. This is not good. I am expected for a late afternoon show, and then another backer's audition tonight for *The Best of New Faces* at Leonard Sillman's Home. Of all things: I was worried about them. I would not make, "Half hour… Half hour, please."

Then, reality set in. I asked my God, to please let me live at least two more years. I needed to take care of my children, somehow.

We had limited resources, and I would be without a job even if I survived.

I had my briefcase with me containing my voice recorder. As the cab was working its bumpy way north, I recorded a personal goodbye to each of my seven children. I realized that my oldest son, Bran, would have to be the new man-of-the-house, now. I began with him and went through the other six. At least I thought I had.

I had a major heart attack. The main artery (the left anterior descending) was completely blocked. And, there was dead muscle. But, I lived. To prepare for the surgery, they pumped dye through my heart to see exactly where the obstruction was. All the other arteries were completely clear. Turns out it was a "single artery disease." "Mazel tov," I was told. The surrounding corollaries would have to, eventually, branch out and take over the workload previously done by that most important artery. The oddest thing... I had to learn to walk again. Lying in bed and not using my muscles left me a little rubber legged.

I had to bow out of the remaining *South Pacific* tour. Never heard from Howard.

By this time, we were running low on money. What was I going to do? Luckily, I almost immediately got a commercial that would bring in a little money... And, possibly, a good sum, too. This was about two months after my heart attack. In this commercial, I was supposed to walk into a drug store, cough, and look sick. That was it. No danger. When I arrived on the set, they had changed my spot... I would be riding a stationary bike off and on for two or three hours. This was a different story. Of course, the ad agency didn't know that I had recently had a heart attack. I considered bailing out, but we really needed the money. I lived. And that was in 1977. Maybe there is a God, who told me to disengage the chain... Whew!

A month or so later, during my recuperation, I remembered making my, thankfully unneeded, farewells to my children on my voice recorder... And, I carefully listened to each message; reliving that cab ride to the hospital. Now, with surviving that possibility of leaving them, I shed a few happy and grateful tears. I even thought that they, one day, might like to listen to how I felt about them at that frightening time. Maybe not. But, there was a problem. I had left out one message. How I could have overlooked it, I don't know since it was the first one that I thought I had made. On impulse, I erased the tape.

Straws in the Wind

Maude Amber Maggart had been born two years earlier during *Straws in the Wind*, a revue, at the American Place Theatre. I enjoyed a wonderful romp there with Josh Mostel and Tovah Feldshuh. That was the third show that I had done with Betty Comden and Adolph Green. And, it was ably and happily directed by Adolph's wife, Phyllis Newman. No one objected when I missed a performance on the occasion of Amber's birth. As stated before... Amber's professional name is Maude Maggart (after my Grandmother, Maude Apple. This also lets you know how Fiona got her middle name.)

What a joy to do material written by many of the very best writers of the time. One of the funniest (by Peter Stone) was called "My Doctor the Box." Tovah and I had a go at that one, only; I was off stage and giving my voice to the box set at center stage. This took being "upstaged" to another level: being "off-staged." Nevertheless, it was great fun. As I say, Phyllis Newman directed..., and much of the material was written by Betty Comden and Adolph Green. All of the writers had a right to pull their material during previews if they weren't satisfied with the execution. My favorite "big" number was pulled by Stephen Schwartz because he wasn't pleased with the performance. Ouch! The night Schwartz saw the number, my backup singers and I were in conflict with the orchestra. Never mind, I still had loads of good stuff to do.

There was a wonderfully funny thing that happened, both on and off stage: During curtain calls, I, sometimes, would give Tovah as we were bowing, a gentlemanly pat on the rump. Okay. Tovah had a boyfriend. A jealous boyfriend, who attended rehearsals and performances. I believe that he was an attorney... A bearded sort... Always in a suit. One night, before the show, Tovah said that the irate gentleman had noticed my gentle butt-caress at the previous performance. Tovah, laughingly, said that I must cease my affections during the curtain call. At the next performance, during the curtain call, I restrained myself. Tovah kissed me on my cheek... Presumably, thanking me for heeding to the proper protocol.

After the curtain, and backstage, the angered barrister (boyfriend) bursts through the door, wielding a rolled-up New York Times. He was yelling and walloping me, punctuated by angry epithets. I realized that he had seen Tovah kiss me on the cheek, but why was he hitting me? I began to laugh. He made a fuming exit.

I told Diane, Maude Amber's mother, about what had happened. At the after-party, on closing night, as the same suited and bearded boyfriend came in, he passed right behind us. Diane reached and pinched him on his rump. He turned, flabbergasted, and was without a response. Turns out, Tovah's relationship with the bearded, barrister, boyfriend, was short-lived.

Saturday Night Live

In 1975, I auditioned for a new television project that would be called *Saturday Night Live*, with the *Not Ready for Prime Time Players*. After my several auditions, I felt pretty confident that I would be hired for the show. I had done revues at The Upstairs at the Downstairs, also, *Put it in Writing*, and *New Faces...'68*. Both being revues... Plus*, America Be Seated*, a mixed-minstrel show. I was, finally, called in to NBC by the brilliant comedy writer, Anne Beatts. I'm all set to sign my contract, when she informs me that: "We're going with a younger cast." But, they would still like to "use me" at different times. Suddenly, I was "old." How did that happen? "Old?"

For their first show, I was given a short sketch that was to be done as a TV commercial. I would be using a new "Grecian Formula" to make me a better basketball player. It would show me missing shot after shot... Until, I used the New Formula that would darken my skin. Then, I would be seen making shot after shot! My call was ten A.M. for makeup, wardrobe, blocking and taping..., to be aired the next night on their very first live show.

I waited in the dressing room that I shared with two young fellows named Belushi and Aykroyd. I had never seen or heard of them. I could see that they knew each other very well...

Always jabbering back and forth. I don't think they ever noticed me beyond a brief, "How's it going?" from Aykroyd. After being there all day, that premier episode was overloaded, and the sketch was bumped. I began rehearsals for *Straws in the Wind* (another revue), and, I never heard from them again.

I heard that Billy Crystal had been bumped that day, too. I wasn't too upset because I knew that, with all my experiences in doing revues…, I knew how much time and work it would take to make one good show. They certainly would not be able to do that week after week. That was in 1975, and the show is still running, in 2014. Who knew? Not me.

By the way, when I read the script for the original *Fiddler on the Roof*, I said to my agent, "Fat chance of people buying tickets to see this!" Which reminds me of another one of my brilliant assessments; LuJan, my wife, had told me that a young chubby actor, we had seen in an Off-Broadway production called *The Indian Wants the Bronx* would become a star. I laughed. His name was Al Pacino. Earlier, she had said that a young singer from Memphis was going to be big. I laughed. His name was Elvis.

Tidbit: One of my most rewarding roles was playing Tevye in a version of *Fiddler on the Roof*, called: *Fiddler on a West Hollywood Roof.* Go figure.

Jennifer Slept Here

I had been told that I would be working all the time in television and film if I would go out to Hollywood for "pilot season." But, I didn't have the money it would take to go out there on-speck. Without getting work right away, I would be up shit creek without airfare. I couldn't take the chance.

I was doing a light comedy, called, *Nurse Jane Goes to Hawaii*, with the wonderful Georgia Engel at a theater on the grounds of Flushing's World's Fair. This was near to where I had worked during the Fair in the short-lived, *America, Be Seated*. The mother of a casting director told her son about seeing me in that little play. That happenstance got me to Hollywood; all expenses paid. She told her son, Joel Thurm, head of casting at NBC that he should see me. He flew me out to audition for a Buddy Hackett pilot. When I got there, Thurm had changed his mind. He wanted me to see the producers of *Jennifer Slept Here*.

My first television series, other than *Sesame Street,* became *Jennifer Slept Here* on NBC, with Georgia Engel, Ann Jillian, and young John Navin.

We followed a show called *Manimal,* on Friday nights. This was not a good spot. After the second week on the air, I asked

Larry Tucker, one of our two producers how did he think we were doing…, all the time, expecting him to say something like, "We're doing great, Brandon." Tucker said, "I don't know. We've got a very sick cat in the timeslot before us." (*Manimal* was part Black Leopard and part other things. He morphed.) We were cancelled, with only nine episodes being aired.

During the summer reruns, we were ranked in the "top ten" each week. Too late.

Sesame Street

Jennifer Slept Here

Chicken Soup

Brothers

Brothers

I was about to return to New York, hat in hand, following the cancellation of *Jennifer Slept Here*, when I got a call from my LA agent at ICM, Joe Funicello. He had an appointment for me at Showtime. Showtime? Cable TV? What a comedown. I almost didn't go. I went. And, was I glad I did.

It was a wonderful show. I loved my role. I got five years, a hundred and sixteen shows, a house at the beach, and a little red convertible from *Brothers;* along with four Ace Award Nominations... Plus, a wonderful five years of playing in front of live studio audiences. And, these audiences, believe me, were alive-live!

First: The major networks turned *Brothers* down because two of the main characters were gay. That was in 1984, and at that time, there were no main characters playing gay on network television. Compared to today's sitcoms, *Brothers* was so tame that you could almost air it on Saturday mornings. Showtime and Paramount Studios picked it up, and we were a great success, although playing in limited markets. In New York, we weren't seen below 79th Street... Crazy. In San Francisco, of all places, we were aired at 2AM. Here, we have Paul Regina, Himself, and Philip Charles Mackenzie, playing: Cliff, Lou, and Donald.

BEHIND THESE EYES SUCH SWEET MADNESS LIES

A whole segment of our society was given something that those families with gay members could identify with. I remember a young man coming backstage with his father... Coming to thank us. He said that his father, when finding out that he was gay, would not even speak to him. The boy moved away, but after *Brothers* began airing, he wrote to his father to please watch the show. Both father and son had come backstage to thank us... And, they were smiling..., together. That was a good night.

I still get mail, asking if there will ever be DVDs available... Or, why doesn't some network pick up the 116 episodes? I did some research a few years back and found out that CBS owned the show. CBS didn't know they owned *Brothers*. Apparently, CBS had bought out Paramount along with their library of shows. But, they were not aware, due to changes in personnel. Usually, new CEOs want to create their own projects. I assume the 116 episodes are still there in some dusty corner. Although, personally, a fan sent to me his recorded collection. RG, thanks. Robert lived in midtown Manhattan and couldn't get the shows. But, he had a friend who lived in Queens who got *Brothers* and recorded them for RG. There were *Brothers* parties all around the country where like groups gathered to watch, and laugh, and cry a little.

Tidbit: While doing *Brothers*, I made a pilot for NBC with a skinny little unknown kid from Brooklyn. Gary Nardino and Paramount put together a fifteen minute two-character pilot called *Sweets*, starring Chris Rock and Brandon Maggart. Yep, that Chris Rock. NBC President, Brandon Tartikoff passed on it, and it went into the dustbin. A week or so ago, I was looking through my old video tapes, and I found my video copy of *Sweets*. I couldn't help but to look at it again. Tartikoff was right. Chris was okay. He wrote his own material, but I was not properly cast as an elderly candy store owner in the Bronx, New York... Even though, I was aged considerably by whitening my hair and speaking with a slight Jewish Bronx accent. I did my best, and I was told that Tartikoff did like me. He was there at NBC when I did *Jennifer Slept Here*.

This was during the time of the big aids epidemic. We supported and gave laughs to thousands of young men during a tragic time. After the show ceased production, I was most proud of playing Tevye in a special production of *Fiddler* to raise money for aids hospice. It was called, *"Fiddler on a West Hollywood Roof."* It was a wonderful show. We had a solid three week run at Harmony Gold Theater here in Hollywood. Great cast. Great orchestra.

Sometimes, it helps to laugh.

During this tragic time, we had another tragic thing to happen. After the first week of play, we were so very happy that we had a good show and that we were entertaining and bringing some joy to a full house of some very ill young men. Bittersweet. On our Sunday night off, the young man playing the "fiddler" that sat and played on the roof was murdered. He was the nicest of men... A school teacher. He and two friends were walking in their neighborhood after having dinner in a nearby restaurant, when a white van pulled up. Young thugs jumped out and demanded money. Robert was a little slow in complying, and he was shot and killed on the sidewalk in front of his home. We were devastated.

The next performance was on Tuesday night... With a new actor as the fiddler on the roof. At the end of each performance, Tevye motions to the fiddler to come down from the roof and walk off, arm in arm. When I looked up and saw were Robert usually was, atop Tevye's roof, Robert wasn't there. I have no words to adequately describe the shock that I knew was coming... And, it came.

We finished the run and raised a good bit of money for Aids Hospice. And, we continued to entertain many of those young men who needed so desperately to be entertained.

I was privileged to be a part of it.

Chicken Soup

I was in the midst of shooting the last few shows of my wonderful five-year-run on *Brothers*, when I heard about *Chicken Soup* on ABC, starring Jackie Mason and Lynn Redgrave. But, it had already been cast, and the pilot made. At the network revealing, during the spring showings in New York, for all the advertisers; *Chicken Soup* was called the only "surefire" prospect for the fall season. Wow! I was a big fan of Jackie's recordings, and I had loved working with Lynn Redgrave years ago in *Hellzapoppin'*... But, too late... Gone... Missed the boat. Hold everything! I got a call from my manager... They were adding two roles. Yowzah! I got the script. I read the script. I was salivating to play that role "as written." I auditioned a wonderfully written scene and... Double Yowzah!! I got the part. I couldn't believe my good fortune. I played Lynn Redgrave's brother, and owned and ran a bar (Irish of course).

The producers sent me a tape of their pilot: the one that had gotten all the advertisers so excited. My son, Garett and I, with great anticipation and excitement, sat down in my TV room and watched... Our elation dwindled... Our hopes came crashing down. The pilot episode, scheduled to be the first to be aired was, to us, to say the least, disheartening... Still, I had the script for the second episode, and it was terrific. I, certainly, looked forward to that. I did... I did... I did... I did have hope.

But, when we began rehearsals in late summer all the punch had been taken out of that very good script. My wonderful scene with Jackie had had its balls removed... Amputated... Gone. What a downer. Somehow the writer-producers had been persuaded to take all the edge off my character's relationship with Mason's character.

Plus, there was some trouble with a highly visible Jewish organization. Their leader and some members from his group were at the first taping. Afterwards, Jackie laughed and said, "They are upset. They called my performance, too Jewish."

I was surprised that Jackie was nervous while doing the show. At rehearsals and during the tapings, he seemed to be unsure of himself. This was surprising because, after the first week of rehearsals, Jackie had taken me with him to watch him do his one-man concert at The Greek Theater. There were thousands of people out there in this outdoor arena with a starlit canopy, and here was this one little man, calm as the proverbial cucumber. Jackie didn't know what he was going to do or to say as he was about to take the stage.

"How can you do that?"

"It's easy. I just talk, and then I... I keep talking. And, I talk. And, they laugh. And, I keep talking. And, that's what I do."

I watched from the wings. He had them from "Hello." He was natural and easy. The audience was having lots of fun. Jackie was having fun. But, he sweated. He sweated a lot. It was hot that night. He did over two hours, seemingly, off-the-cuff. His act seemed like a "stream of consciousness."

Later, when thinking about how Jackie had gotten his audience within the first minute, it reminded me of a remarkable night watching Jack Carter do a show. I had done a play with Jack called, *Operation Mad Ball,* at The Bucks County Playhouse. It was unusual in that it was first a film and then a play. Usually, it was the other way around. I realize I'm off subject here, (as usual) but stick with me. Jack Carter had been a huge star in the fifties and on into the sixties. He was big on *The Judy Garland Show* and *The Ed Sullivan Show.* And, Jack is one Jack that did know Jack about comedy. Too much?

In *Operation Mad Ball,* I played a character named Ozark (I believe). I had the biggest laughs in the show. Ozark came equipped with his southern witticisms, such as, "Sir, pleasin' that woman is like tryin' to push hot butter up a wildcat's behind with a hot darnin' needle." When, first, I said that line in front of an audience and had gotten the laugh, Jack, facing me, whispered:

"Don't move... Don't move... Don't move... Don't move." The original laugh came and then it rolled into an even bigger laugh. Then he whispered, "OK." And, I went on with the scene.

Again: I stray. But, I must continue; otherwise, I'll forget to write it down. After *Operation Mad Ball*, I did *Damn Yankees*, starring Tony Perkins, at The Framingham Music Tent just outside of Boston. I read that Jack Carter was performing at a nearby nightclub. After my show, I went to see Jack's club act. The beautiful and talented, Paula Stewart, Jack's sweetheart at the time (Paula had been in *Operation Mad Ball*, too) was there. I sat with Paula during Jack's show.

The place was packed. There was an opening act as I recall... Then Jack. Jack came on and did his first joke. Nothing. Nada. He quickly followed with another and another... and another... and another... Nothing. I'm beginning to get "flop-sweat." Jack kept going like a juggernaut. Nothing. I looked at Paula, who seemed to be... unbothered. I was dying for poor Jack. Jack was plowing ahead... And sweating. The audience didn't boo or anything like that. Quite a few were still eating their dinner. They were just... unresponsive. Finally, after an eternity, there came a laugh. Then another... And another... And another, rolling into an unstoppable wave. And, by the time Jack finished his show, the audience was exhausted from laughing so much. He got laughs like you'd want to put under your pillow to dream on. He must have told fifty or more jokes before one laugh. It was as if he had been fishing all day, not even getting one little nibble, and, suddenly, he was catching one after the other... As fast as he could bait and fish. Finally, he didn't even need the bait... They just kept biting the hook. A boatload of fish. The turnaround was amazing... Simply, amazing. His boat was headed straight for the rocks, and suddenly, the doomed boat became an airplane, soaring off into the land of happy endings.

Jack Carter had to work much harder than Jackie Mason, but both got it done. With Jackie, it was easy. With Jack, I was worn out, but I had seen something akin to a miracle.

Forgive me. I had to pass that along. Those two disparate events are forever chiseled into my memory.

At the same time I was doing *Chicken Soup*, my best friend, Ronny Graham had been cast in the musical, *Annie Two*. We couldn't believe our good fortunes happening at the same time. Both shows were forecast to be hits!?! Ronny was looking to buy a new house. I said, "Ronny, you've been in show business long enough to know the nature of show business! Have you forgotten we're in show business? Wait 'til the checks clear! Get back to reality!"

In about the third week of being on the air, I ran into Tom Poston (I had just done a guest spot on Newhart), and Tom asked me, "How is it going with Jackie?" "Fine," I said. Tom said, "Don't worry, Jackie will find some way to fuck it up." Jackie had always been controversial... And funny... but this time, through some social or political blunder, involving Jackie and Mayor Dinkins of New York..., ABC pulled the plug. To be honest, the show hadn't come up to expectations. Chicken Soup was cancelled after only nine airings..., even though we were still in the top ten rankings. Within a couple of months, Annie Two had closed before reaching Broadway, and both, Ronny and I, were "at liberty." (Out of work.)

I didn't see or hear from Lynn until a few years later, when she was going through quite a devastating divorce. She called me. We had lunch. And, that was it. Lynn Rachel Redgrave joined me, in Venice, for a few happy and cherished years. "Cherish," was Lynn Rachel's favorite word.

Ronny Graham

A very, very small percentage of actors make a living in our industry. I have been extremely lucky, especially with having a large family. Believe me, there were many times that it seemed I'd chosen the wrong profession, for a man with seven children. Again, luck has been pretty much a lady with me. Without being a huge star, I've gotten all these years out of several dozen stage productions... Over a hundred TV commercials... Episodic television... Movies for television... And, movies for theatrical release. And, let me not forget LuJan teaching school in the early years. I, also, did a few "Industrial shows," where I would sing about fabrics. That's where I met Marshall Barer... In one of his *Men's Sportswear* shows. Doing one of Marshall's *Men's Sportswear* shows was when I had my heart attack. I was forty-four years old. And, here I am, now, at eighty-one years of age. Ronny was my best friend, while, Marshall came in a close second. And, both of these extraordinary, brilliant, and exasperating iconoclasts were part of our extended family. Marshall had no children. Ronny had five, but, only son Ron, and daughter TJ (Timothi) got to spend much time with Ronny here in California.

I knew Ronny for forty years. Before that, while, in college, I had seen him in the movie version of *Leonard Sillman's New Faces of 1952*. Then in 1959, I saw him in New York at the Upstairs at the Downstairs: the cabaret hosted by debonair impresario, Julius Monk. I was a waiter and "standby" for the show in the Upstairs room. Any chance I got I would sneak down the basement stairs and crack open the exit door to watch this "crazy man" do his act in the Downstairs room. I'd never seen the likes of this. I hadn't realized that when I saw the *New Faces of 1952* film it was a film of a "stage" performance practically filmed on a dime and a wish. In fact, I didn't like Ronny in the film. But, what a revelation here... Live! This was Ronny's world, in this intimate, smoke-filled room packed with his fans. This was his home. He was mesmerizing. Like watching a spider hypnotize a room full of flies. He sucked them right into the mood of each piece with his personal magic and piano underscoring. And the subject matter: "Vera the Vending Machine." "Harry the Hipster." "Truman Capote." And, "The Unrequited Lover's March."

Some not so good times came as Ronny aged... With emotional problems, memory loss..., and pretty women. Marshall, Pamela (Ronny's wife), and I watched a live taping of a television show... I believe its star was Nancy Walker. The audience was filled with young African American children. They were a well behaved and enthusiastic audience until the show had to do a few too many retakes. They became impatient and tired of watching reset after retake. This did not bode well for Ronny, whose big scene came at the end of the evening.

Ronny was playing a very high energy, fast-talking character opposite Nancy Walker. On Ronny's first entrance, he flubbed his lines. Reset: He got a little further, but again, messed up his lines. The young audience began to "boo." This went on until the audience was asked to leave. Ronny and Nancy finally, finally, finally, got the work done. It was excruciating. We, Marshall, Pamela, and I were suffering for poor Ronny all the while. It was not a happy night for Ronny. Ronny suffered more. So sad and even painful for all concerned.

There were a few other same such trials for Ronny. The worst time came when Ronny was doing a character that he was so excited about, on *Cheers*. After each rehearsal day, Ronny would drop by our house and give glowing reports about how things were going. He was truly happy... Or, so it seemed.

On Ronny's day of taping *Cheers*, I was working on another show at the time (can't remember which one). I called home afterwards to check in with Amber (Maude). Amber said, "Daddy... You'd better come home. Ronny is sitting in the front yard mumbling and crying."

After the run-through before taping in front of a live audience, Ronny had left the lot and come home to our house. Ronny told me that he could not go in front of the audience. He knew that he would literally die if he did. He had just left. This was not good. This, in fact, was very, very, bad... And, he knew it.

This presented many problems. We knew that *Cheers* would have to cancel the show, and send the audience home. Ouch! Among other things, the money involved would be enormous. They could sue Ronny. Ronny didn't have money, so that would be the least of his worries.

"Ronny, you said you thought were going to die?"

"I knew if I went back onto that stage in front of an audience; I would die. I knew it. I was going to die. I had to leave. I got into my car and drove here."

"OK. Let's go over to the hospital in the Marina and check you in."

We went and had him checked out by the ER doctor there.

"Could he have died?"

From the attending physician: "Possibly."

Neither *Cheers* nor Paramount pressed charges. The part was recast, and the show was taped the following week. I don't know what happened, but Ronny never heard from them. No repercussions whatsoever. Whew!

We did have it on record that Ronny went to the hospital in fear for his life.

Ronny was married to Pamela during these bad times, but he always called me to take him to the hospital. We did this routine several times. He would always think he was dying.

"I'm dying, Buddy. I'm dying."

"Ronny, you always say that, and yet you're still here."

However, the last time I took him to the hospital, he was right. The last time I saw my friend smile came near the very end. I asked the attending nurse if she knew who "that man" was... "No," she said. She had no reason to know who Ronny was. To her, Ronny was just another old man in his last few hours. I could understand how she might not want to know anything personal about this elderly, dying man. She, being a nurse, sees it every day. She might prefer that the dying remain anonymous to her. But, in this case, I think she sensed that I needed to talk... And, I did. I looked over at Ronny and saw the remnants of a once very animated and very special man that was my friend... And, my children's friend. I said, to the nurse, "You don't know this, but that old man over there in that bed, was once known as Mr. Dirt."

The nurse remained stoic... Just a deadpan gaze over to Ronny.

Ronny had made over sixty appearances on *The Tonight Show with Johnny Carson*. He was, occasionally, making movies with old friend, Mel Brooks... And, had been in, and/or directed, a few

Broadway shows, including the *New Faces* that I was in. And, during the 50s, Ronny had been the toast of New York's cabaret scene. Capitalizing mostly on those *Tonight Show* appearances, Ronny hit the road, starring in one of Neil Simon's plays. I believe it was either *The Odd Couple* or *Prisoner of Second Avenue*. He was playing a dinner theatre somewhere in Florida and having a grand time doing so... With star billing... His name on the marquee... Always a reassuring validation.

Ronny would often take his breakfast at a diner just a few blocks from the theatre. One of the young waitresses smiled at Ronny the first time Ronny walked in, and from the way she smiled he assumed that she had seen him in the play. And, she had seen the play just the night before. The girl smiled and said, "I liked you in that play last night." Ronny could rarely pass on a smile.

According to Ronny, soon after one of her breakfast shifts she invited Ronny to come home with her to her nearby apartment. Ronny did, indeed, accept her invitation, which seemed to make the young woman very happy. Once inside, she asked if she might kiss Ronny. Ronny could rarely pass on a kiss from a pretty girl. She appeared to be overjoyed with the kiss, and immediately began disrobing. In no time at all, they were in the throes of making "the beast with two backs." Pretty soon, as passion was building, the girl said, "I can't believe this!" Then, she began muttering some sort of a passionate mantra..., over and over..., punctuating each thrust... Finally, Ronny said, "I can't understand you, sweetheart... What are you saying?"

Keeping her rhythm, and in a rather high-pitched, raspy-giggly, southern voice, she was saying: "I'm doin'... Mister... Dirt...... I'm doin'... Mister... Dirt..., in my own..., little bed..." And, on reaching the ultimate peak of ecstasy; one final, "I'm... doin'... Mister... Dirrrrrt!!! Oh, my ever-loving God... Mister... Dirt!" And, following a brief afterglow, she said: "Someday... Someday, when I get old, I'll have this to tell my grandkids about... About me fuckin' the famous Mister Dirt."

During the 1970s, Mobil Oil ran a campaign of commercials featuring Ronny as "Mr. Dirt!" Mobil Detergent Gasoline would, theoretically, keep that terrible Mr. Dirt from clogging up your car's engine. Mr. Dirt would appear, grumpy, nasty, and grimy, from under the hoods of various cars, growling, "I'm Mister Dirt!" Only to be thwarted, once again, by Mobil Detergent Gasoline. Of course, this series of commercials were seen time and time again across the country. Ronny was "Mr. Dirt!"

The nurse smiled and said: "I think I remember that Mister Dirt."

I thought I saw Ronny smile... A little one... But a smile. Maybe he'd just taken one final pee. Ron Jr. got there, and the three of us were with Ronny when he drew his last breath. And, Ronny flew away... As if he were late for a gig with Oscar Petersen, in some lofty gathering. That would surely be a bit of Heaven for Ronny. Ronny had "left the building." Did Ronny linger for a parting birds-eye look down at me, Ron Jr. and the nurse? Who knows? I know he was no longer in that used up carcass on that hospital bed.

Yes, talented and seductive females, in the past, could, on occasion, "sidetrack" Ronny. He was a great admirer of those who were great admirers of him, and he would sometimes comfort his admirers... And, he was always enthusiastic about it... And always... Always... A gentleman.

Ronny truly loved talent and was encouraging to those possessing their own unique talents. The lovely, talented, and extremely sweet, Mona Abboud, spoke at Ronny's Memorial, of the encouragement and guidance he had given to her. Ronny had cast Mona in a show at the Upstairs at the Downstairs called *Graham Crackers*. Ronny paid an unexpected 3am call to Mona. Ronny entered her apartment carrying a suitcase and insisted that his visit was urgent. Mona was concerned that he might be moving in. But, he immediately dumped the contents of the suitcase onto the floor. The suitcase had been filled with books, records, and sheet music. He spread Stravinsky's *"Rites of Spring"* over the floor and on his hands and knees, began going through the music, measure by measure, sounding out all the various instruments. The "urgent" part of the visit was for Mona, "to experience such work." On other occasions, he would take her through some of the all-night bookstores or record shops, saying, "You need to know this... And, you need to hear this... This is important... And, don't miss this."

At another time, when Mona was visiting Ronny, Ronny was on his hands and knees with music, lyrics and sketches spread across his floor..., when a very attractive woman bursts through Ronny's door (apparently, she had a key) and shouted, "I have a gun, and I know how to use it!" There's more to the story, but you get the idea... Never a dull moment.

Mona, in her own words, said: "I loved Ronny Graham with all my heart, and will be forever grateful that fate allowed me to experience his friendship, his instruction, and his unique wisdom and that I was blessed with the gift of having shared some of the most-meaningful moments of my life with that remarkable man."

We held Ronny's Memorial at Bud Freedman's Improv in Hollywood, where Mona told that very touching story about how she felt. The witty and very sexy Gloria Bleezard followed Mona's touching tribute with: "Yeah... Ronny pulled some of that same crap on me." The house, full of comedians, including Mel Brooks, roared.

Now, for my soirees; on the last Thursday of each month I continue to schedule "fight-nights." Ronny is always here. The next one scheduled will be a rematch between Sandy Saddler and Willie Pep. Willie had won seventy-three fights in a row before losing to Sadler in Madison Square Garden. Saddler upset Pep by knocking him out in the fourth round. In all, Saddler and Pep fought four times with Saddler winning three of the four. These were huge fights, taking place in The Garden, and then in Yankee Stadium and The Polo Grounds. The last two fights were called "vicious brawls." The New York State Athletic Commission even revoked the fighters' licenses for months. In one of the fights, even the referee got knocked to the canvas.

Willie Pep, called by some as one of the best fighters his time, wants to redeem himself. We will begin with the first fight, the one that was held in Madison Square Garden in the fall of 1948. Chances are that Pep will not fare any better, but it promises to be entertaining as all hell. And the fact that Ronny and I didn't get to see those fights, "live," this promises to be a good one. Marshall wasn't fond of those evenings... And, even now, he does not partake of our violent entertainments.

After the fight, Ronny might sit in with Oscar Peterson on the "88sx2."

America, Be Seated:

A Modern Minstrel Show

The first time I worked with Ronny Graham was in a "Modern Minstrel Show," written by Ronny, Sam Pottle, and David Axlerod. Ronny cast me in *America, Be Seated,* scheduled to play at the Louisiana Pavilion at New York's World's Fair in Flushing Meadows, NY, in 1964. The show was loaded with talent: Ronny, Timmie Rogers, Mae Barnes, Lola Falana. Lou Gossett Jr., Bibi Osterwald, Val Pringle, Jack DeLon, Rico Froehlich, Peter Conlow, and more wonderful singers and dancers of the musical comedy ilk. Mike Todd Jr. had mortgaged his house to finance the show. After quite wonderful reviews in New Haven and Boston, we were excited to open at the Fair. Actually, in Boston, we hit a little snag. Ronny became ill. I went into Ronny's dressing room to rehearse new material that was going into the show in about thirty minutes. Ronny was "off the wall." I don't remember what we did after that. He must have muddled through the remaining performances. Ronny played the Interlocutor for the show. He was the compere or the host. After that, Keith Charles took Ronny's role. And, we headed for Flushing Meadows and The World's Fair of 1964. The World's Fair press release called it an "all-stops-out slapstick pageant of American History."

This was during the hard-fought struggle for Civil Rights era. C.O.R.E. the Congress of Racial Equality was staging a huge demonstration at the entry to the Fair. We, being a "Modern Minstrel Show," had an integrated cast of black and white performers. Some from CORE had seen the show in New Haven or Boston, and objected to some of the material and the show in general.

On the other hand, the show received support from the NAACP. They were upset by the label, Minstrel Show, but after seeing the show in Boston, they praised the revue to be an "asset for integration." The President of the Jamaica, Queens, NAACP branch said: "I have no serious objections. There is nothing in this show detrimental to or ridiculing Negroes. In fact, it is a satire on the old-style minstrel show."

Nevertheless, when we made an appearance on the *Ed Sullivan Show*, we had to present a couple of numbers that were without any of the edgier and funnier content. Guess that Sullivan and CBS were being less than progressive. (Stevie Wonder was on the Sullivan show that night, only then he was still, "Little Stevie Wonder.")

So, the bottom line was that when we opened at the Fair, it was cold and raining throughout our week's stay. We had been scheduled to run through the summer and into the fall. Unfortunately, the Louisiana Pavilion was at the far end of the grounds. So, one had to be bound and determined to see the show, to brave the foul weather and the long trek to our venue. There had to be walk-in traffic, of which there was none.

I envisioned a dark curtain descending. Why? On opening day, we were scheduled for afternoon and evening shows. For the matinee, at nearly show time, I stuck my head out of the tent (Yes, it was a tent) and saw a Nun and ten or twelve children tagging along in the wind and rain. After those out-of-town raves we got, we never imagined such a quick and sudden death by foul weather. This was "my shot." (Well, one of my shots) My shot was a dud.

I believe it was Metro-media that televised the whole show on their local station in New York. Apparently, there was no market for it in the outer boondocks. Then, it flew away to entertain at various venues deep into the ether. And, Mike Todd Jr. lost his home and his dream. As I recall, Mike had at least six children and a wife. Years later, I saw Mike on the Boardwalk at Venice, Beach. He seemed to be schmoozing a prospective investor for one of his projects. Mike didn't see me, so I didn't interrupt his pitch.

Ronny spent some time in the hospital, finally returning to the real world; he lived with LuJan and me and the children for a while. He used the little room down the hall with the half-bath. Later, his son, Ron Jr. lived in that room. Years later, I inhabited that little room down the hall with the half-bath.

Two years later, we toured in a pre-Broadway production of *New Faces of 1966*, before opening in 1968 at The Booth on Broadway. But, that's another story. Ronny moved west, where he got back in stride performing and writing. He wrote for some time on M*A*S*H and appeared regularly on The Tonight Show with Johnny Carson.

BEHIND THESE EYES SUCH SWEET MADNESS LIES

Check out those rave notices from New Haven and Boston... With those notices, the show was a "sure-thing." With Eliot Norton and Kevin Kelly, it can't miss, right? On to the World's Fair in Flushing Meadows, and then transferring to a Broadway theater. I had wonderful material to do. And, it was, indeed, a "mixed minstrel show." In one of our big numbers, Lou Gossett Jr. played my father. He was Uncle Sam, and I was Young Mister America. Here, we got a brief history of our country. Bibi Osterwald was The Statue of Liberty.

Timmie Rogers was very funny: "Oh, Yeah!" And, "Yummy. Send over some more of those UN troops. That last batch was delicious." We had great voices, with Val Pringle, Jack DeLon, Rico Froehlich, and me singing a rousing sea chanty... A quartet of lusty men, robust and riding the waves. And, me (with the help of a green gel) becoming more and more seasick... With Mae Barnes and her unique bluesy sound. And, Lola Falana, with her Lola Falana self.

We were a theatrical Titanic. Everything was on course, ship-shape, smooth sailing with laughter and singing... and... "**Iceberg**!!!" There were survivors, but the ship went down. And, it took Mike's house down with it. Was it bad luck? Was it a confluence of negative vibrations? No. It was the nature of "show business." And, well yes, extremely bad luck.

After twenty years of cabaret, Off-Broadway, and Broadway shows, I moved west, but not on "spec." I had a job. Ronny had been there for all that time. After not being in touch for years, we picked up where we left off: Best friends. Also, my friend

Marshall Barer had moved west. Ronny and Marshall, both, spent a lot of time at our house. Great friends, both. Getting Ronny and Marshall Barer together for an afternoon... As Marshall said, "We have three geniuses here... Me, Ronny, and Fiona." You'll notice that I was not included and rightly so. On one of Marshall's recording sessions, he had time left in the studio, and he asked Fiona if she would like to record one of her songs. She did. And, that was the beginning of many extraordinary recordings and concerts, worldwide. That was her genesis as an artist. Fiona has been recognized as the premier female songwriter of her generation, paving the way for the many who would follow.

Marshall Barer

Marshall Louis Barer was an artiste unique, calling himself, "The irrepressible, wafer-thin Anglo-sexual, psycho-Semitic, and almost unbearably gifted, Marshall Baer."

Defining a category occupied only by himself, he was Seattle Slew in a one horse race… A man totally embracing the art of being Marshall Barer. Painstakingly putting a string of words together and letting them laugh and sing and dance with talented composers was what he did best.

At my house in Venice, CA; most times, Marshall, knowing there was quite a turnover of my children and friends coming and going, would arrive at the gate, unannounced, saying, "Hi, I'm here for a few days. Do you have room?" He actually preferred it when all the beds were taken. That way he was sure to get his favorite; the couch in the living room where he could keep the TV going all night and stay near the refrigerator. He loved the refrigerator. If you sneaked in and turned the TV off, he would shortly wake up and turn it back on so he could sleep.

This photo was taken after Marshall had moved to Santa Fe and found turquoise.

Once Marshall is through the front gate, he's off headlong into the refrigerator. "What'cha got to eat? Don't get up. I'll help myself." -- A minute later he's standing in the middle of the living room chomping and dribbling from what he says is a tuna fish sandwich. Now, how the hell did he open a can of tuna and make a sandwich that fast? Marshall, chomping away, says, "It's quite unusual. Rather sweet. I like it... Sweet tuna fish... Interesting." My daughters had left a bowl of cookie dough in the fridge.

His Sunday songwriter-singer evenings, his soirees, when he lived near us in Venice, were wonderful, and, like Marshall, always interesting and usually quite bizarre. A number of singer, songwriters would gather for Marshall's Sunday Soirees: Anita Nye or David Ross, both of whom wrote beautifully with Marshall. Ronny Graham, sometimes dueling parodies with Marshall... Carl Anderson... Plus, the enchanting Melissa Converse, the wonderful, dear, Betty Garrett, and one of Marshall's favorites, Laurie McIntosh. Laurie knew the lyrics to every Marshall Barer song, and sang most of them at Marshall's request... Along with Andrea Marcovicci and Michael Feinstein.

Marshall always kept his front door open... with neighbors and some of the local homeless drifting in and out. You might see a few shabbily dressed, unbathed, and mystified nomads grazing Marshall's food table, and overhear some first-look comments on one of his "guess-what's-in-this" dishes: "Do you think it's safe to eat that? I don't like the color of that. That's an odd color. Taste it! You taste it!" When, in fact, the food was always tasty and quite often safe.

Marshall would plan elaborate events, with special-effects. His "Infinity" room, a small mood-lit-room, mirrored wall-to-wall, above and below, in which he often traveled, was indeed, a non-chemical based excursion, and not to be missed. It's been said that, without ever physically leaving the "Infinity" room, some trips, "without destination," were often experienced without too much anxiety. Aided by some mild pharmaceutical, it would be classified as travel-at-your-own risk.

I can see Marshall now; endlessly plugging and unplugging and plugging and tracing down cords to amplifiers. Often he would disappear then later return with a change of costume and a newly focused dedication to finding, through a M.C. Escher-like maze of useless cords, the end of yet another useless cord. Then, frustrated, he would go for a somewhat "edgier" costume change.

Once, I recall his wearing of a voice-activated brooch, he said he had invented, down about "there" on his brief briefs that lit up and twinkled when spoken into. He walked over to my visiting lady friend, Susan, who was somewhat conservative, and new to Venice Beach, meeting Marshall for the first time, and seated eye-level to Marshall's brooch. Marshall, with dancing eyes, said, "Speak into this!" She hesitantly managed a rather shaky, "Hello." The brooch twinkled like a Christmas tree, and Marshall twinkled off to twinkle elsewhere.

Nothing technical ever, or rarely ever, worked. After glitches and delays, the one who could accompany on his white, baby-grand piano would sometimes have to leave for a paying engagement. Following the string of complicated technological failures, the evening would completely fall apart, and then, before our very eyes, rise from the ashes, somehow morphing into a special, wonderful evening, with Marshall telling stories, and singing a cappella, or along to tracks from a pink boom-box, dueting with himself.

As if waiting in the wings, a talented tickler of ivories would stroll in. Michael Feinstein would come in late, from a performance elsewhere. Andrea Marcovicci the same... Or Dale Gonyea... Or Michelle Brourman. My daughters, Amber and Fiona, might duet. Fiona, at the age of eleven, and encouraged by Marshall, started playing and singing her own highly personal and sophisticated songs at Marshall's soirees. Once, when Fiona was playing and singing one of her songs, I happen to look over at Andrea Marcovicci, who had tears running down her beautiful face. Marshall, praising Fiona; soon to be known to the MTV world as Fiona Apple, said that at that age he'd written only one song... A song about his little dog. Of course, Marshall, later, followed his "little dog" song with a "little mouse" song; "The Mighty Mouse Theme," it's called.

And my daughter, Maude Amber Maggart, made her professional debut at Theater West, in Marshall and Hugh Martin's musical, *Happy Lot*. The musical was originally called, *A Little Night Music*, and was written before Sondheim's, *A Little Night Music*. It was written for Jeanette MacDonald and Liza Minelli. But, unfortunately, set aside after Jeanette MacDonald's death. I was in the show, as well. And, you can imagine my thrill, at being on stage in my friends' musical, with my daughter, Michael Feinstein, Melissa Converse, Betty Garrett, and members of the Theatre West Company singing those beautiful songs..., and, with my friend, Shelly Markham playing and conducting.

But, Alas! Somehow, once again, plugs weren't plugged into the right places. Cords snaked off into Pasadena! Microphones sputtered. It opened like a "train-wreck," with Marshall, as the "Master of Ceremonies," getting his pages out of order, and extemporizing off into at least three other librettos relating vaguely to the one at hand. But, fear not! Deus Ex Machina and his assistant, Mighty Mouse, arrived just in time to "save the day," and pull off yet another magical-Marshall-musical-miracle.

When Marshall moved to Santa Fe, a few years ago, I insisted that he let my son, Brandon (Bran), drive him there. And, I insisted that Marshall should he have any illegal substances, God forbid, to please jettison such substances before leaving. Because, should the Highway Patrol observe this denim-patch-covered-Mercedes, a younger handsome man driving an older gentleman, with the older gentleman wearing a tie-dyed parachute-like ensemble and listening to a pink boom-box, and red kerchief tucked in the pocket of the right rear window, the law enforcement officers might possibly, I repeat: might possibly, become curious enough to pull such vehicle over for a closer look!

Marshall agreed, but reneged, even before reaching the end of the block, as I later found out. I was, what one might call, "really pissed." Much later, it became a long, hilarious story that my son loves to tell, concerning a long side trip to the Biosphere and several scary stops at diners along the way. Bran and Marshall weren't fond of each other before the trip, and they loathed each other afterwards.

Certainly, he was, along with Ronny Graham, a member of our family and treated as such. One afternoon I heard my actor son, Garett, from an upstairs bathroom, cry out in his best Shakespearian anguish, "No! No! No! No! Noooo! Marshall's heeeeere!" He didn't even know Marshall was in L.A. until he opened his new jar of a special hair gel. There, a perfect handful of gel had been scooped out. Besides the refrigerator, Marshall was fond of using other people's toiletries. I told Garett that at least Marshall had put the top back on. Garett shot back: "But couldn't he have put the top back on with his non-gelled hand?"

Marshall and Amber adored each other, while, according to Marshall, he and Fiona were the most alike and the most at odds. "We're both true eccentrics," he said. "We're very much alike." But Fiona, being a vegan, kept her food sealed and in its place in the fridge. Marshall was, shall we say: "Not like that." Besides helping himself to her special juices, non-dairy and meatless dishes, he would leave his prey out on the counter top and uncovered. Fiona's reaction: "Expletive deleted." And that girl can really "expletive delete."

Over the years, Marshall allowed me to video-tape hours and hours of himself talking about his life and how he perceived his curious world. Sometimes, I could get both of my best friends together; those being Marshall and Ronny. Their mutual admiration and respect was a joy to behold. I highly recommend such friendships for whatever might ail you.

On his first trip back after moving to Santa Fe, he shows up at my front gate all bedecked in cowboy duds. The Kid had gone "cowboy," full tilt boogie; complete with cowboy hat, long "Shirley Temple" ringlets, leather fringed jacket, cowboy boots and lots of turquoise. At first glance, one might think it was Buffalo Bill Cody himself. But, as he posed, I blurted out, "Well, I do believe it's Mister Annie Oakley!" --That was not the reference he was looking for. But, he gave me a reluctant smile of recognition.

On one of the last tapes, Marshall said, "This, Brandon, will be a 'Now this can be told' session." Marshall said that he had loved and/or had affairs with at least four women. The first (I'll only give first names for obvious reasons) was Rosemary. Rosemary and Marshall were madly in love with each other. This was before puberty. Puberty changed the relationship, but they loved each other until Rosemary's premature death.

There was also, (I will give her name) Anais Ninn. Yes. He had "been with' Anais Ninn" in Paris. "She liked young beautiful boys," Marshall said. And, there was Jill. She with, "the most beautiful and saddest eyes."

And finally, Mary. (No last name here, but Marshall referred to her as "Dorothy's daughter.") Mary and Marshall had been successful creative partners, friends, and finally lovers. They planned to be married. They had already told Marshall's parents, who were quite happy. And surprised. Although his sister, Natalie, according to Marshall, was not so sure. Natalie said, "Look, we know we're a good and fine family, but we know little to nothing about them. There could be all sorts of skeletons." Marshall said he admired Natalie greatly for saying that.

On the other hand, Mary's parents, extremely prominent in New York society and the theatre world, presented another problem. Marriage to Marshall might well come as a shock to them. After a while, Mary thought it best to break the news, first to her mother who would in turn present it to the father. Marshall tells the story with the greatest, painful, and almost child-like glee. The father had no immediate comment but told the mother to tell

Mary to meet him in his office the following day. Now Marshall is roaring. The father, an icon in the American musical theatre, said, "My God, Mary! Why don't you just go the whole way and marry Truman Capote?" By now, Marshall is laughing so hard he's near tears. In the end, of course, they did not marry. But that's yet another story involving another celebrated lyricist who seemed to be constantly, though not intentionally, stepping into the hem of Marshall's gown.

I'm quoting here from a cabaret review printed in the New York Daily News on December 1, 1977, and written by Patricia O'Haire: "The world's first, and possibly last, performance of *'An Evening with Marshall Barer,'* took place Monday evening at the Ballroom, as part of its continuing Composers' series. It was a howl."

It goes on to give some of his credits and that Marshall "Was so nervous in the spotlight that his hands fluttered more than a flag in a windstorm. He held onto his tape recorder as if it were a security blanket. He had some friends to give him moral, and vocal courage; people like Anita Ellis, Indira, Tally Brown and Roberta Ross to sing, and Ellis Larkins to play piano, but it was one of those times when nothing worked right. Still, the result was charming and frequently hilarious." -- Does that sound vaguely familiar?

O'Haire's review continued: "For Example, the show opened with Marshall and all the women singing while holding aloft flickering votive lights. His went out, and he couldn't read his music. On stage, he had trouble with his mike. -- "I don't like this much anyway," he said. His hands trembled so he couldn't read the list of his songs, so he decided just to muddle through. He went to sing with his tape recorder only to find he had the wrong tape on; at one point, Larkins sat down to play for Anita Ellis and discovered that it was Tally Browns's song time. (Here comes my favorite) Craig Zadan, who had put the show together, stood on the side divorcing his hair from his scalp."

And the review winds up with: "It was a stew of a show. Everything was thrown in; without regard to its mix-match qualities; yet the result was a delectable dish that I am sure could never possibly be recreated."

Not so fast there O'Haire! Is it possible that Marshall got such a "rush" out of that nights' performance in 1977 that he did recreate that same chaos the rest of his life? Did he, there, on that winters night, become instantly addicted to the intermingling of disaster and triumph? I know I saw endless versions of that (whether by design or not) when he would enter the stage with precious gems in hand, trip and fall, tossing the stones into the air, and have them land as if by magic, to be his diamond bejeweled crown for the evening.

One final item, or as Marshall considered it, one final honor, that I'm sure he would like everyone to know. He was very, very, proud that he was "barred for life" from The Comedy Store. On an open-mike night, years ago, Marshall had made an attempt at "standup" comedy. He performed some bizarre act involving a string of small wieners. After stripping down to his jockey briefs, he apparently pulled, quite slowly, said string of wieners from his frontal nest. This act, perceived to be lewd by even the very liberal Comedy Store, got him "Barred for life!"

In an effort to make me understand the "lewdness," he performed the "act" in my living room, one night. Roaring with laughter. I never did figure out what the hell the act was about. He was laughing too hard to be understood, except for the part about being "barred for life." He loved that.

The visual alone was probably enough to get him tossed out. And to be honest, I thought about asking him not to come back myself! He was laughing his ass off, "You can't get banned from the Comedy Store! Nobody gets banned from the Comedy Store! But I DID!!" No. I didn't really think about banning Marshall from my house. But, sometimes… Close… For various reasons. At the time, Andrea Marcovicci and Michael Feinstein had called Marshal, "…Our greatest living songwriter." To which, I added, "…and our worst living houseguest"

Marshall traveled light. Marshall had money, but, if he needed a change of wardrobe, he would pay a visit to the nearest *Thrift Shoppe*. He came in one day with a shopping bag stuffed with what he was going to wear to an important meeting, the next day. He dumped the contents onto my dining room table, proudly saying, "Armani suit, shirt, tie, cufflinks, felt hat, and flip-flops… Seven bucks!" Next day, he looked fairly nice. Although, when he left, I noticed the back of his suit jacket was held together by two large safety pins and some gaffers tape.

Marshall's "pitch" meeting was with executives at Disney... The Mouse House. He got there a half hour late, driving in his start-stop, bucking style, in his denim covered Mercedes, with a red kerchief hanging from the right rear window. The Disney "suits" were not receptive. He might well have frightened them. Marshall was known to be quite animated, and, oftentimes offensive, if under stress. But, as the story goes; on that infamous day, Marshall Barer became a minor legend within certain circles around the Mouse House. At the conclusion of his disastrous meeting with the Disney "suits;" it's said that Marshall, in his slightly distressed Armani suit and flip-flops, had climbed atop the conference table... And, had relieved himself there. Others say he left in such a huff that he forgot to take a much-needed trip to the men's room. So, once in the Disney parking lot, he opened his car door, partially shielding himself, and took a big pee right there in the parking lot.

And, of course, as legends grow, word quickly spread around the lot about Marshall's meeting, with some reporting that Marshall had, indeed, made an artistic comment by climbing atop the Disney conference table, and had taken his big pee right there on the table. Marshall denied the table pee but owned up to his parking lot relief. By the way, the show Marshall was "pitching" that day was a musical that he had written with Dean Fuller. The name of the show was, *Appearances...*, based on *The Emperor's New Clothes*.

LuJan

While at school at The University of Tennessee, I met a gorgeous girl named LuJan Hudson. LuJan, to me, looked a little like the movie actress, Gene Tierney. The first time I saw her was at a school dance. I noticed her back... Her bare back... Her bare, toned, and tan back... She was dancing with her bare, toned, and tan back to me. LuJan was dancing with her dance partner, Guillermo "Billy" Hidalgo. They were doing some Latin dance unfamiliar to me at the time... Something, akin to some of those Fred Astaire and Rita Haworth numbers. I had the nerve to ask her to dance with me. She accepted, and we did the Jitterbug. The waltz, the stand-and-sway, and the jitterbug were my full arsenal. She was smiling and laughing, and I was smiling and laughing. Doing the Jitterbug, I swung her around, landing her on my right knee. Then, I swung her around and neglected to provide my left knee. I dropped her, landing her on her butt. Oops. She laughed, got up, brushed off her butt, and we continued on into the night..., and for years after that. We jumped from the Jitterbug to marriage and five children in no time all. Besides, being gorgeous and a good dancer, she maintained A's and B's without ever being caught studying: Excellent breeding stock.

Here, we posed for an ad: Lujan, Himself, Bran, and Garett on the way.

LuJan was a music major, and I a journalism major, but I spent a lot of time in the music building. Both singers; with the Knoxville Symphony Orchestra, we did the operas, Carmen, Der Fledermaus, and La Traviata together.

Again, it must be noted that during those early years, I did not carry the financial burden alone. LuJan, my noble ex-wife and mother of my first five children, Jennifer, Justine, Brandon,

Julienne, and Garett, for much of that time, taught music in two private schools, one of which was the Walden School in Manhattan and the other: Adelphi Academy in Brooklyn. LuJan was, and is, a courageous and determined woman, who, after our divorce, met and married a fine fellow; making a better match..., both being conservative Republicans. I respect her very much, and we remain on good terms, notwithstanding our political differences and my less than honorable behavior. She certainly didn't win the lottery by marrying the likes of me. But, our union did produce those five wonderful offspring.

I'll never forget calling her, from backstage at Radio City Music Hall, and telling her to watch me on the *Jack Paar Show* that night. She asked me what I was going to sing... And, I said, "I'm not singing. I'm calling hogs."... And, hung up. And, I was. And, I did.

Musical Chairs

So, *Musical Chairs* was my last show on Broadway. The show was an unwieldy sort. We, the cast, were the onstage audience being observed by our house audience who were watching us as we were watching the show that was taking place behind us, while we were facing the audience in front of us. Let me try that again... We faced our audience, but we were supposed to be seeing the show that was taking place behind us. So, the actual house audience watched us as we watched the show that was taking place behind us... Well, somewhere between those two, is the best I can do. The show had some good tunes and some interesting characters. My character didn't want to be there. Neither did I want to be there. I quit the show during rehearsals. I felt useless. I did have one duet with the wonderful Joy Franz, but it needed jacking-up! And, the writers were not around as far as I could see. There were no improvements... And no word that rewrites would be forthcoming. I left. I quit.

Susan Stroman, (Yes, that Susan Stroman) the assistant choreographer and cast mate, called me at home and asked if I would reconsider. I said to tell the invisible "them" that I would come back if "they" would permit me to infuse some laughter into the show for me and others. I would do this without credit or monetary compensation. Susan came back with, "OK... Come back." I did, and I added some much-needed laughter for myself and others.

Besides Susan Stroman, Scott Ellis was also in the cast. (Yes, that Scott Ellis)

Although we had only a brief run at the (now long gone) Rialto Theater, Earl Wilson of The New York Post, said that I was "one of the funniest men in the world!" I wondered if he had been on the phone with my mother. In a following interview with Wilson, he was mostly impressed that I could remember all seven of my children's names and birthdates.

Immediately before *Musical Chairs*, I had closed, in previews, with the Jule Styne, Herb Gardner musical, *One Night Stand.* My name was still up on the marquees of two Broadway Shows at the same time... And, I had no job... Not even a job waiting on tables... Zounds!

(I think maybe I already told you that. It's like saying, "goodbye" twice.)

Hellzapoppin' and Lynn Rachel Redgrave

Hellzapoppin' was another of my huge flops. Bob Williams and Louie (his dog) were featured in Alex Cohen's last production of *Hellzapoppin'*: with Jerry Lewis and Lynn Redgrave. Bob and Louie were the biggest hit in the show. The act was about Bob's efforts to get Louie to do a few tricks. Louie failed at his tricks, but charmingly so. So, did our show, fail. But, not charmingly, so. I had done the previous Alex Cohen production of *Hellzapoppin'* ten years earlier with Soupy Sales. Neither show made it to Broadway. But, I had loads of fun in both shows, especially when I got to write and do my own bits and to sing my own number, "The Jug Song." I had written the song and used it in several revues and a pilot for a TV series, with me, Robert Klein, and Hines, Hines, and Dad. The pilot did not sell. "The Jug Song" was my "money-in-the-bank-go-to-number." I wrote some bits for the earlier one with Soupy, too. I played, on my trumpet, "I Can't Get Started," while dressed in a gorilla suit… high class stuff.

Zany is an overused word, but *Hellzapoppin'* was the epitome of the word. One of the favorite bits used in the original show in 1938, with Olsen and Johnson, was called *Mrs. Jones.* In one of our versions, we had a diminutive English busker doing the *Mrs. Jones* bit. I forget his name but; he could finish, in ink, the London Times Crossword Puzzle as fast as he could write. Anyway, the first time he's seen and heard, he is walking around the audience, carrying a small potted plant, and calling out, "Mrs. Jones! Mrs. Jones! For... Mrs. Jones." He does this several times during the show... Each time, the plant has grown a little... Then bigger... Then even larger, in larger pots each time... And it gets more urgent... Calling out, "Mrs. Jones!!!! Mrs. Jones!!!!" Finally, after the show, when the audience is walking out through the lobby, he is sitting in a tree... Muttering "Mrs. Jones... Please... Mrs. Jones."

Lynn Redgrave was given a bizarre and tasteless bit to do while singing a rather generic ballad. I didn't think it should be in the show... And, I let my feelings be known. During the song, a baby begins to whimper..., from the balcony. The audience sees that Lynn is not pleased and becoming more and more annoyed as the baby continues to cry. First, let me say; we had a cast member positioned in the balcony, named, Tudi, who could cry exactly like a baby. Lynn stops singing and, addressing the balcony, asks if someone could, "Please, quiet the nice baby? Thank you." Lynn, again, in her stately manner, resumes singing. The baby cries even louder. Again, Lynn stops. "Usher... usher... Perhaps you, yourself could take care of the sweet baby... Thank you." As Lynn begins to sing once more; the baby begins to wail...double *fortissimo*... The audience is really laughing... And, a loud gunshot rings out; followed by dead silence... And then, a seismic boom of a laugh. I had been afraid that the audience might turn on us. I was wrong. Go figure.

HELLZAPOPPIN' AND LYNN RACHEL REDGRAVE

It was in that last production of *Hellzapoppin* with Jerry Lewis, in 1977 that I met Lynn Rachel Redgrave. I had a great time with Jerry, Joey Faye, Bob Fitch, Lynn, and a fun cast... Including a dozen or so of gorgeous, gorgeous, gorgeous, girls. But, at the same time, Lynn was having a very tough go-of-it with Jerry, on stage. He surely wasn't himself. Jerry suffered bad neck and back pain, but continued doing his pratfalls; ergo, the need for taking painkillers. Jerry did one fall to perfection: Bob Fitch enters, in-one, and spots Jerry across the stage. Bob takes an imaginary lasso from his imaginary belt. Bob twirls the lasso over his head... Jerry patiently waits for Bob to finish his imaginary rope trick... Bob tosses the imaginary lasso across the stage, and it slides down around Jerry's feet. Jerry looks at Bob as if to say, "So what?" Bob jerks the imaginary lasso. Jerry does the greatest fall I've ever seen. This was performed exactly as it would have been if it were a real lasso around his ankles. Jerry did not brace one bit for the fall. All this time, Jerry's back was killing him... For a laugh.

Lynn and I had a wonderful burlesque-farce-sketch with slamming doors and a very large bed. It was called, "Husbands, Lovers, and Wives." (I think) As the husband, I would knock on the door and say, "Honey, I'm home," before entering. During that brief time before I actually opened the door, a lover would scurry under Lynn's bed. I always carried a briefcase. This went on through three or four lovers scrambling under her bed each time I would enter. Each morning as I was leaving, I would pick up my satchel that I had placed beside her bed... and exit, saying, "Goodbye, Dear." She says, "Goodbye, Dear." The final time... (This was closing night, when stagehands were apt to pull pranks.) The final time, having forgotten my briefcase, I knock and say, "Honey, I'm home!" Six or seven lovers scramble under the bed. But, one has to go into the closet. I reenter saying, "I forgot my briefcase." During the blackout, the stagehands switched satchels, replacing my satchel with an identical satchel, now loaded down with fifty pounds of stage-weights. All this is done with the lightning-fast pace of any good farce. On leaving, I say, "Goodbye, Dear." She says, "Goodbye, Dear." I pick up my satchel. I'm surprised by the heavy weight and try to disguise my tilt to one side. This strikes Lynn to be hilarious, and she falls backwards onto her bed, laughing uncontrollably. I had never seen anyone break-up like that..., on the legitimate stage. She couldn't speak. I guess, after all the trouble with Jerry, she just released everything on a burlesque bed, center stage, in Boston. The audience was aware that something unusual had happened. And, Lynn's uncontrollable laughter was contagious. She would sit up only to fall back with uncontrollable laughing as I was listing to one side. I stepped forward and dropped my satchel onto the deck... Sounding to the audience as if a bag full of iron had been dropped there, which it had. I, then explained to the audience that mischievous stagehands had switched my satchel. I told the audience to "Hang on; we've got a big laugh coming." On each previous exit I had said, "Goodbye, dear." This time I said, "Goodbye, dear." then, I knocked on the closet door and said, "Goodbye, Sam!" on my way out. But, I slam the door and do not exit. Sam comes out of the closet, and all other lovers emerge from under the bed. "Ah, Ha!!!" -- Blackout.

That show was a "doozy." (Aren't they all?) There was a lot of bitterness between the west coast faction and the east coast faction. Alex Cohen had invited several directors up during the final weeks to give their assessments on whether or not they could right our badly damaged vessel. Tommy Tune came. Even, Dick Cavett. There were others. Ah, life in the vortex of a disaster, with our stage manager/now director Jerry Adler shouldering the brunt of the everyday conflicts. We closed at that storied old Colonial Theater in Boston. Sound familiar? But, through it all, most have stayed friends... Or, friendly. Though, I didn't see Lynn Rachel for several years until I was cast in the TV series, *Chicken Soup* with Lynn and Jackie Mason. Which, as we all know, was not successful either. This time, we closed in LA on the Universal lot. I've closed in some of the better theaters and studio lots around.

I did not hear from Lynn until another few years, when she gave me a phone call. She was about to go through a very messy and very public divorce. We had lunch. After her lengthy divorce battle, when we both were free, we became more than just friends... We became sweethearts. We grew to love each other... And, began sharing our lives together. Those were happy years.

BEHIND THESE EYES SUCH SWEET MADNESS LIES

After a year or so, living with me in my house, Lynn grew weary of my somewhat bohemian household, sometimes occupied by a few children and maybe a stray friend or two. Marshall Barer was there from time to time. She might find Marshall or a total stranger cooking up something in the kitchen. She didn't mind the dogs. In fact, she loved Bucky, a small black junkyard dog who adored her. One day I came home to find Lynn Rachel gone... Moved out. She had taken a small cottage just across the street. It was like a doll house. Order. Everything in place. Sanity. She needed her privacy, and she got it. She was writing a new play. She was happy. I was happy. She could spend time with me across the street in bohemia, and then go home to sanity and order. And, she got to bring her beloved two cats out here to be with her. Those two cats soon owned the neighborhood.

Lynn Rachel had returned from Australia upon completion of the film, *Peter Pan*. She went to her doctor, here in LA, for a routine checkup; and got the shocking news. She wanted to and did go back east and bought a house to be nearer her children and grandchildren. She fought the cancer with a vengeance for seven years; while, all along, writing her last play, performing in productions on stage... On television... And, in films. Lynn's daughter, Annabel Clark, documented that fight using her mother's journal, along with her own photographs. It was published as: *Journal: A Mother and Daughter's Recovery from Breast Cancer*. During the roughest times, she said she only got total relief when she was onstage. Dr. Theatre was her big help. Dr. Theatre meant being totally focused; *going on* and not stopping. With Dr. Theatre's adrenalin, she never stopped. In her last solo performance in New York, in her new play *Nightingale*, as seen by my daughter, Julienne, on closing night... "She didn't appear to be ill in the least." But, she was.

Lynn Rachel had called me during the rehearsal period and said that she was in a bad way... She was having trouble remembering her lines. Her treatments were interfering with her memory. But, after opening, she called me (I'm here in Bohemia) and said that, oddly enough, this had improved her show. She and Joe Hardy, her director, had removed all staging except that she would enter and go to her center stage desk and sit. From there, she would tell her story; referring to her text only when, if ever, needed. She got glowing reviews!

On the sad spring morning of Lynn Rachel's funeral in 2010, I was having a cup of coffee while writing down a few, hopefully proper and dignified words that I might later say at the church service. I was failing. For this dark occasion, I wondered what Lynn Rachel might have suggested. I was about to take a sip of coffee, when I noticed the mug I was using had been handpainted purple and blue, with tiny blue flowers all around. It was from Nashville, Music City USA, with a banjo and a guitar painted within an oval frame. I remembered that she had picked it up, a few years ago, when we were visiting my family in Tennessee. It was as if Lynn Rachel had placed that particular mug into my hand for a reason. Written on the mug were the words:

"I think you're gonna like this mug..., cause' it's got a lot of flowery shit all over it."

"Is it okay if I say shit in here?" "Anything you want to say," the minister said. With permission from the Lady Minister (whom Lynn adored) at the church, I related the story. Thank God, it broke the heavy gloom a bit. I wondered if "shit" had ever before been uttered in that or any other house of worship.

This prompted me to pass along one of her favorite stories. It was about an old actor/manager who, along with his wife, toured their small company, and at each curtain call, the old actor would announce the play and players for the next performance:

"Tomorrow evening I shall once again undertake the demanding role of King Lear..., in the Bard's great masterpiece... And, the good wife will take on the role of the daughter, Cordelia."

Someone from the balcony shouts: "Your wife is a whore!!!" (Pause) "Nevertheless... Curtain at seven."

About a year later, Lynn's daughter Annabel, produced a wonderful memorial honoring her mother in a Broadway theater. An impressive Broadway audience of actors, directors, writers, and theatre folk from both sides of the pond, all, spoke, sang, and read from Lynn's work. Maude Maggart Sang one of Lynn's favorites, Sir Noel Coward's, "I'll See You Again."

The Culture Project's theater formerly known as 45 Bleeker Street is now named: Lynn Redgrave Theatre. Lynn had performed there many times during her worst of times, when

Dr. Theatre assisted her on stage and off. She appeared in the original run of Culture Project's *The Exonerated* and was last seen on the Culture Project stage in 2007 with her sister Vanessa and brother Corin in *A Question of Impeachment.*

I miss my dear, Lynn Rachel Redgrave.

Losing My Fastball

But, Still in the Game

During the past few years, more than once, I've caught myself repeating parts of the same stories that I had previously told or written about. (As you may have noticed) This is not a good sign. At one time, my idea was to present some of my works, not just at my soirees, but on other stages as well. But, I found that I could no longer retain my own words sufficiently enough to do so. Someday, with proper wood-shedding, I might chance some select bits of it for public scrutiny. If not, I will contain all live performances within this safe attic stage beneath my brow and behind my eyes.

Sometimes, with *traveling without leaving*, I am apt to go to another scene right in the middle of experiencing the intended story. (Again, as you the reader may have noticed) I, sometimes blissfully, and sometimes aggravatingly, do go astray from my intended narrative to where times of clarity do not reign in cohesive concert. A treacherous adventure, to be sure. During some of my REM sleeps, I am often panicked by my condition as it deteriorates. Not to mention some old cracks in the wall of my character. I have certainly not been an angel. A few years ago, according to my sister, Honey; I unzipped my fly and exposed my brains to the temptations of life on the wicked stage. I have no rebuttal. LuJan says it all began with "the sixties." My son, Bran once said that he was the only kid in school whose parents were divorced. And that within six months half the kids in school had divorced parents. There was that whole 'free love" thing "in the air," or in my case, "in the glass."

And, since turning seventy, I have been known to say inappropriate things at inappropriate times. As with my mother and with one of my daughters, whatever enters my mind usually comes out of my mouth, *tout de suite*. Also, when writing, if something enters my mind, I am prone to write it down. I am loathe to censor my thoughts. As I have previously noted, I have been called bizarre, eccentric, unusual, strange, a galactic transient, a consummate liar, and the ideal lover. Here, in rebuttal: "I am not a liar. However, I do write fiction."

I have taken and considerably rewritten parts of this book (and two others) from my autobiographical odyssey called *Papa's Footprint*. *Papa's Footprint* covered four million years from my birth in Africa to my present home in California. However, *Papa's Footprint* was written primarily for my family and friends. It was meant to be read, spoken aloud, and at times, speak-sung (singspiel). The book is rendered in prose, poetry, paintings, personal letters, versified expressions, and family "tater stretching" folklore. It is Papa's tale of his many footprints, as he ponders the baffling mysteries and fascinating wonders of life on this earth.

Here, in, *Behind these Eyes Such Sweet Madness Lies*, I play Himself on the convenient stage behind my eyes as well as my life off stage as I push the pen and confess these words.

Rex Reed, John Simon, and Fiona Apple

(Added on October 7, 2013)

The following is an attempt to arrive at some explanation for a recent remark made by my daughter, Fiona Apple. It begins with that Broadway musical I was in at The Palace Theater in 1974. It was called, *Lorelei*; starring Carol Channing.

I had an old friend of the theatre who usually began his show-biz tales by laughing and saying: "This, I think, is very funny." He would tell his story and, then, end it with, "Which, I thought, was very funny." The following is one of my show-biz stories, "some of which, I think, is very funny." It all depends on how you look at it; I guess.

Lorelei was a heavy dance show with two of the best in Tamara Long, and my old friend from *Applause* (also at The Palace) and *Potholes* (at the Cherry Lane), Lee Roy Reams... Plus a whole line of terrific hoofers, including Bob Fitch and John Mineo, in support. They tapped their asses off. By this time, after having my songs and most of my dialogue cut, I had nothing much to dance about. At one point in the show, I took center stage, with

Dody Goodman, for a brief turn..., and that was it. However, I must have impressed Pulitzer Prize-winning critic, Walter Kerr, who had liked me in *New Faces of 1968*. Kerr, of the Herald Tribune, concerning the dance numbers said:

"The first tap... is agreeable, especially as spun out by Tamara Long and Lee Roy Reams, but the second and third and fourth fast taps don't uncork much that is new (except when the skillful Brandon Maggart is briefly applying his own instant stylization)." Kerr's brackets, not mine.

However, not agreeing with Walter Kerr was critic for *New York Magazine*, John Simon. Simon, reviewing *Lorelei,* had given me a quote to remember:

"Brandon Maggert and Dody Goodman are both untalented and irritating."

This quote appeared every week in the magazine. After six months, Dody Goodman left the show for greener pastures. The following week, the quote read:

"Brandon Maggert is both untalented and irritating."

I'd had enough. I called the magazine, and was put in touch with Ruth Gilbert, who edited the weekly John Simon reviews; reprinted there for as long as a show is running. I introduced myself and said that I was calling about Simon's review of my performance in *Lorelei*. She said, "Oh, I know... I'm so sorry."

I said, "Please, don't be sorry. I wear John Simon's review as a badge of honor. But, would you please correct the spelling of my name? Mr. Simon has spelled my name incorrectly. It's Maggart... Not, Maggert."

The following week, there I was, for the rest of the run... Brandon Maggart remained "untalented and irritating." But, my name was spelled correctly... "All of which, I think is very funny."

Fiona was not yet born at that time, but years later she had heard me tell about John Simon being known as a critic prone to pointing out negative physical appearances of some actors, especially, actresses whom he did not find esthetically appealing to his discerning eye. He preferred beautiful young actresses; and was known to escort a few of the chosen around town. Those failing to qualify *should not be allowed onstage*. This was odd for a man who often appeared on television squeezing out an off-centered smirky smile, revealing to my eye, his unsightly gray-green teeth. This was quite distressing to my delicate sensibilities. He *should not be allowed on television*.

Other than that, I had great respect for the man as a critic. And, his reviews were always smart enough and insightful enough to keep me running for the dictionary. (We used dictionaries back then.)

One year, producer Alex Cohen, for whom I had appeared in four failed productions, including two productions of *Hellzapoppin:* One in 1967 with Soupy Sales and ten years later with Jerry Lewis and Lynn Redgrave, along with a play called, *We Interrupt*

This Program, and a TV Special with Dick Van Dyke and Carol Channing called, *The Fan,* or *I'm a Fan,* or something like that. One Christmas, Cohen gave out rolls of toilet paper as presents. John Simon's picture was on each tissue.

Now: On October 7, 2013, Fiona Apple, Blake Mills and their band (of two), gave a wonderful concert at Disney Hall in Los Angeles. A few nights earlier, in Portland, Oregon, towards the end of what some called "a magical night," until someone in the audience called out for Fiona to "get healthy." And, "I saw you twenty years ago, and you were beautiful." This heckling broke the "magical" spell and evoked an emotional reaction from Fiona. She called for the house lights. And, the heckler was escorted from the theater; along with a few blistering words from Fiona.

Then, according to Bran, her brother, "She lost it, Dad." She had only two songs left on her set, but becoming emotional and reduced to tears; she cut her haunting ballad, "I Know," and finished with her last song, "The Waltz," while sobbing. She, then, left the stage. There was some concern about whether or not she would continue the tour.

But, the following night, gathering herself, and with equilibrium restored, in Seattle, Fiona and Blake Mills with Sebastian Steinberg, Fiona's great bassist and one-liner man for many years, and Barbara Gruska, a new-to-me and extremely talented drummer did a flawless performance; sans hecklers. By happenstance, Dave Chappelle, who recently had experienced some of his own disruptive hecklers happened to be playing in Seattle that night. Fiona, Spencer (Bran), Blake, Sebastian,

Barbara, and others caught Chappelle's late show. Yes, the shows do go on.

Then, on to Los Angeles and Disney Hall, which is the best performer and audience friendly concert hall I've ever experienced. It's a Frank Gehry masterpiece configured so that there is not a bad seat in the house; with the audience seated all around and over. It reminded me of the Globe, in London..., except much nicer and more comfortable.

I hadn't seen this show... And knew not much about it, except, going by what Fiona and Blake called, *The Anything We Want Tour*; one might venture a reasonable guess.

Right away, they began to build something from scratch. Judging from the title of her last album, *The Idler Wheel Is Wiser than the Driver of the Screw and Whipping Cords Will Serve You More Than Ropes Will Ever Do*, I figure that Fiona feels free to follow her instincts. On that recording, at a brief moment, she had used the distant sound of children playing in a nearby schoolyard. Here, she uses, for percussion, things that she might have run across during one of her walks: like an empty wine flask, or a piece of palm frond, or a wooden sculpture, or a collection of sticks.

Without fanfare, the group of four enter. They pay little attention to the hearty entrance applause. It was as if they were beginning their day in a rehearsal studio. Fiona begins the show by writing on a blackboard these words: "Teach me how to be free." What did that mean? Maybe it means that she would, by example, teach us how to be free. Or, maybe, she wants the audience to teach her the same. It seems to me that Fiona already forges her path, unencumbered. Maybe, this is meant to encourage other artists not to be sheep. And, to set the stage for what she is about to do... She looks about the stage deck, and from a selection of percussive objects; selects a few thin sticks as if preparing to interpret her *I Ching* for guidance. Will she hold them perpendicular and then let them fall where they will for her to contemplate? Is this the art of work creating a work of art?

From there she, Blake, Sebastian, and Barbara ease into and unfold and build their unique work of art. Blake barely touches the strings of his guitar as he quietly introduces something that the others pick up and gather from this pianissimo intro through scorching lyrics, spreading the wings of a musical thread into a crescendo until, finally, landing it gently at its proper rest. To steal from Sondheim: they had cobbled together a work of art where there had been no work of art; referring to his, "Finishing the Hat."

Fiona, Blake, and Barbara Gruska prepare to launch. Sebastian is off camera.

This was not presentational. We, the audience, were included as passengers on a private and personal flight. It's an unusual, often spell-binding, venture; with Fiona being sensitively focused, and vocally and dynamically at the top of her game.

Personally, I likened it to a meditation with dynamics that rise and fall and rise and soar without losing its calm center. I was transported.

Blake Mills had opened for Fiona on her last tour and is now sharing the bill with Fiona on this one. Blake is a marvelous guitarist, making the guitar say what Blake is thinking, or else the guitar makes Blake play what the guitar is thinking. It's a Fiona Apple and Blake Mills unique ride through the evening at Disney Hall.

I and several members of our rather eclectic family, along with a packed house were enjoying this experience..., when just before her sad and haunting, "I Know" ballad... Fiona stops the show for an aside... Perhaps for something relating to her words earlier written on the blackboard? "Teach me how to be free."

Fiona takes a moment. She scans around the audience. Suddenly, I feel that this moment might be a "Fiona moment." I was right. She says: "Sometimes, there are things you just want to get off your chest... I've wanted to do this for a long time: Daddy, this is for you: 'Rex Reed: You're a cunt."

Holly shit! Did Fiona just call Rex Reed a "cunt" from the stage of Disney Hall? Yep, she sure did.

She went on to explain this specific naming by saying that I, her Daddy, many years ago, had been given a negative review by Rex Reed, saying that he had even misspelled my name… And, then she continued with how Rex Reed had offended her with his negative physical descriptions of women performers.

Now, to me, Rex Reed does appear to be a tired and bitter old Regina with a poison pen, but Rex Reed was not the critic who had given me a bad review and misspelled my name. Though of little import to the world at large, that critic would be John Simon. I assumed that Fiona had confused the two, due to both having been guilty of bullying women from their respective bully pulpits. Most recently, Reed, in reviewing a film, starring Melissa McCarthy, had used tasteless terms in describing McCarthy's girth, which is probably what caused Reed's name to come flying into Fiona's mind and out of her mouth. (Sadly, Reed continued to pound McCarthy in her next film, *Tammy.*)

After having attached that graphic assessment to Reed, Fiona went into her beautiful and poignant ballad of resignation "I Know," bringing to a close a wonderful and unique concert and evening at Disney Hall.

However, I must say this, in John Simon's favor; Simon was, and is, much smarter and a far, far better critic than Reed. To me, Reed is merely the queen of "snarky." And, Simon's goof has supplied me with a good story to tell. And, I do tell that story at the drop of his name, such as "A Christmas gift for John Simon."

REX REED, JOHN SIMON, AND FIONA APPLE

Rex Reed was a critic at the *Observer* (I believe that's the name) who, about eleven or twelve years ago, on Maude's New York debut at Danny's Skylight Room, had taken issue with my daughter, Maude Maggart, for having parents who had named her "Maude." Saying: "The only thing worse for her would have been if she had been named... Fiona." (Fiona was right. Rex Reed is a cunt.) Obviously, a retort had been fermenting in Fiona's arsenal for these many years. Yes, there's where Reed as the villainous hen had committed her unfortunate clucking and the laying of his rotten egg. This, I'm sure, was what was lurking in Fiona's mind. Also, Reed had continued about Fiona's sister, Maude with: "She sounds like Little Lulu and looks like Margaret O'Brien in *Meet Me in St. Louis* on Halloween night wearing her big sister's gown with her hair piled on top of her head like a Gibson Girl."

On the other hand: Following Maude's debut at Danny's, the Association of Cabarets and Clubs (M.A.C.) recognized Maude with its Best Female Debut Award.

Reed must, also, be without vision and hearing because Maude and Fiona are both considered to be quite gorgeous, with exceptional voices and talents... Both having appeared separately on front covers of, *Time Out New York*, and, in the same year. I don't know if that has ever before happened. I wonder.

Perhaps, Reed had envisioned himself playing Margaret O'Brien's role in that scene from *Meet Me in St. Louis*. Dear fellow... Heartbreaking... So very sad... Poor Myron. Perhaps he's never gotten over the tragic fact that he will never become

Raquel Welch. Alas, poor fellow. I will say that back in the time of *Myra Breckenridge* Rex was uncommonly pretty.

Following Reed's review of Maude's show at Danny's, I wrote a note to Mr. Reed, at the *Observer*, explaining to him that my daughter, Maude Maggart, had named herself, "Maude," after my dear grandmother, Maude Apple. Also, Fiona was named after her as well; opting to use her middle name, Apple. However, I wrote that I was going to overlook his mean-spirited review of my daughter, Maude, and his snide aside at my daughter, Fiona. I would overlook that in light of an embarrassing week that he had endured. Rex Reed had been arrested for allegedly stealing CDs from Tower Records. Reed said that he just had "a senior moment." And, for possibly plagiarizing another critic's film review, his excuse was that he wanted to eat his "Dove Bar," and he had to step outside to enjoy it. I guess he was so taken by the Dove Bar that he missed the film and just took a shortcut. That would tend to make most anyone a bit grumpy. Rex Reed did not reply to my note. Yes, Rex Reed might be a shop-lifting plagiarist and a... Stop. Don't say it. It's been said.

So, Maude opened to rave reviews and, immediately, began a successful yearly run of from four to six-week engagements at the storied Oak Room at the Algonquin Hotel for the next seven years. This, apparently, did not sit well with Reed.

Sadly, before playing her eighth year at the Algonquin, the Oak Room was closed... Gone the way of corporate greed; under the ownership of The Marriott chain. I believe Dorothy Parker and the other regulars of The Round Table might well expire once again.

Maude Maggart, Himself, and Lynn Rachel Redgrave at the Algonquin

Thousands of New Yorkers and others signed a petition in an attempt to save the Oak Room, but the Marriot has the keys. It is New York's sad loss of a bright star in its colorful nightlife history.

Maude, including Stephen Holden of the *New York Times*, always gathered excellent reviews from the critics..., except for dear Rex, who continued to drip sulphur from his pen. It must have wilted his hothouse lilies to see that the crowds were not influenced by his irresponsible and shabby drivel.

After about the sixth or seventh year, on an opening night for Maude, I watch the puffy doughboy stroll into The Algonquin and into the Oak Room, where he proceeds to wet his whistle and to dine on some of the fine cuisines served in the Oak Room. It seems Miss Otis has no regrets.

I must say that I have several learned friends who do admire the man. After all, he is the best of all possible Rex Reeds. And, what good is a proper tale without a good villain?

"All of which, I think is very funny."

I agree with Fiona that sometimes there are things one needs to get off one's chest. Critics have their bully pulpit, and sometimes this performer makes use of her bully pulpit.

"As a person who performs on stage, it's good to be emotionally open. If you mess with someone when they are in that state, it's like you're messing with an animal when it's eating. What do they expect me to do?"

-fiona apple

I believe the above quote concerned the concert in Portland when she was interrupted at a particularly vulnerable moment.

Over the mantle: That's Maude and Fiona as featured, separately, on covers of *Time Out New York*. On the mantle: That's Garett on the left... a few rhinos 'neath the ladies of words and music, and on the right: Himself hawking a possible new show to people who invest in such endeavors.

Before I was in Africa

Many years ago, when I was in college at the University of Tennessee, I came across a little book called *God's Trombones: Seven Negro Sermons in Verse*. It was a collection of seven poems by James Weldon Johnson. The first poem, written in 1919, was called, *The Creation*. I guess it might be called a folklore telling about the creation of the world and its inhabitants. I was moved and inspired by *The Creation*. For me, it had resonance and was a much better way of telling the story as opposed to the book of *Genesis* in the *Bible*. I decided, considering today's knowledge of science that I would attempt a fable along those lines.

(My fable: *Before I was in Africa*)

Before I was in Africa, I'm not sure I was anywhere. All the pieces must have been around, but they hadn't been put together yet.

According to my Grandpa's grandson, which turns out to be me; before everything that is and everything that ever will be; there was nothing. And, as my story goes, within this darkness and void stood only the two of them, the two Mem-Branes, Mr. and Mrs. Huckleberry, contemplating; were there any facets of darkness and void that they had failed to investigate? After lengthy consideration, the Huckleberrys agreed that darkness and void were without merit and thereby scheduled no future ventures into the void; whereupon, the Huckleberrys began to assess their relationship to each other and to define their purpose of being.

Side by side, the Huckleberrys took a lengthy stroll. The Huckleberrys experienced only emptiness as they moved through the darkness until they decided to turn their search inward. Deep inside, they came upon something; waiting to be found. On the instant of discovery, a strange feeling of attraction came over them. Mr. Huckleberry said, "Let's call this attraction 'Gravity.'" Mrs. Huckleberry said no, "This is nice and warm and tingling... We'll call this 'Infatuation.'" Mr. Huckleberry acquiesced. They had come upon a bright glowing light around a pinpoint of space that radiated a powerful new sensation. From this warm, circular glow, they experienced a growing urge to become closer... To be creative... And, to fully investigate that tiny centered space without dimension but equally related to the whole of its circular aura. Huckleberry had a very strong impulse. Mrs. Huckleberry had a like impulse. Huckleberry said, "Woman..., let us fill that little 'Whatchamacallit' and nourish it. Let us make a 'Whatchamacallit' in our image... After our likenesses. And too, let us make a grand plan for it, and a world in which it might thrive."

On Huckeberry's words, their incredible energy of intent, fueled by heated desire and passion, became such that by summoning their two separate streams of photons from opposite directions, and by colliding them at the speed of light, there came a grand climax! Holy Photons! Holy Mackerel! Holy Cannolis! And Yowzah!!! They spewed forth their very own, newly born, and violently expanding, infant...... universe.

Included in their "can do" plan, were the laws of Gravity, Electricity, and both Strong and Weak Forces (among others). These were the makings for everything that is, and everything that ever will be. The Baby Huckleberry Boson emerged by way of a will and a faith infinitely smaller than a mustard seed. Totally exhausted... Mr. Huckleberry fell asleep, while, of course, the Missus made plans.

Emerging from their quickly expanding Universe came a special planet that they named, "Terra." But, later Mrs. Huckleberry changed the name to "Earth" because it had a special "earthy" feeling about it. They placed it revolving around a nice big star they called, "Sun." Sun was very warm and would keep Earth warm enough within a very cold space. It took a while to fine tune things; the tilt, the spin, and the orbit must work like clockwork with the warm Sun to support necessary plant and animal life, dependable seasons, and a well-balanced carbon-oxygen cycle. The Huckleberrys made use of mathematics, physics, biology, chemistry, and all their sciences. They used these tools to explore; continually finding new combinations and new doors to open. Creating and perfecting the first cell, with its infinitely exacting combinations, was essential for life.

Once that was done; the blueprint of that first cell, with slightly varied blueprints, led to higher forms. Constantly evolving and improving led to male and female organisms (Two circles often sharing a common radius) that would eventually become the intended likenesses of their parents.

From that point, these offspring came upon the most pleasurable way imaginable to continue the lineage. This seductive act caught on quickly. It became and remains extremely popular. Yowzah and Shazam!!! In fact, the Hucklberrys sang out, in sweet harmony, "Do-re-mi-fa-so-la-ti-do." Hold everything! That sounded so good that the Huckleberrys said, "Good God..., that was good." And they added music! And that felt so good..., they danced! And they told each other stories about what they had done that day... And they laughed! Yowzah-Zaroonie! Singing and dancing and laughing and fun on the planet! And they decided that enjoying this together was the best of all possible worlds. And, they retained these stories for the telling at later dates. They called this process: Theatre.

They soon realized the joys of *"work,"* hard work, with attention to detail..., evolving towards, but never reaching perfection was their path. This mode of operation, they called: trial and error. They went about making mistakes and improvements on what they deemed to be the mistakes. By always having somewhere to go and something to do..., to work on; they held any creeping ennui at a distance. Proper maintenance became quite a chore. However, each day's hard work, well done, they found to be quite fulfilling. Things were up-and- running.

And the Huckleberrys said... "This is good... Now, let us turn everything over to the kids and see what happens. Of course, after a much-needed vacation, followed by a lengthy slumber, we'll look in on them to see how they're doing.

And too, we must and will, assign a BIG ROOSTER to constantly keep an eye on things. This will require constant 'eye-balling' on BIG ROOSTER'S part, to be sure. And, we'll let them know that BIG ROOSTER is watching every little thing... His eye on the sparrow... And they will be able to bring all their problems, big or small, directly to BIG ROOSTER. And BIG ROOSTER will listen..., intently. And, hopefully, BIG ROOSTER will be able to help guide them along in various and mysterious ways. Also, instructions will be in a BIG BOOK, written in nano-script, which will be translated into various languages as they emerge. Extreme care must be taken in making the translations; avoiding any possible confusion. So, be it."

The End of the Beginning

So, what possibly could go wrong with the children? - I need more popcorn. OK. Back to work... Back to the Huckleberrys...

"Oh, Shit!"

After a fourteen billion year nap, the Huckleberrys arouse themselves to check on the kids. On BIG ROOSTER'S report, they were, in many ways, elated. However, they were extremely disappointed and gravely concerned on other counts. They wondered what to do, if anything? They decided to not give up on their offspring. But, the kids would have to sink or swim on their own. Tough love. During BIG ROOSTER'S long tenure, the young universe had, indeed, been rife with innumerable failures, along with many successes. The number and nature of the disasters sent Huckleberry and his Missus reeling. The absence of harmony within the human family, and the failure to make proper use of their Sun's ample supply of energy were both: huge disappointments. BIG ROOSTER, Himself, had stumbled badly. But, now, the Huckleberrys are bound and determined that their kids will make Earth a successful place to live, grow, enjoy, appreciate, and to love and respect each other while here orbiting our energy source..., our Sun... Or, else they will get their asses kicked from on high.

Yep... I'm expecting some tough but considerate love from Mom and Pop. I expect that, after a lifetime, and on a day of reckoning, all souls will gather in spirit form, with BIG ROOSTER standing at a gate. Beyond the gate will be a place somewhat like Horse Shoe Bend was in the 1930's and 1940's when I was growing up along the Cumberland River. For all those having lived their lives on planet Earth, and then recognized by BIG ROOSTER at the Gate, the Huckleberrys will greet them with; "Come on in... We know you've been through hell already... some of you more than others... Take a load off... and welcome to Huckleberry Heaven!"

But, as I see it; there'll be some folk that'll still need a good ass-kickin'. I hope Huckleberry has got some good ole ass-kickin' boots for the job. I'd be willing to assist on a few of them. I imagine a lot of folks would queue up for that job. Perhaps, some of us will be dropped through worm holes and sent back to clean up any nasty spots and blemishes remaining on our records. I wouldn't mind that. That might be a relief. To be sure, there's some settling-up to be done. I suspect Huckleberry won't terminate them, for reasons known only to Him. But, Huckleberry, I suspect, will give them a chance to apologize and say, "I'm sorry." However, they'll know they've had a prime, grade-A-ass-kickin'. Mrs. Huckleberry might give'em that look, the one she calls on only in case of emergency. That look could wither a Redwood. But, always the liberal, she'll probably minister to them and get them so they can sit down without too much prolonged, and extreme agony... Nothing over a century in Earth's time.

I'm pretty sure that I'll have a mighty strong urge to kick BIG ROOSTER's ass... And a good one too. I might hug Him first, and then kick Him a good one... Then hug Him and ask for forgiveness... He, probably, did His best. Then, kick Him a good one for the road. Kate taught me that. BIG ROOSTER has been cursed plenty of times before, to be sure, but, I don't know if He's ever been kicked in the ass. However, I've always been reasonably good at controlling my urges. So, wisely, that won't be happening. Once, having kicked old John Barleycorn's ass back in 1980, I have been pretty much in control of my many temptations and shady behaviors. Except for a few, truly amazing women that I did bend to with blissful abandon. Surely, women have been my most blissful and painful downfall... Time and time again. But, I do heartily stress the word "blissful."

Rumors have been floating around that both Branes, Huckleberry and Mrs. Huckleberry, did indeed come from mothers and fathers of their own and that we might possibly have some relative

Universes out there somewhere in numerous other dimensions. We do know that our precious life-giving and sustaining star is only one sun of the billions of suns in our galaxy alone and that there are billions of other galaxies other than our own. It seems like there ought to be a great deal of extra real estate to explore out there. Maybe the Mound People have a homestead on a colony out there somewhere. Of course, they might not want to see the likes of us again.

I'm kind of hoping, too, that Mr. and Mrs. Huckleberry will have something like "fireside chats," so that BIG ROOSTER will, finally, talk to us and maybe, using some self-deprecating humor, tell us about some of the times He's not too proud about… Like where He'd failed at His job, and that He's deeply sorry for. I mean, let's face it; BIG ROOSTER's job is tougher than being the President of the United States… Impossible to please everybody. Then, He could tell us about some of the funny and interesting things that happened along the way… Things we might have missed… Those would be well worth the listen; I'm sure… Especially, with the exception of George Burns, and of the time I played God on the stage in my attic, we have never heard BIG ROOSTER speak a single fuckin' word. (In this case "fuckin'" doesn't mean coitus. It doesn't mean anything really. Used sparingly, it just has a good sound for stressing an extra emphasis.) Maybe some heroic stories, narrow escapes, and such… And gentle stories, like stepping over a ladybug, as my friend Karen did so as to not squish it. And lots and lots of funny stories… I do favor a good story with a few delicious laughs, and maybe a tear or two… And, every once in a while, we should talk about some of the bad stuff we did, that we're not proud of. (But, ending a sentence with a preposition ain't all that bad.)

There's one big question I'd like to ask: Are some people just born mean, or do they get that way through the rigors of life?

And to think; none of this would have happened if Huckleberry and the Missus hadn't had that original urge and powerful intent (in this case, thought does have mass... Thus creating something out of nothing) to start the ball rolling in the first place. Indeed, with birthing their singular, all-rolled-into-one-Huckleberry Boson..., they created this whole "razz-ma-tazz of... lots of pretty girls in a... just for you... kind of blue... old-time... burlique show." And, they just thought we ought to know.

But, on the other hand; what if, after life here on this orb, there is only darkness and void..., with virtue being its own and fleeting reward? Zounds... We're screwed.

I'll admit that I have, in the past, doubted both BIG ROOSTER, and the story about Mr. and Mrs. Huckleberry as told by me. Maybe, I have just dreamed all that shit up (Please, excuse the mild profanity) as the most reasonable opiates I could come up with. Or, maybe, on the other side of that birthing canal, where they birthed Baby Universe, there isn't just darkness and void. Maybe, that's where we're headed; back to the center; surrounded by that beautiful aura. That might be another great adventure... A great fractal adventure. A mathematical fractal seems to be a never-ending journey into its like self. Maybe we'll all continue, using that Golden Ratio structure... And, go on and on like Pi... Like a circle sharing its radius with its twin evolving circle... Going on and on like a stage actor repeating the same role night after night; while still evolving and making every performance a new and unique realization; a controlled spontaneity within the musical measure. And, with my *traveling without leaving* repertory company, we'll have endless lives to lead and to present on some heavenly stages.

Wherever I'm headed, I trust that Kate (My "Kates" are Lynn Rachel Redgrave and every other woman before her that I might have loved) will always be with me. We'll always sing and tell each other tales. And, if we can get up a crowd, we will put on some kind of a Razz-ma-tazz of a show for them. Maybe we can get everybody to share their stories... Using poems and songs with lots of happy tears... With even a goodly amount of Tater-Stretchin' allowed. That Tater-Stretchin' part would necessarily include Grandpa, who will surely be there with Grandma, and Irene, his other wife he took after my Grandma passed. That would be somethin'!

And, Grandpa will be telling the story about how Earth is but a young Huckleberry, and we are tiny little Huckleberries within the Big Huckleberry Family. And at the end of his story, I expect, he'll dance his Huckleberry Jig... Maybe we'll all join in... Including FDR, and the great physicist, Stephen Hawking, and Kirk too. (The story of Kirk and how we got Kirk laid is in my next book: *The Trunk in my Attic*.) I especially look forward to meeting President Roosevelt and thanking him for giving my generation such a good start. And, I do certainly hope President Roosevelt will get his young legs back so he can join in on the dancing. That goes for Stephen Hawking too. Of course, I imagine that Hawking will be busy trying to figure out how in the hell he got to a place that doesn't exist. Well, he'll always have something to work on. That process of working on something might be what Heaven is. "It's the doin' of it." I can truly understand that. And, Kirk, our young friend, bound to a wheelchair, will be dancin' and going Aeeeeeeh with joy! Jessica, a wonderful human being who happened to be a prostitute, certainly deserves to be there. Jessica might be reunited with those she has loved..., and those who have loved her.

I do hope Ronny finally gets to play piano with Oscar Peterson... And, maybe with that little French jazz pianist, named Marcel Petrucianni, who got dealt a bad hand, physically. He had a condition that made his bones brittle. And, he was very small, weighing about fifty pounds. He had to be carried to the piano (by his wife, the one night I saw him play)... And then, Marcel played the shit out of that piano. I can only imagine what he might do in Heaven with a better deal in the physical department. He wouldn't need more talent or heart. He had that covered.

Ronny's life did certainly parallel a wildly varied and intricate venture within a jazz form; and, at the same time, cause laughter and some tears. Marcel was surely magic. Amazing.

And, I expect my dear Lynn Rachel, whom I loved so very much, and who loved me in return, will be teaching Shakespeare classes, as she did at Ten Chimneys. And since I didn't grasp it too well before, when I come, I'll be attending all her classes. I still might not cotton to Shakespeare, but I would be happy just to watch Lynn Rachel work, and teach. Maybe she'll take us on some of her long walks along something like a Heaven's Appalachian Trail to explore some of nature's beauty that we might have missed. I expect that her dog, Viola, will soon be with her.

I haven't the foggiest idea how the internet works... Or how words and pictures fly with integrity and precision from one place to another on my push of a button. And, I'm still thinking about that "trial and error" way of progressing. Maybe that's why it takes millions of sperm in a single ejection to penetrate the one female egg. Only one of the millions swimming upstream will get the job done. Yep. Looks like "trial and error" to me. Also, If Earth is the only place where there is life, and there is a googolplexian number of galaxies out there..., sounds like big-time trial and error case to me. So, there should be no fear of failure. Just do the best you can with what you've learned by failing. Am I afraid of failure? Good question. As an old football coach once said, "We weren't beaten... We just ran out of time."

One lesson I have finally learned: When a woman tells you her problems, she usually does not want you to solve them. She, more often than not, only wants you to listen while she talks. This concept was extremely hard for me to comprehend. A man should only attempt to solve her problem if she specifically asks him to do so. I had a hard time learning that. However, Athena did some good coaching with me on that one that served me fairly well.

I have a feeling that BIG ROOSTER will get better at His job. Lord knows; He needs to. He could pitch in on conversations. Those one-way conversations suck. And He needs to let all the people know that they have to stop fighting over who He or She, is! He's got to make it perfectly clear, exactly, who He is... And that He is doing the very best He can..., by trial and error. And, He only expects folks to do their best, as well. And, if BIG ROOSTER can't handle this..., maybe Mr. and Mrs. Huckleberry should man-up and step in and clear things up... And get all their kids on the right track.

So, was, and is, life just a series of plays within plays within plays? Fractals?

The way I see it: progress by trial and error is evolution. Mutations in the fractal evolvement continue to have mutations on previous mutations. The mutations that survive become steps to the next evolvement. Mutations on mutations to mutations that, hopefully, will mutate an advantage for survival. The same with creating a work for the stage. During initial thoughts and drafts, creative changes are made. During the following rehearsals, changes are made to the work that is already changed during previous rewrites. Evolving.

Unlike legitimate productions, the work in my small attic stage behind my eyes is never "frozen." Usually, the producer, along with the director, will "freeze" a show a night or two before opening. As a general rule: No changes for the complete run. No "improvements" by the actors. But, in my productions, the show evolves as life evolves.

Certainly, a collaboration of the best producers, writers, actors, composers, lyricists, choreographers, stage managers, stage crews, lighting, sound and costume designers, the best PR folk, and deep pocket investors could be an asset. And, if everyone makes their very best effort, the show still might not succeed. Millions lost. Dreams dashed. On the other hand, if the stars are in their proper alignment, it could mean a big hit. A huge hit. A monster. And, artistically gifted and stage-struck investors will continue to take that leap, as a group; intoxicated by their show-biz success. Just being a part of the venture is exciting… And, can be very expensive. And, once more as Jule Styne told me: "It's like gambling. It's not so much the winning or the losing… It's the action."

Soirees, Artists, Glitterati, Cognoscenti, and Me

After extensively mulling the meanings of things, I look forward to one of my soirees; a festive evening with a large all-star cast of interesting characters. On these occasions, with the mingling of the uniquely talented, the compulsive and best thinkers, and the vivacious and often raucous personalities, one gets infused by an overflow of special vibrations. By merely walking through the crowded room, I am elevated. So, I'll just write it in, here:

The idea for my soirees came to me, after having enjoyed many enormously entertaining soirees at my friend Marshall Barer's home here in Venice Beach. Tonight, I will be visited and entertained by a somewhat eclectic group, including Louis Armstrong, Leonard Bernstein, Leo Tolstoy, Hedy Lamarr, Moondog, Glen Gould, Madeline Kahn, Vivien Leigh, Margaret Mitchell, Christopher Hitchins, Janis Joplin, and Richard Feynman... After, Glen Gould plays the Goldberg Variations; who, will be first to spark lively conversations? Tolstoy and Hitchins might toss around a few lightning bolts. I'll be listening in on that. Moondog: reading his poetry to Bernstein and others. Richard Feynman and Janis Joplin might jam a bit. Later, Hedy Lamarr will corner Feynman and impress him with her mind while Feynman continues thumping his own tom-tom along to her speech pattern... Moondog will join in. Vivien Leigh and Margaret Mitchell will surely speak of their collaboration. Maybe not. I'm not sure. It could be that they never actually met. Even so, that project certainly turned out well. Vivien will send me a knowing smile from across the stage that will temporarily affect my equilibrium. I have extended invitations to both Gore Vidal and Norman Mailer. William Buckley will referee if needed. Madeline Kahn will sing, "Das Chicago." And, Leonard Bernstein will conduct the full New York Philharmonic in the overture to *Candide*. Then, Madeline will sing "Glitter and Be Gay."

And, things will surely be lively on Friday night, with Ernest Hemmingway and Marlene Dietrich, Hume Cronyn and Jessica Tandy, Alfred Lunt and Lynn Fontaine, Laurette Taylor, Jack Paar, Sherry Britton, Michael Jeter, Grace Kelly, Isadora Duncan, Truman Capote, and Tallulah Bankhead. Cronyn, Tandy, and the Lunts will swap tales of life on the road. Tallulah will share, wittily so, on Shakespeare, the Bible, her many past lovers, and why she has no use for underwear. Joe Louis and Jimmy Catusi will play gin rummy. Max Baer will watch. Laurette Taylor will make her entrance, unnoticed. Jack Paar will lure Sir Noel Coward into sparkling conversation with Sillman, George Burns, WC Fields and Sherry Britton. Sherry will dance, seductively so, to the Warsaw Concerto. Joey Faye will walk across the stage, and everyone will laugh. Hemmingway will report on bravery and the running of the bullshit... While "the Kraut" will be eyeballing Sherry Britton. What might Grace Kelly and Isadora Duncan talk to us about? Whatever it might be, it will cease if Gary Cooper shows up.

SOIREES, ARTISTS, GLITTERATI, COGNOSCENTI, AND ME

Probably, the real "hoot" will be on Saturday night, with Elsa Maxwell, Mae West, Dorothy Parker, Nikita Khrushchev, Karl Marx, Moss Hart, Thomas Paine, Jacqueline du Pre, Pablo Casals, Houdini, Carl Ballantine, Lenny Bruce, Ronny Graham, and Marshall Barer. After Bach duets for Cello and Violin from Casals and du Pre; Elsa Maxwell, Bobby Fischer, and Khrushchev will stare at each other until Nikita removes one of his shoes and bangs it on the table. Marshall Barer will do his "wiener" act that got him banned from The Comedy Store. Lenny Bruce will interrupt: "For that? For that, you got banned from a comedy club? Fuck that!" And, we will thoroughly enjoy Casals sensitive playing of Elgar's Cello Concerto in E Minor... although, I prefer Jacqueline du Pre's playing of it. After which, Truman Capote will mumble something. It will most likely be something gossipy about Babe Paley. Ronny Graham will take to the piano and play his jazz version of "Ding Dong; The Witch is Dead." Mae West will, more than likely, tell us about her many conquests of handsome young men. Capote will be taking notes. Elsa Maxwell will join the Paar group and be much happier. Well did you evah? Sinatra and Crosby will indubitably bring the house down with "What a Swell Party" this is from *High Society*.

But, "the-eleven-o'clock-number" will be Michael Jeter with someone of his own choosing, doing, "We'll Take a Glass Together," from *Grand Hotel*. Mickey, Billy, and Whitey will get here just in time to catch Frank, Sammy, and Dean close the night. Bobby Fischer will be on a straight-back chair in the corner, waiting, impatiently, for Boris Spassky.

For reasons that are beyond me... Galileo has not responded to my many invitations. Oh, how I would love to hear from him about his bucking up to the Catholic Church and the established thinking of his time.

"In questions of science, the authority of a thousand is not worth the humble reasoning of a single individual." - Galileo Galilei

Now, for Sunday: I will have many from the three previous evenings back for Sunday Brunch, to be provided by Toots Shor. Mayor Fiorello LaGuardia will read the Sunday funnies to us. Followed by a special concert: Jeanette MacDonald and Nelson Eddy will sing. The eternally vibrant Jeanette MacDonald and her stoic singing partner, Nelson Eddy will sing some of my favorite duets: "Wanting You." Then, "Will You Remember" and, "Ah, Sweet Mystery of Life." Finally, with a nod to Sir Noel: "I'll see You Again." At one time, I admit, I was in love with Jeanette MacDonald. Things will really get rollin' when the Original Dixieland Jazz Band plays "Livery Stable Blues," and "Some of these Days." Sophie tucker will surely join in on that one. And, to put a lid on it... Louis "Satchmo-Pops" Armstrong will join in and improvise on a few numbers... And, finally, "Pops" will sing, "What a Wonderful World." What a swell party, indeed.

Of course, I will, once again, invite Gene Tierney. But, so far, she has avoided me like the plague. You'd think that, being the writer-director-producer, I could just write her in, but no... The pen will not write an entrance for Gene Tierney. 'Tis a mystery beyond my understanding. Perhaps, she is insecure..., not liking crowds. Maybe she'll drop by some afternoon when I am alone and not expecting Vivien.

I will have to ask Bobby Fischer to leave, telling him, "Not yet, Bobby. Be patient."

Bobby will answer me with, "Spassky is afraid to die because he's afraid of me. But, someday he will come. I've got all the time in the after-world." At that point, Bobby will crack a self-congratulatory smile and leave.

Vivien, after charming or alarming us all, will stay the night. As usual, we will enjoy sweet bedroom madness until we are limp and soggy noodles. Exhausted and sated, we will, eventually, visit the Land of Nod.

I will arise early Monday morning to give yesterday's Sunday Times Puzzle a less than adequate try. But, as Jule said, "It's the action that counts." After which, I might consider possible productions for the week ahead. Actually, I don't consider. I just follow the pen and smile. I smile a lot. It's good to live in Utopia.

Vivien will arise in a burst of energy, looking disheveled and incredibly beautiful. Almost... Almost as beautiful as I imagine Gene Tierney to be. It's true that I have no idea of Gene Tierney's off-screen temperament... And, it's also true that I am attracted to women who live on the edge of sanity. Oftentimes, there lies genius. It's well known that, on occasion, my fiery Vivien Leigh has an extremely short fuse.

Nevertheless, Vivien and I will rehash the previous evening's gathering of the muses, and laugh; recalling how Mae West turned out to be a drag queen that no one knew. Very funny. He'll be invited back… Maybe, with Mae West.… Even W. C. Fields was amusing. Houdini did not understand what was so funny about The Amazing Ballantine's failed tricks. Dorothy Parker spent most of the evening in conversation with Robert Benchley and Moss Hart. Karl Marx and Thomas Paine exchanged some time together discussing Tolstoy. By the way, Paine had gone missing for years. Some thought he was in Paris. I don't know. Maybe, he will fess up concerning his mysterious whereabouts during that time. He'll let us know when and if he wants us to know.

About midnight, Vincent Van Gogh stumbled in muttering, "I sold a painting; one painting, in my whole life. I sold it for four hundred francs. Today, a country; an African country bought one of my paintings for over a hundred and fifty million dollars. Merde." Zero Mostel jumped at the chance to say, "Oy. With a good agent, you could have been a rich man." Van Gogh said, "Right now, I will settle for cheese and bread and some libation of the grape variety."

One of my all-time favorite theatrical experiences was on the previous Sunday afternoon, following another Toots Shor brunch, when Laurette Taylor and the original cast of Tennessee William's *The Glass Menagerie* performed the complete play for us. Word got out that Laurette Taylor was going to be performing her role as Amanda on my attic stage, so, I had to enlarge my seating capacity, while, at the same time, keeping the production onstage behind my eyes and between my ears. The crème de la crème of New York actors, plus, Clurman, Adler, Strasberg, Durante, Cantor, and Gleason, and from London: Gielgud, Richardson, and Redgrave, all came to see the most natural and effective performance ever on any stage, anywhere, at any time. They marveled and wanted to know, "How does she do that?" Maureen Stapleton's jaw was hanging at half-mast. We were all flies-on-a-wall... Witnessing a great actress, not acting.

I'm told that Laurette Taylor and others had been using the Belasco for brush-up rehearsals. David Belasco had allowed them to use his theater from midnight to six in the morning. Also, at my request, Jason Robards, Colleen Dewhurst and Ed Flanders have been rehearsing *A Moon for the Misbegotten* there, and plan to have it ready for us soon. I have no hand in the production. I especially look forward to seeing Ed Flanders repeating his role... Wonderful performance. But, the tragic ending to his offstage life was a shock. Hidden pain, gone unnoticed by the public.

Making for a perfect Sunday afternoon; just as Marvin Gaye was ending the song, in walked our old friends, Abraham, Martin, John, and Bobby.

During these entertainments, I, mostly, just listen, look, smile, and enjoy.

I understand that Lauren "Betty" Bacall and Robin Williams will be attending my next soiree. As with Ed Flanders, a shocking ending for Robin Williams. With Bacall: she had quite a remarkable run. I'm sure that I'll have to schedule a special evening for

Robin Williams alone. Then, another special evening with Robin and Jonathan Winters together. Many sides will split from laughing. I'm looking forward to Bacall's entrance, too. No one makes an entrance like Bacall. Bogie and Bacall will arrive together, but all eyes will be on Bacall.

You the reader have noticed that all of my guests have been missing from Broadway and New York and planet Earth for a while. I bring them back for return engagements and intellectual intercourse... and, funny-business intercourse, I imagine. We enjoy these magical evenings, here in my attic theater. And, my guests come alive (so to speak) with meeting some of their birds-of-a-feather that they missed during their earlier romps through the New York and Broadway scene. They are comfortable on my stage, while being in this nest of like-birds. And, I do believe that everyone will continue to return. And, possibly..., just possibly..., after my personal theater goes dark for the last time that others will invite me back for similar gatherings. I would heartedly appreciate that.

Many of my younger readers will, possibly, not know or even be aware of, but a few of my guests. Maybe, some names will sound familiar. But, for me, these guests, from my time, are indeed stars shining brightly above the chandeliers in my frescoed sky. I would imagine that these young readers will someday have their own indelible icons of their time. And, the world turns. They have theirs. I have mine... with some overlapping. I do hope that theirs will include theatre folk and outrageous personalities that have inhabited and enhanced their times. Dare I say, "Circles sharing the same radius?"

Beginning on Thursday night of the coming week, there will be an entirely different cast of great minds and unique personalities, with the exception of Vivien. If Vivien is not going through one of her "troubled" times, she will be back. Vivien Leigh is the desired mistress in the minds and the shorts of the many. At times, she is incredible. At other times, poor dear, she is incredible, but the hell-on-earth kind of incredible. However, when Vivien comes to me, she is usually warm, funny, charming, and insatiable. I venture that Vivien is a much better mistress than a wife. I understand that Peter Finch is my competition. Sir Lawrence is off doing what he does best. Hopefully, not another, *Betsy* kind of embarrassment for that great actor. Terrible American accent. I do believe that he is the only English actor ever to speak the language that could not act with a respectable American accent. He needed the money; I trust... As most actors do from time to time. Remember that he was the first big star that stooped so low as to do a television commercial. That made it somewhat acceptable for some of the rest of us to stoop. When it was revealed that Lawrence Olivier received a million dollars for one commercial, other "big names" followed suit. Yes, big stars have to eat as well.

The entertainment for the evening will be a special concert, given by Ethel Merman and Mary Martin. I expect I'll have to enlarge my audience seating to something the size of the Winter Garden for that. Every available dapper lad from that era will be in attendance. Maybe, we'll have to schedule two nights... Possibly, three. A few friends from "Forgotten Musicals," will be here. I hope that when the current members read this book they will not do anything rash just to attend this concert. They should rest assured that there will be many return engagements by Merman and Martin.

BEHIND THESE EYES SUCH SWEET MADNESS LIES

My dear, Ruby Dee has joined her husband, Ossie Davis, and will be available to attend. I love and admire those two wonderful people of the theatre. They made a difference in helping to change the world; especially in the civil rights movement. Maybe, I can get Ruby to do her one-woman show, *My One Good Nerve: A visit with Ruby fDee.* I saw it in Los Angeles, and was moved to tears and laughter. I did a daring play with Ruby, called *Wedding Band*, by Alice Childress. And, I did a musical that Ossie co-wrote the book for, called *Purlie*; a musical version of his play, *Purlie Victorious.* I and my other guests will certainly welcome Ruby and Ossie to our evenings on these attic boards. They will have much to share with Hume Cronyn and Jessica Tandy... And the Lunts... And, everyone else.

I do not expect that Gene Tierney will come, or even acknowledge my invitation. A conundrum, indeed. Although, I do know she is happily married now and lives in Texas, of all places. Garbo is also a routine no-show. But, she doesn't go anywhere as far as I know. If Garbo and Tierney should walk in together... now, wouldn't that cause a stir. Ha. Lively conversations would suddenly become muted, with special area lighting required... All eyes on the two... Making for dramatic tension here on my cozy attic stage 'neath the proscenium arch of my brow, behind my eyes, and between my ears.

I wonder how many people know that in the movie, "Garbo Talks," that the woman in Central Park, 'neath that Garbo hat, was Betty Comden... True. Ha. And, a good likeness, too.

SOIREES, ARTISTS, GLITTERATI, COGNOSCENTI, AND ME

Here's another thought: Wouldn't it be interesting if Garbo would miraculously show up on a night that Dietrich was here. Conversations would not only become muted; they would stop. Again, special lighting. As I understand it, they "knew" each other before either one became a big star.

And too... Rocky Marciano has agreed to go another fifteen rounds with me, giving me four months to get into fighting shape. Of course, I am at a disadvantage in this. I don't want to hurt Rocky. He's my idol... Undefeated heavyweight champ while weighing only 185 lbs. Nevertheless, a fight is a fight. And, I won't throw a fight..., not even for Rocky.

Though, I am looking forward to seeing Joan Rivers arrive at one of my soirees, I feel the country got robbed. Had Joan pulled through, and come out of that coma, just to think about the material she would have mined from her near-death experience boggles the mind. What a tragic loss. But: Lucky us! Here, she'll be SRO for more than one show, I'm sure.

Yes. I am a lucky, lucky man. All this from my small attic stage and living quarters, nestled here behind my eyes. Years ago, I came to New York for a life on the stage. And, now, I have my own stage. Traditionally, my theater is dark on these Monday nights. Tonight, I have had my favorite dinner of skinless and boneless sardines in olive oil, doused with my Cholula hot-sauce, with chopped raw onion and garden-fresh tomatoes. Yowzah!

Later, I'll put in a couple of hours on a venture that I'm calling: *Casting the Troubled Waters of Coleman Ainsworth Cobb*.

It's about how life goes on, even on a week when the world might very well come to its earth-scorching end. This would be the week of the Cuban Missile Crisis back in October of 1962. What's more important: The success of Cobb's play on the little stage atop Riverside Church, or a nuclear holocaust that could very well end life on earth? Cobb has written his play, and its performance is about to be judged. And, of course, there's this other bothersome thing about missiles and the end of the world. And, there too, is this woman Cobb had made love to when she was married and pregnant and in college. She and her husband pay Cobb a surprise visit. There's more: Cobb has brought a mentally disturbed giant of a young man, who has threatened to kill him, home for lunch. Oh, and Harold Clurman has come to give Cobb's play the once-over. What a swell gathering this is! A lovely day in October, and it's coming along nicely.

Presently, as I muse about things in total, suddenly, for no apparent reason, I remember what my Aunt Ella had said to me, many years ago: "Think about this, Buddy. (She as did most, called me, Buddy) If you could walk for say ninety years in the direction of the setting sun, and you kept walking and walking and walking; you would eventually end up right here where you now stand. Think about that." Why would that pop into my head? Don't know. Yes, I do.

So, for now, I sit in my *travel* chair and appreciate my good fortune. I hear the young soprano in the next building, running her pianissimo vocalizes. She stops. Finished for the night, I guess. In this "city that never sleeps," at this very moment, there stirs not one sound. Not the sound of one cricket. Except, now, in the distance, I hear the elevated subway, at 125th Street, roll in and screech to a stop. After a minute or so, it rumbles off into the tunnel and into its long night of screeching and rumbling. Again, there is an almost tactile quiet. Delicious. I am about to put on my recording of Tibetan Bowls for gentle transport into my tunnel and into my night...

A phone rings... I do not have a phone. I removed it from the premises. And, yet there it is. It continues to ring... I am, immediately, overcome with anxiety. I look at this ringing phone as if it were a poisonous snake about to strike... Something terrible has happened... Is Vivien calling? I pick up the phone...

"Hello."

"Hi. This is Gene Tierney. I hope you won't mind if I drop in at this late hour. I'm in town for the night, and I'm quite anxious to meet you. Would you please tell me where you live?"

"Certainly... I'm quite easy to find. I live on the small attic stage behind my eyes. It's just beneath the proscenium arch of my brow... You can't miss it... The door is open."

Again, the phone rings: "I'm desperate to see you... I'm on my way."

It's Vivien.

I stare at the blank page before me... Now, I ask myself, "What, possibly, could go wrong?"

Again, the phone rings... I watch as it fairly well rocks in its cradle...

"Hello."

"I've been given your address by Larry Olivier, and I'm coming right over to kick the shit out of you, you son-of-a-bitch!"

Let me think... I could wait for what portends to be a disastrous end to a wonderful day. Or, I could hop onto my *travel* chair and get my ass out of Dodge.

I put my pen down, and I mull this over... I think on the plot what's in the pot... I pick up the pen... Again, the reluctant pen will not move... I sense that someone is here. Who?

I look up from my blank page, and standing before me, is a bearded gentleman, I do not know. He is dressed in a toga. He smiles and says:

"I would like to introduce myself. My name is Galileo Galilei. (He pauses) All truths are easy to understand once they are discovered; the point is to discover them."

"Tell me then, sir; what is my truth?"

"You sir, are up shit creek. That was Peter Finch on the phone."

My pen aches to move... Nothing... I am frozen...

SOIREES, ARTISTS, GLITTERATI, COGNOSCENTI, AND ME

Galileo Galilei stares at me as if awaiting my reply.

In the distance, I hear a subway train rumbling along and screeching to a halt at the elevated station at 125th Street. Following a moment of complete silence, it rumbles off and into the tunnel at the north end of the elevated tracks. It is gone.

"Take your time," he says. Then, "Oops, your time is up. Someone is here."

Falstaff enters. I know what he'll say.

Yep. Tomorrow is another day. I hop onto my *travel* chair... From my window, I am overlooking a small park in Paris. The young woman, playing her cello, is the most beautiful woman I have ever seen. The music is new to me. I can't decide which is the more beautiful; the young woman or how sensitively she bows her cello. She glances up at me, and she smiles.

There is a knock at my door. I am not in Paris. I open my door, and there stands a be-speckled older gentleman sporting a well-groomed snow-white beard. He speaks:

"My name is Sigmund Freud. We have work to do."

"Don't take this personally, Herr Freud, but..."

I close the door and continue to enjoy the beautiful young woman with her cello. I am in Paris. I am overcome with the beauty of it.

She stands and, once again; she smiles. She places her cello in its case. She quizzically studies my face, and then:

"You don't remember me, do you?"

Shit! I am not in Paris. Bursting through the door is Peter Finch... Followed closely by Vivien. His face is about to explode redness all over the place as he shouts: "I'm mad as hell! And, I'm not going to take this anymore!" He grabs a chair; holding it above his head, he charges... as if to bash it down upon my head. I'm frozen.

Gene Tierney walks in. She makes a quick assessment of the situation and exits without saying a word. The expression on her face was that of exquisite beauty and sheer terror. My clock stopped when she entered and began again when she exited. I don't suppose that Gene Tierney will be coming back... At least, not anytime soon.

"Was that Gene Tierney?" asks Finch.

"Vivien says, "Yes. I believe it was."

Finch changes the expression on his face to one of resignation. Now, he swings the chair about and places it gently on the floor, before me... He sits there on what once a weapon but now is merely an accommodation. He laughs as if to be thoroughly enjoying himself. Then, he stops laughing, and stares at me.

"Sorry, old chap. It seemed like a fun idea at the time. It seemed like the perfect time for me to revisit that iconic line once shouted

SOIREES, ARTISTS, GLITTERATI, COGNOSCENTI, AND ME

by me in the film, *Network*. You see, Vivien and I were having a late supper at Sardi's. After dining, she was beginning to look rather gloomy, so I said, "Let's have a bit of fun. Let's go over and scare the shit of that boyfriend of yours! It'll be fun. And, I'll get to say that iconic line of mine: 'I'm sick and tired of this! And, I'm not going to take it anymore!' I love hearing myself say that line... It did win me an Oscar."

Vivien pipes in: "Buddy, my dearest... It did seem like a fun idea when Finchy suggested it. But, you're not laughing, so..."

There's a somewhat awkward silence.

Finch stands... Offers his apologies... Kisses Vivien on her cheek and exits; saying that he had a flight to catch.

Vivien walks to me and hugs me... Saying that she is sorry but that she was afraid she was beginning to have the gloomies... Not the dreaded in-the-dark-cave-gloomies, but just down a bit. And, that Finchy's idea seemed just the thing to do. Rather mischievously, she utters, "You must admit, it was fun. You should have seen your face."

"Fun? Yes. It was a riot."

"Buddy, could we just spend the rest of the evening together. We'll cuddle and canoodle in your chair. We'll be together. We'll listen to music."

(Note: Here, my chair is now wide enough for two.)

I begin to take off my clothes. Vivien stops me.

"I can cuddle in the nude," I say.

"No, you can't," says she.

Vivien insists. And, we settle down comfortably in my chair. Vivien nuzzles under my arm and across my chest. The beautiful girl with the cello begins to play ever so softly *The Viennese Waltz*. Her selection strikes me to be unusual, until our chair lifts off, and we waltz into the night sky. The music stops, and there is only the low drone of a plane and the whistling sounds of the wind. We are in the yellow two-seat bi-plane that Redford and Streep flew in *Out of Africa*. We are over Central Park and heading south. As we fly over the theatre district, Jule Stein's brassy overture to *Gypsy* startles us and lifts us higher.

We look over the side at the Broadway lights below. Straining over the drone of the plane and the distant sound of that big Broadway brass, Vivien calls out: "I can see The Broadway Theater. Dear me; that's where I played in the musical, Tovarich. I won a Tony Award for that. Did you know?"

"Yes, I knew that."

"What?"

"I said, yes, I knew that."

"Did you see it?"

"No. No, I didn't see you in Tovarich. Sorry."

"Why, not?"

"At the time, I couldn't afford the ticket. I did see you exit the stage door one night. You smiled in my direction. I thought you might have been smiling at me."

"I was."

"Really?"

"Of course, not, Silly. But, maybe I was and just didn't know it."

For a while, we circle above the whole of Manhattan Island just drinking it in and laughing and singing tunes that are wafting up from the glorious past.

Then, Vivien reaches her hand back to hold mine. I'm not ashamed to say that tears are cascading down my cheeks as we continue holding hands, and sharing this wonderful flight amongst the stars over Broadway. Sharing what is pretty damn close to ecstasy. And, without fasting, sleep deprivation, or by the use of hallucinogens… Only by the lights on Broadway, the wafting sounds of Broadway brass, and by my extraordinary friend and lover, Vivien Leigh.

The morning sun wakes me. My dear, Vivien lies beside me. She looks so incredibly beautiful and peaceful. Life is good.

My curtain speech

Years ago (In the mid-sixties) when I was attending the First Annual Playwright's Conference in Aspen, Colorado, with Harold Clurman who simply radiated artistic intelligence as our resident celebrity director, there was at the same time another gathering in Aspen... A gathering of some of the great scientific minds from the world over. They were not a part of the Playwright's Conference. They were gathered for their own separate conference. But, we shared the same sidewalks on our ways to and from various meetings and rehearsals. As I walked amongst these men and women of brilliant minds, all but rubbing elbows with physicists, biologists, economists, and other heavy hitters of that community, I experienced a definite sensation... A transfer... An exchange... Due to the proximity..., a tactile experience... But, more from them to me than from me to them, I'm sure. But, who knows. Matters not.

Here, at my soirees where some of the great creative talents mingle, there seems to be a similar transfer. What kind of transfer? What do I mean? In both communities, there are energies that radiate from one to the other. Is this another variation of quantum entanglement? I have been the recipient of that radiant wealth. I felt it in Aspen and most recently here on my stage. The first time that I was aware of such exchanges was when I first reverently held my sister's high school history book in my small five-year-old hands. It was as if I were cradling something sacred... This, even before I could read.

The book had a faded red cover that featured a silver line-drawn American eagle. I suspected there were endless treasures inside those faded red covers. I remember holding the book to my chest and feeling something from within. And, that once I could read, I would find all the secrets of the world. I often fell asleep while holding that book. It was special. It was my first book.

Yes, my being a bibliophile all began with coveting my sister's faded red history book. I find comfort being surrounded by books... And great minds... Intelligent minds... And minds of warmth and compassion... And minds of considerable talents. I feel it, almost as if I could hold it in my hands and rub it into my very being: Good for my mental health and enjoyable as a banquet table of delicious comfort foods.

When Robert Benchley is near, I feel wit and charm. With Galileo, I feel uncluttered perception. With Tallulah, I feel a dramatic and flamboyant abandon. With my dear Vivien, I do not feel trapped by stale convention. Mostly, I feel a wonderful obligation to respect and protect her fragility and to enjoy her strength and her beauty and her pure unapologetic lust.

I think it's something akin to fans touching the hand of a Rock Star... A transference from a strong and compelling energy... The same as with autographs... Touching certain iconic statues... Being said "Hello" to by the President of the United States of America... Or, not wanting to wash a cheek recently kissed by someone special. A favorite that I have to mention is when my high school classmate, Billy Buxter asked to shake hands with an old actor from Hollywood, who had come to see me in a play at school. The old actor (Olin Howland) mentioned that he, when playing a schoolmaster, had spanked young Elizabeth Taylor's bottom.

"I'd like to shake your hand, sir."

The old actor said, "Why, sure young fellow."

Later on, I teased Billy: "There's no telling where that old hand has been and just what it might have been doing."

"I don't care where else that old hand has been. I'll just be thinking that I touched the hand that had touched Elizabeth Taylor's bottom," was Billy's reply.

I write more about that in my next book that will be the third in this series. It's called, *The Trunk in My Attic.*

I was still five when I went to my first-grade classroom. My teacher was Mrs. Allen. I heard she had been ninety years old since my uncle William was in her class. Mrs. Allen sent me home and told me to come back the next year. What had just happened? Well, when she asked what we would like to study; with an abundance of enthusiasm, I erupted: "History!"

"We won't be studying history in this class," she said.

I was crushed. Why? What did she have against history?

Did she send me home because I wanted to study history?

That year I spent a lot of time with my dog, "Spark."

In truth, the class was too large, and I was not yet six, so, I was banished from my educational pursuits for another long year. Years are incredibly long for five-year-olds.

The next fall, I went back to school for another try. Mrs. Allen was still the first-grade teacher as she had been since the beginning of time. Then, the school burned down. The fates were against me. But, we did hold classes in the Nazarene Church.

I did manage to get through the first five grades without studying history. And, then I found that I liked girls better than I liked history. When I held a girl in my arms, I certainly felt a strong energy, but an energy of a different kind. An almost intoxicating energy. My asset at the time was that I could sing. My singing did seem to give me a slight edge with the girls. And good women are like good books. Even though many years have passed, you want to enjoy them again.

Important recurring question: By writing this book: Is this a selfish thing to do? By relieving some of my guilt, but at the same time, ushering in a somewhat needless regurgitation for my family to deal with, is my truth that important to me? And, to my family? Although, they have not been kept in total darkness, will this book be of any positive value to them? I don't know, and yet

I continue to write. I can dodge the question and present the book to them. If they object, I might consider discarding these writings and banishing them back into my theatrical trunk in the attic.

What did I think about not really knowing very much at all about my own father? The answer is: I would very much like to know anything... Everything... No matter what blemishes of character he might have had. Perhaps, that would give to me some insight into my own character. My friend of over fifty years, Gary Haber, made a terrific documentary honouring his bigger-than-life father. In the film, Gary had made his father out to be a virtual saint. (Which he was from time to time) But, I knew his father to be a much more interesting and complicated character. (See, there you go: I just wrote the word "character" rather to than to write the word "man.") The question is: Is everything a play to me? And, not life...? A play? A theatrical production? Will Shakespeare thought as much.

Let's see... Where was I? I was considering the energy radiating from my library of books... Dozens and dozens of dog-eared and only partly read books surround me. It has now been seventy-five years since I first held my sister's high school history book. I recall that the last page was blank. There was the one blank page. Why? No writing... Just a blank page... Being receptive to more history?

Now, in early January of 2015, I walk across the crimson clover and the alfalfa fields. I lean against Big Oak. Azaleas and grapes and squash and tomatoes and beans and all sorts from nature's bounty are all around and under. I see them and I feel them. This is all familiar to me. Why? I look into the vast starry heavens. A sweet angel's voice tells me to fly, to soar aloft on butterfly wings. With aging Monarch wings, I take to flight; soaring through the starry night until; finally, I float softly to rest on the near side of the moon. I look back in awe. I am near overwhelmed with the wonder of it. But, have I been here before? I see my Mother Earth; now a seemingly small, near perfect sphere. It hangs and rotates in space. It is alone in a vast sea of stars. Not a sound... Only, quiet. I have no words for this. I am not aware of time... Minutes... Hours... Years... Or centuries. All are one.

I sit in my father's straight-back chair by the potbellied stove in Grandpa's General Store. I see my Grandmother, Louisiana. She sees me. She smiles at me. I am pleased that she is quite beautiful. She does not speak. Her smile says that she loves me. I love her. I love her, and yet I have never met her. I whittle long curls of shavings from a nice cut of red cedar. This act of whittling and the smell of cedar always pleases my senses.

I lie on my back, on the soft grassy spot between the apple trees and the grape arbor, and I look to the heavens as I am prone to do. I see cotton-candy clouds floating in a pale blue sky. I lie here until darkness comes, and the once blue sky is now black and covered with twinkling stars. I meditate on what wonders there might be out there within that bejeweled canopy of galaxies. I venture deeper into that seemingly endless space; deeper than even the most powerful telescopes can see. I am there, and I am here.

The magical stage beneath my brow and behind my eyes is abuzz. The house lights are down. Orchestra instruments are tuning up. This is somewhat akin to the first time I saw a Broadway musical. It was *The Most Happy Fellow*. When that Frank Loesser overture began, back in 1956; I was about to jump out of my skin with excitement. Now, here I am in 2014, and on the tap of my friend, Milton Rosenstock's baton; there is an overture coming from behind the curtain that is beyond all imagination. I do recognize overlapping strains from my favorite composers... Classical, jazz, spiritual, and good old Broadway, (heavy on the brass.) What a show! What a show there might be here!?!

And, I do, very much, aspire to be booked into such a show, along with a troop of other fine actors and singers and dancers and storytellers and lovers. And, of course, with my sweetheart, Lynn Rachel..., all will be sharing stories and bringing laughter and tears of recognition to all the other attentive and appreciative minds and hearts!

I would be hard put to ask for more.

I do hope that this book, *Behind These Eyes Such Sweet Madness Lies*, will be of some interest and value to my children and grandchildren. If they dare not read my books, for fear of embarrassment, or for any other reason, I would ask them to, at least, hold the books in their hands... Get the feel of them... Giving them a few minutes, each. Hopefully, by doing this, they will be able to absorb some of the personal essences that I want to pass along to them. And, that they should know well that I have a tub full of love, admiration, and respect for them all. I am honoured, and take great pride in being their father and grandfather.

Before My Attic Stage

Brandon Roscoe Maggart

Before my *traveling without leaving* chair from the small attic stage behind my eyes was required, I ventured into the light quite a few times. Since 1958, I have been an actor/singer on television and on Broadway (Tony nomination for *Applause* with Lauren Bacall)... Winner of the *Theatre World Award* for the musical revue, *Put it in Writing*. The original cast of *Sesame Street* (Buddy and Jim)... Four-time Cable Ace Award nominee for the TV series, *Brothers* on Showtime... Starred in TV series *Jennifer Slept Here* NBC... and *Chicken Soup* ABC... Over 50 yrs., guest starred on shows like... *Naked City, The Defenders, Route 66, Newhart, Murder, She Wrote, Murphy Brown, Married With Children, ER, Ellen, Madeline, Love, Sidney, The Sentinel, Boy Meets World, L.A. Law, Who's The Boss, Simon, Bakersville P.D., Babes,* and *Brisco County Jr.*... TV movies: *Daughter of the Streets, The Man Who Corrupted Hadleyburg. The Betrayal, Running Mates. Spiritual Warriors, Living in Fear, Mars and Beyond, Intrepid, Running Out, Dream Date,* and *My Old Man*.

Other Broadway and Off-Broadway shows include, *New Faces of 1968, Lorelei, Purlie, Musical Chairs, Put it in Writing, Potholes, Straws in the Wind, Sing Muse, The Long Valley,*

BEHIND THESE EYES SUCH SWEET MADNESS LIES

The Mad Show, Gems of Burlesque, Lil Abner, South Pacific, Romance: But Not for Me, and Eugene Ionesco's *The Killer.* Big flops were *Kelly, One Night Stand, We Interrupt This Program, America be Seated,* and *Hellzapoppin* (twice). Films include *The World According to Garp... Dressed to Kill...* and the cult film, *Christmas Evil.*

Some of the most memorable actors, in one way or another, I've worked with have been, (in alphabetical order): Albert Hall, Andy Garcia, Angela Lansbury, Ann Jillian, Anne Baxter, Anita Gillette, Arlene Dahl, Ben Johnson, Betty Garrett, Big Bird, Bob Newhart, Burt Reynolds, Candice Bergin, Carol Channing, Catherine Cox, Charles Kimbrough, Clarice Taylor, Debbie Reynolds, Debbie Weems, Diane Keaton, Dick Van Dyke, Dody Goodman, Don Francks, Don Scardino, Earl Holliman, Ed Harris, Eileen Heckhart, Ella Logan, Ellen DeGeneres, Estelle Parsons, Franchot Tone, Garett Maggart, Georgia Engle, Gerry Mathews, Glen Close, Howard Keel, Hume Cronyn, Jack Carter, Jack Paar, Jack Weston, Jackie Mason, James Catusi, Jane Alexander, Jane Powell, Jerry Lewis, Josh Mostel, Judith Light, Julianna Margulies, Julie Newmar, Karen Morrow, Landy Sten, Lauren Bacall, Lee Roy Reams, Leonard Sillman, Lily Tomlin, Linda Hopkins, Lola Falana, Lou Gossett Jr., Lynn Redgrave, Madelyn Kahn, Mae Barns, Margaret O'brien, Marilyn Child, Marshall Barer, Maude Maggart, Melba Moore, Morey Amsterdam, Michael Feinstein, Mickey Rooney, Penny Fuller, Peter Palmer, Phil Silvers, Polly Holliday, Rhetta Hughes, Robert Guillaume, Robert Kline, Rose Marie, Renee Taylor, Robert Preston, Robin Williams, Ronny Graham, Ruby Dee, Ruth Buzzi, Shelly Berman, Sherman Hemsley, Sherry Britton,

BEFORE MY ATTIC STAGE

Soupy Sales, Tamara Long, Timmie Rogers, Tina Louise, Tony Danza, Tony Perkins, Tom Poston, Tony Randall, Tovah Feldshuh, Van Johnson, and my dear Vivian Vance.

During the early years, I appeared in over a hundred television commercials. Money from those commercials and seven Broadway shows paid the rent. One hit TV series bought the house: My home is in Venice Beach, CA, where I continue to write and to spend a lot of time on the small attic stage behind my eyes. After amassing over seventy paintings, I stopped painting when I ran out of wall space. I write in stretches of have two more books in the offing. I am thrilled to wake up each morning. At night, I say aloud, before going to sleep: "Thank You."

I am the father of musical artists, Fiona Apple Maggart and Maude Amber Maggart, actor Garett Maggart, writer Spencer (Bran) Maggart, R.N., C.C.A.P.P. Recovery Counselor, Jennifer Louise Maggart, Contract Administrator, Julienne Joy Maggart, and five grandchildren: Ian, Mack, Kylie, Loren and Lindsey. And, hopefully, saving me a seat in the afterlife, Justine Marie Maggart.

I am a graduate (Notable Alumni) of the University of Tennessee's School of Journalism, class of '56. I, also, attended Sewanee, The University of the South, and Columbia University. My artwork was featured in the Venice Centennial Art Walk in 2005. Also, I had the honor of reading my poem, "Diversity in Venice" at The Venice Carnivale, the Venice Centennial Celebration, and the Venice post office Abbot Kenney Mural Dedication in 2007.

BEHIND THESE EYES SUCH SWEET MADNESS LIES

Thirty years ago

"A book is made from a tree. It is an assemblage of flat, flexible parts (still called "leaves") imprinted with dark pigmented squiggles. One glance at it and you hear the voice of another person, perhaps someone dead for thousands of years. Across the millennia, the author is speaking, clearly and silently, inside your head, directly to you. Writing is perhaps the greatest of human inventions, binding together people, citizens of distant epochs, who never knew one another. Books break the shackles of time — proof that humans can work magic."

Carl Sagan

Made in the USA
Lexington, KY
18 January 2015